Looking Away

LOOKING AWAY

HOLLYWOOD AND VIETNAM

BY
JULIAN SMITH

Charles Scribner's Sons
New York

Copyright © 1975 Julian Smith

Library of Congress Cataloging in Publication Data

Smith, Julian, 1937–
    Looking away; Hollywood and Vietnam.

    Bibliography: p.
    1. War films—history and criticism.
2. Vietnamese Conflict, 1961–   United States.
3. Moving-pictures—United States. Title.
PN1995.9.W3S6   791.43'0909'3   74–13520
ISBN 0–684–13954–5

For Monica and Willie and Joe and Monty and all the other support troops and for anyone else who has suffered that this book might live.

ACKNOWLEDGMENTS

My thanks to the many producers, directors, and filmwriters who have answered my questions and provided scripts; to the many people who helped at the Museum of Modern Art, Lincoln Center for the Performing Arts, and (most particularly) the Library of Congress; to the students who sat through all those films with me; and to my editor, Patricia Cristol, for giving me room to run.

CONTENTS

ILLUSTRATIONS

INTRODUCTION

I'm not entirely happy with the title of this book, but it will do.
Looking Away does suggest my basic concern: how Hollywood has
averted its eyes from the war in Vietnam.

If I were starting out fresh and were clever enough (and had some-
one not beat me to it), I might have chosen American Graffiti. *The*
films I will discuss are part of a national writing-on-the-wall, and my
basic technique is to surround major films with little bits of graffiti
gathered from diverse sources: quotes from contemporary reviews
and public relations handouts, snatches of conversation overheard in
the dark of theaters, money earned, Oscars won, the public and pri-
vate statements of filmmakers themselves, the random memories and
joys of some thirty-odd years of moviegoing, mostly without prejudice
in mind or pen in hand.

I have piled up what has come to hand or eye or ear in the hope it
may all build to a meaning greater than the sums of the parts, to more
than a mere heap of broken images.

This book is film-generated. It started with a movie, and it seeks to
document the tremendous interpenetration between life (personal
and national) and the movies. Looking Away *began in early 1972*
when I went to see The Last Picture Show. *I came home from that film*
and in a few hours wrote the first draft of the following essay, which
I duly sent off to the New York Times. *Though the essay, like* The Last
Picture Show, *has nothing to do with Hollywood and Vietnam, I re-*
print it here because it establishes who I am, where I come from, and
how I feel about the movies.

I went not long ago to Peter Bogdanovich's *The Last Picture
Show* under the mistaken impression I would find a nostalgic
reminder of what it was like, really like, to go to the movies in
a small town a generation ago. Instead, I found that the last
movie at the Royal picture palace was a metaphor for the passing of the old order—or something like that.

Coming out of the theater in Ithaca, I remembered another
theater in the little Louisiana town of Covington, where I grew
up. It was called the Star Theater, and it doesn't exist any more.
But the Star was *my* first picture show.

I cried at my first picture show in 1941, and I still remember
the scene that did me in and caused my father to drag me out:
it was under water—a man in a diving suit was writhing in the
tentacles of a giant octopus. And somehow I too was caught in
the tangles of film, in loops of celluloid reality.

My father swore I was too young to go to movies, but my mother, still too young in those days not to go herself, took me back a week or two later to see *Dumbo,* a far more terrifying story (for a three year old) than that of a mere adult caught by a nightmare octopus. I wept for hours. My father was disgusted; my mother promised she would never die or leave me or be locked up like Dumbo's poor mad mother. And when she did die, a quarter of a century later when I had children of my own, I was moved far less.

But back to the Star Theater. Tickets, as I remember, were 25 cents for adults, 14 cents for children under 12, and 9 cents for children under 7. Typically, you were given a nickel and/or a dime to present at the box office, and you traded your penny change for candy inside—it might be only a penny, but it got you used to standing in line, and a penny habit quickly became a nickel habit. Mr. Salles, the owner, was a dapper man with a kind of Central Casting European elegance, but he took the tickets himself and kept his eye on the popcorn sales.

Ah, how Mr. Salles had us all conned. The marvelous way he remembered birthdays—when I was about 6, he started reminding me to tell him when it was my birthday so he could give me a present. So each year I got a movie poster or a set of stills. It was years before I realized his solicitude was intimately linked to profit, for when you announced your birthday, out came the "present" and the damning question, asked loud enough so Mrs. Jahrus, the box office lady, could hear: "And how old are you *now?*" By the time I was ready to make the big leap from 14-cent childhood to quarter adulthood at the age of 12, I had learned to keep my mouth shut. But Mrs. Jahrus knew or suspected and shook her jowls at me when I presented the dime and nickel, shook and stared so hard I dug deeper and found another dime, the one for popcorn, and entered manhood. Well, almost.

The reason Mrs. Jahrus knew my age was not simply that she had a better memory than Mr. Salles, but that she was a real stickler for detail and fine at bluffing. Besides, she had also been my first-grade teacher, had taught me my letters during the day and guarded the palace of dreams at night.

Looking back, it strikes me as somehow significant that my first teacher was also the box office lady, for the majority of my teaching today centers around film. Come to think of it, though, I am typical of that generation of students in the forties and early fifties when film firmly entered the classroom, in the days before television *became* the classroom.

Our school was not far from the Star Theater, and at least once a week during World War II we trekked over for an afternoon benefit showing of a purported literary classic like *The Prince and the Pauper* or a historical biography, as Sister Phillipina called them, like *The Story of Louis Pasteur.* Instead of admission, we each brought a can of food, and these we stacked in the lobby of the Star to be shipped to beleaguered England or, after V-E day, starving Germany. The good and grateful citizens of Liverpool and Leipzig must have gotten the impression that Americans thrived on canned beets, lima beans, and green peas. The trick, you understand, was to snitch something awful from the shelf. But then there were those weird children, those true Christians, who deprived themselves of cling peaches in syrup, of fruit salad, of Vienna sausage, in the name of sweet charity.

And there was the time we saw *The Good Earth* and each of us tried to out-do the other in chipping in to buy a Chinese baby. For the uninitiated among you, this meant there was a chart with little stars representing our individual contributions: a nickel bought a silver star, a dime a golden one, and $20 was the going price for a Chinese baby in those days. We didn't actually get to take possession of a genuine Chinese baby, unfortunately, but we did get to choose the name under which "our" baby would be baptized. Twenty dollars, you see, was what it cost to save a baby from starvation and bring it into a mission where its body and soul could be saved with holy water, soap, and soup. Now that President Nixon's been to China, I hope to get there soon myself to see if I can find some 25-year-old orientals with strange first names out of the calendar of forgotten saints.

Ah, it all comes back. Thank you, Peter Bogdanovich, for not doing it all for me in *The Last Picture Show,* for making *me* remember. Now I recall right after the war, when the Italian film industry started exporting again, that for weeks the lobby of the Star bore a most seductive poster of a lush Italian woman in a gauzy gown over the legend "Coming Attraction."

Then one night, my mother saw the previews of coming attractions and she swore this was one Italian movie I was not going to see. I was at least 10 then, and the argument we had on the subject of what I could or could not see began to break the bonds of sentiment welded by *Dumbo* and *Bambi.* My father told her not to bother fussing with me: the gossip at his drugstore, just down the street from the Star, was that the Eyetalian sex epic would be banned.

The whole thing was so scandalous that somehow the outrage didn't get back to the good sisters at St. Peter's, for the afternoon before the film was to open we were all marched over to the Star to see the very same spectacle our parents forbade us, and it was all about Christian martyrs and how they were treated by the pagan Romans, about virgins who refused to join the terrible orgies and were thrown half-naked to the lions. I date my own latent sadomasochism to a fleeting scene in which a Roman centurion raked the naked breast of a crucified virgin with what looked for all the world like the kind of gardening prongs my grandfather stocked in his hardware store.

Good old Mr. Salles—with an ear to the ground for prevailing community standards, he singlehandedly established the doctrine of redeeming social value. If the nuns brought the whole combined student body of St. Peter's and St. Scholastica's, could the rest of the community not but follow?

Movies brought the world to Covington in those days, and Covington gave back what it could. I remember the excitement when a local girl, Peggy Varnadow, made her Hollywood debut back in the late forties. Peggy Dow they called her, and she was Arthur Kennedy's girlfriend in *Bright Victory*. I saw Peggy just a few weeks ago, and she looked not a day older than the last time I saw her in the flesh in Covington 20 or more years ago. There she was, frozen in time on the Late Show, playing opposite Jimmy Stewart in *Harvey*.

Harvey, Harvey. . . . That reminds me: Lee Harvey Oswald, a year or two behind me in school, lived in Covington in those days. Did Mr. Salles's programming somehow undo JFK?

And Walker Percy, who won the National Book Award for *The Moviegoer* ten years ago, has lived in Covington for 30 years. Did he see most of the movies that led him to the conclusion that we find our reality in film, right there at the Star?

Or maybe he went to the Majestic, the other picture show in town. It was on the same street as the Star and also belonged to Mr. Salles, but it was older and somehow less memorable, and so were the movies shown there. The father of my best friend, Jigger, was the last projectionist there, and when the Majestic closed for good during the Korean War (at the same time as Bogdanovich's last picture show), when the projectors had been carted away to the new drive-in, Jigger and I spent a happy afternoon sailing old phonograph disks from the projectionist's booth out into the cavern of the theater. The screen would never light up again, and we were trying to slash it with records, but try as we would, we couldn't get the thick old 78's to stay in the air that far. Jigger's dad raised hell, but Mr. Salles never did find out who made that mess.

Mr. Salles is dead now. Mrs. Jahrus has moved to California, and the Star is gone forever. The building was gutted last year, and in the shell were crammed two smaller theaters, the Twin Cinemas. No longer do the colored folk sit upstairs and the white folk down; instead, the races are mingled and the audiences segregated: one house is for adult films, the other for family shows. The new realities, the new dispensation.

But it's the Star that glimmers in my memory, for of all my picture shows, it was the first, and will never be equaled by the plastic-fantastic of the shopping center cinemas that spring up around us as we all, movies and people, grow older.

Every piece of entertain-
ment, like every political
speech or swatch of adver-
tising copy, has nightmar-
ish accuracy as a triple-dis-
tilled image of a collective
dream, habit, or desire.
    —*Agee on Film*

Looking Away

FANTASY
MONTH OF OCTOBER
JOIN THE SCRAPPERS CLUB
MANAGER FOR

ONE

LOOK AWAY LOOK AWAY LOOK AWAY MOVIE LAND

Psychiatrist: "You want to talk about Vietnam?"
Violent black veteran: "Some other time."
—*The Stone Killer*

The movie starts. The title appears in letters formed with stars and stripes, but I am too young to read them. Nor do I recognize the music, "My Country 'Tis of Thee." The first scene is in a church where an old man is spinning out a sermon on the parable of the lost sheep while outside some young men are raising hell. I've heard that story about the lost sheep in my own church, but I'm still too young to know what point this preacher (or my own) is drawing.

I'm not too young to enjoy the whole thing thoroughly, especially a drunken fight in a tavern, the scene in which the hero gets knocked off his horse by a bolt of lightning, another in which he goes "gobble-gobble" at a turkey shoot to make the dumb bird stick its head up over a log. And when he goes "gobble-gobble" on a battlefield and a German pokes *his* head up, how I laugh! And my mother and father and my father's own parents and my father's sister and *her* husband and *their* little boy. We all laugh, knowing the German is going to get his head shot off.

The movie, of course, is *Sergeant York,* and we are seeing it at the Star Theater on Sunday, the fourteenth of December, 1941. I know the date because it's my fourth birthday, exactly a week after Pearl Harbor. It is my birthday, but my father is the focus of attention at this little family gathering. He does not want to go to the new war. My grandfather, who heads the local draft board, thinks his only son should enlist and set an example. An experienced campaigner in domestic warfare, my grandfather has commissioned a patriotic birthday cake: a big flat affair with a field of chocolate holding two rows of little tents. There's a tiny toy soldier in front of each tent and a little American flag between the rows.

After the cake and ice cream, the head of the draft board takes us all downtown for a special treat, the matinee at the Star Theater. *Sergeant York* is a good movie for Covington in 1941. The opening scenes show familiar places—a neat farm cabin, church, tavern, general store—the simple habitats of a simple people. On the screen and off, the same realities hold.

The men in the movie stand around the general store and argue the merits of intervention, just as they have done all through 1941 in my grandfather's place (H. J. Smith & Sons, Est. 1876—Farm Supplies, Hardware, Sporting Goods, Staples, and General Merchandize). Like my father, Alvin York doesn't

2

want to go to war. The preacher, Walter Brennan, stops him from being a draft resister—that's not the path of righteousness, he warns. Put your faith in the Lord and let Him decide whether or not you should go into the army. So York goes off to the foreign war, kills a lot of people, captures half the German army (or so it seems, the line stretching across the landscape, a really Big Parade), comes home to find all his dreams fulfilled: a farm in the bottom land and a nice little house (a gift from his neighbors) and the girl who said she'd wait. "The Lord sure works in mysterious ways," Gary Cooper mumbles.

My father is not immediately converted, but soon enough he gives in to the inevitable, enlists in the navy, and spends the war in San Diego. All told, he is to admit later, he had a pretty good time of it.

So what are you doing, friends ask, knowing I'm not teaching this year. Writing a book, I mumble, dreading the next question. Oh? What's it about? If I say I'm working on a study of how a changing America is reflected in a limited cinematic genre, they'll nod judiciously and ask me how the kids are doing, which means I've got to ask them about *their* kids. If I say that I'm writing about the recent American film, they'll say it sounds too broad. If I say "war movies," it sounds too "pop" for a serious academician who has held research grants and hopes to go to the well again.

And if I say "Hollywood's response to the war in Vietnam," they frown, collect their wits, and ask how I expect to write a whole *book* on a John Wayne movie. In the minds of most Americans, Vietnam has produced little popular art: one major popular song, "The Ballad of the Green Beret"; one major popular book, *The Green Berets;* and one major popular film, *The Green Berets* (making a total of three artistic disasters—four, if you count the war itself).

But there is more, much more. Though there have been few combat films set in Vietnam (only four since 1962, when Americans started dying there on a regular basis), Vietnam's effect on the American film has been pervasive. The way movies look at past wars, especially World War II, at the taming of the West (i.e., genocide), at the military, at our government, at our national identity and destiny, has been drastically affected by Vietnam. This book will only begin to touch on some of these issues.

Vietnam did not generate a great many films,* but it may have been America's first film-generated war, the first (and hopefully last) war to grow out of attitudes supported, perhaps even created, by a generation of movies depicting America's military omnipotence. "I remember all the movies, *Dawn Patrol* and stuff like that," a forty-year-old infantry colonel told Ward Just. "It was something inculcated in me at a very young age. I became a super patriot, a hero worshipper, and perhaps I wanted to be a hero myself." "His hero was James Cagney, recklessly courageous in *Ceiling Zero,*" writes Steven V. Roberts of a forty-five-year-old Navy flier who spent over seven years as a POW in North Vietnam; "He still holds the beliefs in American power and wisdom which he got from the textbooks and Saturday matinees of his youth." "Americans like to think that war is John Wayne," Lieutenant Calley told John Sack. "To get a grenade and a VC's throat, to shove the grenade right down it." "I felt sorry," a veteran confessed to Robert Jay Lifton. "I don't know why I felt sorry. John Wayne never felt sorry."

Not surprisingly, the contrast between movies and reality sneaks into novels about the war. Here's a passage from William Wilson's *The LBJ Brigade,* describing the feelings of a frightened American soldier, an incipient Sergeant York, upon finding himself surrounded by Vietcong:

There must be a way to capture them, I have heard stories, I have seen it in movies, one man capturing a whole army of Japanese soldiers, all it takes is brains. . . . they are my prisoners, all ten million of them, I march them towards the base, they make a line twenty miles long, it goes up and down the hills. The Brigade is waiting at the base, thousands of GIs, all at attention, they have been unable to capture a single Vietcong but I have them all plus ten zillion Chinese to boot, they are my prisoners, somehow I have tricked them into surrendering. The President appears, he is waiting with dozens of generals, there is a truckload of medals, another with girls, hundreds of photographers scurry about, guys from Hollywood want my story, they are already preparing the movie.

If for no other reason than their ability to shape new generations of warriors, the movies that preceded, depicted, or evaded Vietnam deserve attention. Thus, this book will range over

---

*If Hollywood has looked away from the war, so did the French when it was their ball game. Joseph Daniel devotes only one and a half pages in his detailed study of the French war film to Indochina's *"films proscrits, films sans public."* (Note: identification of articles and books dealing with war films will be found in the Bibliography.)

thirty years of war films in which Hollywood, by affirming certain values and reinforcing certain fears, helped to create the state of mind that led to Vietnam.

It's conventional to cite Siegfried Kracauer's *From Caligari to Hitler* at this point: "the films of a nation reflect its mentality in a more direct way than other artistic media." I'll go one step further: the treatment of *war* in a nation's films provides a crucial index to popular concepts of patriotism, national purpose, and relationships with the rest of the world.

And one step further yet: that the surest index is to be found in feature-length commercial fiction films made for a mass audience, and not in documentaries, underground films, or short films produced by church groups, the military, or any other organization with a vested interest in supporting or criticizing a war. Because I am concerned with the purest expression of what we think of ourselves—with stories shaped free of the demands of historical accuracy—I have restricted myself to fiction films about Vietnam or its impact, to fantasies. This book will ignore (or mention only for the purpose of contrast) such American documentaries as *Winter Soldier, Vietnam! Vietnam!, Interviews with Mylai Veterans, A Face of War,* or *In the Year of the Pig.* It will give no more than passing reference to foreign films, to homegrown radical fantasies, or to films made in Europe by Americans—Burr Jerger's *General Massacre,* for example, or William Klein's *Mr. Freedom.*

Howard Sufferman, speaking for the War Anti-Defamation League: "Hollywood let us down miserably. In order to have a good war you have to have dozens of motion pictures showing our brave American boys with their backs to the wall, wiping out hundreds and hundreds of the ruthless yellow enemy. If you want to know the truth, what we missed more than anything was Errol Flynn. Perhaps if he were alive and we had him on the Ho Chi Minh trail with a machine gun and five hand grenades, the entire attitude toward Vietnam might have been different."

Art Buchwald: "We had John Wayne."

Sufferman: "Americans are more sophisticated now. One film on the Green Berets is not enough to sell the people on a war."

—Art Buchwald, "Vietnam Gave War a Bad Name"

Every war has given war a bad name, and Hollywood has looked away from other conflicts, particularly divisive ones, or looked at selected scenes. Not surprisingly, American brutality in the Philippines has been ignored, and the war with Mexico is an annex to the Western. The Civil War exists chiefly as an excuse for costume drama *(Gone With the Wind)* or as a background to Westerns in which the warring factions unite for a common good *(Major Dundee, Rio Lobos, The Undefeated).* Surveying 3,234 American films made between 1950 and 1960, Garth S. Jowett found only four about the American Revolution. Since then, as far as I know, there has been only *1776,* a song and dance act.

The main years of our involvement in Vietnam fall between the Centennial of the Civil War and the Bicentennial of the Revolution, but there was no rush toward celluloid celebration of those two milestones. Perhaps intelligent and honest treatments of the complex tragedies wrought by our own wars of national consolidation would have been embarrassing in a time when we were expending great amounts of money, energy, and morale to bolster the heirs of a colonial régime and prevent the unification, no matter how bloody, of a divided country.

Though the newsreels, radio, and press documented the growing threat of the Axis powers in the late thirties, Hollywood resolutely averted its eyes. When *The Mortal Storm,* one of the first American films to directly criticize the Nazi régime, appeared in 1940, Bosley Crowther asked: "Where Was Hollywood When the Lights in Germany Went Out? . . . the most distressing thing about this heart-rending picture is that it reaches the screen too late. *The Mortal Storm* is the sort of picture we should have seen five years ago."

Though the war in Vietnam is over as far as most Americans are concerned, it may not be too late—no, it will never be too late—for American filmmakers to present the war in such a way that we will begin to understand more fully its meanings within our dream lives, our sense of ourselves. This cannot be done in one film, probably not in a dozen, maybe not in a hundred. But it must be done. Hollywood, the saying goes, is our dream factory—and we need the dreams it can give us, for if we don't dream about what is troubling us, we may go mad.

Vietnam brings night thoughts, even at the movies. David Halberstam titled his Vietnam novel *One Very Hot Day,* but the most revealing thing happens one night as combat troops watch *The Guns of Navarone.*

It was a fine movie filled with action and handsome mountains and beautiful color and Gregory Peck and Anthony Quinn on the same side, though not trusting each other. It went very well until someone discovered Peck's defection and shouted: "He's a damn VC."

There was a slow sense of shock when he said it, and then slowly it dawned on everyone that it was true, that Peck was a Cong, and from then on the complexion of the picture changed sharply, and the loyalty to Peck ended abruptly, the hearts did not beat so fast when the Germans came near, and the beautiful girl, seemingly loyal to Peck, then step by step obviously betraying him, in the movie a fink, now a loyal government agent, drew occasional cheers. From then on they shouted encouragement to the German sentries, and when Peck and others repeatedly slipped by the sentries, Raulston ordered one of the sergeants out of the mess hall where the movie was being shown to check the perimeter and make sure that no Vietcong had slipped past the sentries. When the Sergeant came back and said that one of the Vietnamese sentries had been asleep there was more laughter, which like the game they were now playing with the movie, eased the tension. On the screen the Germans, tipped off on the whereabouts of Peck and the others, were arresting them in the market. There was some cheering, but someone, sensing that it was too early in the movie for Peck to die or disappear, shouted: "Don't take any prisoners." Peck did escape and continued bravely on, putting down the revolt among the civil libertarians in his own group. Steadily they passed obstacle after obstacle, finally entering the guerilla-proof gun batteries and, miracle of miracles, silencing the guns.

"Hell of a good movie," said Lieutenant Anderson, as they walked out.

"Yes," said Captain Beaupre, annoyed to find how little pleasure he had gotten, annoyed to find that Vietnam took the pleasure even out of Gregory Peck killing Germans.

When I was a child, Hollywood kept us warm, covering defeat with a storm of remembrance, feeding a little hope with big tubas, banging drums, waving flags. Victory surprised us, thirty seconds over Tokyo with a shower of bombs. We were children then, but we were not frightened, for the movies made us feel free, and we came to believe that there was a connection between going to the movies and ultimate triumph. Perhaps it was something as simple as those war-relief matinees where we brought canned food as the price of admission, but the war movies seemed to feed us as we, in turn, sustained the world.

They don't make movies like *Sergeant York* any more, and you could starve before the movies inspired by Vietnam could offer sustenance. When Elliot Gould's draft-dodging friend suddenly enlists in *Getting Straight* and announces in all trembling seriousness that he has found religion, that he must purge himself of deceit in order to be *worthy* to serve his country in Vietnam, it is funny in a horrifying way. A lot of things in *Sergeant York* were meant to be funny, but Alvin York's discovery of scriptural revelation (the pages of the Good Book blow in the wind until it lies open at the right verse) on that back-lot mountainside was not funny in 1941 nor did my students laugh in 1973 when I screened it for them.

Seeing *Sergeant York* today, even the generation that lived under the guns of Vietnam are able to overlook the clichéd jingoism and appreciate, perhaps even covet, the world the film reflected or invented. The world of *Sergeant York* is a better world than that of the 1970s, a better world, too, than 1941 (and, I assume, than 1917). From the perspective of Vietnam, World War II seems an exciting time when the nation managed to retain a cheerful confidence in the face of awesome challenges.

To a large extent, this is a view created by the films of the period and now resurrected by a flood of new movies hankering after the apparent certainties of the era. As Andrew Sarris observed recently, World War II had something for everyone: "Hitler and Fascism for the Bolshies, slant-eyed Japs for the racists, a sneak attack on Pearl Harbor for the patriots, gas chambers for the humanitarians, and gifted phrase-makers at the helm in London and Washington." Almost as soon as Vietnam began to seem a lost cause, Hollywood consoled us with nostalgia for the best war of our lives. The Disney people got in the act with *Bedknobs and Broomsticks* (a good witch and cute children chase off German invaders). *Slaughterhouse-Five* turned American guilt and anguish over the devastation of Vietnam into gentle remorse for a doomed German city. The makers of *Patton* found a perfect way to serve two masters—stand George C. Scott in front of the world's biggest American flag and have him snarl that "All Americans love the sting of battle—that's why we've never lost a war" and "No bastard ever won a war by dying for his country—he won it by making some other poor bastard die for his country." Those who hate what Patton stands for saw Scott's portrayal as simply a step beyond his Buck Turgidson, while those who admire Patton probably didn't see *Doctor Strangelove* in the first place. Either way, the film raked in awards, critical acclaim, and money.

Perhaps it is the whole era of that war that attracts us. How much of *The Godfather*'s blockbuster success is related to the period clothes, cars, songs, to the whole ambience of the time, to young Michael Corleone in his Marine uniform, bobby-soxers swooning before a crooner, Michael and his girl coming out of *The Bells of St. Mary's* in December 1945?

Hitler has become a fairy tale figure, an evil but fascinating stepfather to the western world, the Andrews sisters are back, and the homefront is being exploited without shame: *Summer of '42, Class of '44, A Separate Peace, Red Sky at Morning, The Way We Were.** Movies are even getting soppy about the people who were in the war, as though they are a national resource or an endangered species. Observe Harry Stoner in *Save the Tiger,* Jack Lemmon's best role since he won an Oscar as Ensign Pulver. Having survived World War II, Harry finds himself in a far worse, more ambiguous war—and finds too that the old one has been somehow lost or misplaced; that Anzio Beach is covered with bikinis, that the war has gotten stuck inside his head.

"Where were you in '62?" ask the ads for one of the most successful films of 1974. *American Graffiti* draws huge crowds to relive the last year of American innocence—before Dallas and Watergate, before Mylai and Tet. The audience is lulled by crew cuts, Edsels, girls who want to look like Sandra Dee. Then the epilog, bringing us back into the flow of time: "Terry Fields was reported missing in action near An Loc in December 1965."

Where was Hollywood since 1963? When will the looking away end, when will the important movies about Vietnam be made, I asked directors and filmwriters, producers and critics and agents. Stirling Silliphant, who has written two Vietnam scripts, is pessimistic: "I doubt that such a film will ever be made." Some other time, the rest answer. Here are some of their replies:

Arthur Penn: "I don't believe the war in Vietnam can be treated in a 'popular film.' We seem to have no capacity to confront events of that enormity head on. They bubble to the surface a generation later as *M*A*S*H.*"

---

* *The Way We Were* is probably the first film since World War II to show a crack in the façade of national unity over America's entry into the war. "I refuse to support the government of the United States in any war it might conduct," says Barbra Streisand at a campus peace rally in the late thirties. Later, even she will look back fondly to those days and to the time of the war as having been less complicated and will have to be reminded that things were never as simple as she thinks they were.

Paul Schraeder, a scriptwriter and critic: "The war is still too close to most Americans for them to sufficiently detach themselves. . . . One must work in metaphors *for the moment* (i.e., Mexico is Vietnam). Give it another five years, though, maybe less, and films will be set in Vietnam."

Stanford Whitmore, a scriptwriter: "I read the other day where some executives from Kaiser Steel are headed, with other moguls, to Southeast Asia to look into opportunities. . . . A brand new gold mine. In ten years they [the Vietnamese]'ll all be in miniskirts and swigging Cokes and the war will be another Wounded Knee until exhumed a century later. Until then it is just a rotten rumor, and will we all please get this country back on the right track and not criticize the economy or scandals or anything. And as in cummings' letter to Aunt Lucy, meanwhile we lie quietly in the deep mud, dreaming of etcetera."

Warren Bayless, a literary agent: "Motion picture interest in a fiction drama on a war theme is best received some time (years?) after the actual conflict, and the reception by film people and then by audiences is a retrospective look. More often than not, the promoters of such films, by word of mouth, are the audience which were too young, unborn, etc. at the time of the actual event."

Someone who asks to remain anonymous: "When we are in another war so stinking bad this one will start to look good."

And so the answers go. Stanley Kramer writes that he wanted to do a film on Lieutenant Calley, but the time was not right, for legal appeals were pending. Josiah Bunting writes about trying to sell his novel, *The Lionheads,* to Hollywood: "The word I get from them all is 'Definitely—but not yet.' "*

---

* *The Lionheads,* a minor-scale *The Naked and the Dead* written by a Regular Army officer and published while he was teaching history at West Point, seems an ideal source for a Vietnam combat film: easy to shoot (mainly indoors— briefing rooms, a general's office, a troop ship, a barge; a brief action sequence; no expensive helicopters, few Vietnamese characters, and an invisible enemy), a relatively small set of characters, and a politically safe dialectic (the villain is an ambitious general who rises at the cost of his men, but other officers are treated sympathetically; the sacrificial figure is a gentle former altar boy who goes to his death without complaining about the war—the kind of figure both hawks and doves find appealing).

Why have there been so few films about the war in Vietnam? Stanley Kramer writes me that he dropped an earlier Vietnam project (before the one on Calley) "because I never managed to understand why we were there and never was able to draw a bead on the subject." Elia Kazan answers "Because it was insane, disgraceful and immoral. We don't even *think*—how the hell are we going to make a film about it?" Samuel Fuller tried a Vietnam story, but could not find a studio willing to finance anything having to do with Vietnam: "It's ironic that the general reaction was 'It's an unpleasant war' since I have never heard of a pleasant one." Most of the answers are very simple, brief. My sources are busy men concerned with making films, not with why certain films don't get made.

Ernest Callenbach, the editor of *Film Quarterly,* volunteers a fuller explanation:

Alienation, as they say, is when your country is in a war and you hope the other side wins; and there can hardly be an American who did not grasp, by about 1967, that something fishy was going on. . . . Under such circumstances, film-makers have only a couple of alternatives: they can pretend not to notice, like the Waynes; they can 'displace' the material, as the Freudians say, into other periods . . . or they can avoid the subject entirely, which is the easiest of all. My own suspicion is that on some basic, biological, territorial level, it is impossible to make a war film that does not assume that 'our' side is right; this was why Truffaut said that the only anti-war film he could conceive would be one that totally ignores war.

It wasn't that people in the industry* didn't try to make films about Vietnam. The war probably inspired a higher percentage of aborted projects than any other issue confronting Hollywood. As early as 1966, four experienced producers, directors, or writers had tried and failed to bring the war to the screen.

---

*"The film industry is not an industry at all," one of my sources corrected me. "There is little or no organization and it is structured much like the White House, with everybody able to say NO and no one able to say YES." The correction was unnecessary, for I use the term "film industry" and "Hollywood" for convenience only and with full awareness that I am not speaking of a monolith, that the industry's chief representatives can change their minds—that Mark Robson and Gregory Peck could direct, produce, or finance such stern calls to duty as *The Bridges at Toko-Ri* and *Pork Chop Hill* during the Korean War, then make the anti-Vietnam *Limbo* and *The Trial of the Catonsville Nine*— that Dalton Trumbo could write a classic anti-war novel in the thirties, script madly patriotic war films in the forties, and turn his thirties novel into a seventies film, *Johnny Got His Gun.*

The most hawkish project was the one Sy Bartlett wrote in collaboration with the Air Force's Curtis LeMay with whom he shared the view "that it was not *our* war. But since we were in it, he wanted it ended, with the minimum loss of lives, both American as well as enemy." Listen to Bartlett, the producer or writer of such military films as *Pork Chop Hill, Twelve O'Clock High,* and *A Gathering of Eagles,* explain his scheme and why he gave it up:

General LeMay and I had the fullest cooperation on a completed story about Vietnam. Surprisingly enough, it dealt with an approach to end the war in Vietnam by kidnapping the Chinese General who called all the shots for Ho Chi Minh. It propounded the theory that this would end further bombing and bring an abrupt end to the bloodshed.

General LeMay and I made the decision that audiences would *not* leave the comfort of their homes and [undergo] the concomitant problems of going to a theater to be entertained by any feature length film that dealt with Vietnam. The public were exhausted by news reels and other coverage showing the grimness of this filthy war, with our youth slogging through the jungle, which was becoming unbearable for an American to watch.

You must understand that General LeMay, however dedicated a man he is, in his professional and personal life, is a very compassionate human being.

The last sentence in the quote seems double-edged: LeMay is compassionate in wanting to end the war speedily; he is also tenderhearted about dragging exhausted moviegoers out of their safe homes.

The same year, 1966, Stanley Kramer took his first look at Vietnam. As with the Bartlett–LeMay project, this one also involved a covert mission that would save American lives. The film was to be based on Irwin Blacker's novel, *Search and Destroy,* an account of a five-man guerrilla team parachuted into North Vietnam to destroy a bridge, a tunnel, a dam, an oil depot, and an airfield (all conveniently located within a short walk of one another) in order to stop a conventional mass invasion of South Vietnam. "I had dreams of telling the fears and inhibitions and reluctances and hate via the five members of the mission," Kramer wrote me. "That wasn't [Blacker's] novel and we became mired in cliché."

Samuel Fuller, the first man to make a film about the war in Korea and one of the first to treat Vietnam during the French colonial period, began to send around *The Rifle:* "Although it was written more than six years ago," he informed me in 1973, "it has all the ingredients of that flavor of war right up to the end—including a Calley flavor." The main character was to be "a symbol of war through generations—who ends up killing a Viet Cong boy—a boy he fell in love with—a boy he wanted to adopt and take back to the States—because the Army . . . commanded him to murder the civilian boy only because the boy represented the enemy."

Stirling Silliphant, who has a knack for seeing things from an odd point of view (as in *The Poseidon Adventure*), came up with *Groundswell,* which involved the invasion of a winter-locked Long Island village by a Vietcong squad put ashore from a Chinese submarine—they had entered the country to take part in the war-crimes trial, by radical students, of the Chief of Staff of the United States Army. "The studios simply rejected the material out of hand—the fastest rejection ever achieved by any piece of material in Hollywood, I'm convinced." And Silliphant was no amateur: he went in with the "top auspices," including Ted Ashley, then head of Ashley-Famous, now head of Warner Brothers, as his agent.

The years fled by, and the studios bought options on literary properties and then dropped them. At one point, anti-Vietnam books were hot. Some said Donald Duncan's *The New Legions* would be filmed. Warner Brothers picked up Daniel Lang's *Casualties of War,* but nothing happened.* John Milius, who later gained fame with the scripts for *Judge Roy Bean, Dillinger,* and *Magnum Force* turned Conrad's *Heart of Darkness* into a script about Green Berets heading up-river in search of a renegade American colonel named Kurtz. *Apocalypse Now!* was the title. Later! was the response.†

SAIGON FINDS FUN IN FILM AND SONG

People Turn to Sentimental and Escapist Fare

Saigon: . . . When their leaders, their finances and the Vietcong permit, the Saigonese still do their best to have a good time in their tense city.

Casualties of War may have been the starting point for Elia Kazan's independent film, *The Visitors* (see Chapter Five).
†Just as this book went to press, it was announced that Francis Ford Coppola was planning to produce *Apocalypse Now,* "which John Milius . . . will direct from his own script. 'It's best described as a macabre comedy set in the midst of the Vietnam war,' Mr. Coppola explained, 'that we feel is very pertinent now' " (*New York Times,* 7 July 1974).

Music and motion pictures . . . reflect these days the escapism and sentimentality that stand out in the Vietnamese national character. . . . Serious drama, whatever its national origin, is unpopular. The Vietnamese prefer American Westerns and Chinese films of chivalry and adventure.

—Jack Langguth, *New York Times,* 19 August 1965

Saigon: . . . Movie theaters reopened here today for the first time since the Vietcong offensive against the cities started 49 days ago.

—*New York Times,* 20 March 1968

Saigon: . . . The South Vietnamese Government has banned the American movie *From Here to Eternity* for "reasons of national defense," it was announced today.

The film . . . has been seen at regular intervals in Saigon for 15 years.

A story of barracks life and romantic entanglements in Hawaii at the time of the Japanese attack on Pearl Harbor, the film is a favorite with Vietnamese movie-goers, both because of its anti-military and sentimental themes.

—*New York Times,* 16 November 1969

"Did many South Vietnamese directors make films about the war?"

"No, not many."

"How many?"

"Very few. Very dangerous to go into the country. When I make my film, I have threats from the Communists."

Vinh Noan made his film, *We Want to Live,* back in the 1950s. Starring his wife, Mai Tram, it depicts refugees fleeing the North after the partition of Vietnam. Production associate on Joseph L. Mankiewicz's *The Quiet American* when it was shot in Saigon in 1957, Vinh Noan later became Director of the Motion Picture Center of the Republic of Vietnam's Ministry of Information. As such, he was in charge of the development of the commercial film industry and the production of government films between August 1965 and January 1967.

In 1967 he came to this country and tried to interest studios in making a film about the war as seen from the point of view of villagers who must choose between turning a group of helpless Americans (including a blond newswoman) over to the Vietcong or fighting to save them.* It was a rather novel approach, suggesting *Americans* needed the South Vietnamese. There were no takers.

---

*Vinh Noan's "treatment" will be found in Appendix I.

Today, Vinh Noan lives in Arlington, Virginia, just a few blocks from the main gate of Fort Myer and the approaches to the Pentagon. On the walls of his small apartment are his own paintings: a Vietnamese girl with mountains in the background; cherry blossoms framing the Washington Monument. There is a huge television, a hi-fi, a large collection of records; on the piano are Greek vases, jade figures, a statue depicting Botticelli's Venus, Japanese dolls, a photograph of his son, who comes in and out with a toy gun.

While his wife serves coffee, he shows me his scrapbooks—there are photographs of him standing with Audie Murphy, with Glenn Ford. His years as motion picture chief in Saigon were those when the American war was expanding almost daily. Through his office came American cameramen who wanted papers for entering the war zone. If any American producers or directors wanted to make films in his country, they would have come to him. None came, he says.*

Walking down a corridor in the Pentagon, I pass an office door to which someone has taped a yellowing full page ad from the *New York Times.* The ad appeared in the issue for 16 June 1969 and is signed by Darryl F. Zanuck. In the interest of bringing you the best in American Graffiti, I print it in full:

WHY
TORA! TORA! TORA!?

Tora! Tora! Tora! is an American-Japanese historical film officially approved by the American Department of Defense as well as the Japanese Department of Defense. It is an authentic film. The basic reason for producing the film, which is the second most expensive film in history, was to arouse the American public to the necessity for preparedness in this acute missile age where a sneak attack could occur at any moment. You cannot arouse the public by showing films where Americans always win and where we are invincible. You can only remind the public by revealing to them how we once thought we were invincible but suffered a sneak attack in which practically half our fleet was lost.

Our film does not attempt to whitewash anyone in the American government or armed forces and this includes President Roosevelt. At the time of Pearl Harbor, America was fundamentally isolationist,

---

*He may have forgotten (or never known of) *Run With the Devil,* a film made in South Vietnam in 1966 (see Chapter Four).

especially in the West and Midwest. Peace parades were common-place in practically every city. However, after the blow at Pearl Harbor, overnight we became a united nation willing and ready to retaliate; but because of the lack of mental and physical preparedness, it was more than two years before we avenged Pearl Harbor.

This is the lesson of *Tora! Tora! Tora!* and the reason for this production. This is not merely a movie but an accurate and dramatic slice of history that should never have occurred but did occur, and the purpose of producing this film is to remind the public of the tragedy that happened to us and to ensure that it will never happen again.

Donald E. Baruch's office is on the ground floor of the Pentagon. He doesn't have a window, but the walls of his spacious cubicle provide their own vistas. There's John Wayne, that's Frank Sinatra. Jack Warner has a sincere smile for all and sundry. There are group photographs of Mr. B., as the staff calls him, with generals, with politicians, with movie people. There is a faded poster from the Festival International du Film Militaire at Versailles. There is an editorial page cartoon sniping at government assistance to commercial film projects and one from the *New Yorker:* a beer-bellied man in an undershirt speaking into a telephone: "You must want the other Baruch."

When he is called away from his desk, I have time to look around the room. On a shelf near my chair are Jack Warner's *My First Hundred Years in Hollywood,* David O. Selznick's *Memo,* and a few novels. On the wall opposite are six autographed photos grouped together: Tony Curtis, Brian Keith, Ernest Borgnine, Ivan Dixon, Don Ameche, and Suzanne Pleshette. What have they in common? Suddenly I realize they were all in *Suppose They Gave a War and Nobody Came.* Later I recollect that I didn't see Tom Ewell and Arthur O'Connell, the actors who played the right-wing characters in that film, in the group—perhaps I am mistaken. I make a note to ask Mr. Baruch about that remarkable little service comedy that ripped off an anti-war slogan and turned it into a film in which the army comes off looking downright pacifist in contrast to civilian militarists. But I forget to ask.

As chief of the Department of Defense's Motion Picture Production Branch, Donald Baruch has been dealing with Hollywood since his office's inception in 1949. He has seen the love affair between two of the most important institutions in the land grow cold, turn bitter. When Baruch first began collecting his mementoes, major producers and studios avoided doing anything in a film—even one made without Department of Defense assistance—that would offend the military and endanger future aid, aid that could spell the difference between financial success and disaster. Those were the days when the military was still in almost universal good graces, when the Strategic Air Command was happy to open its bases and cockpits to camera crews, when marching bands performed at premieres of service films, when patriotism was marketable.

The terrors of the House Un-American Activities Committee hearings were still alive in those days. Writers and directors who had not been willing to discuss whether or not they were tough on communism had gone to jail. There were blacklists in the land. "So you got a new kinda bomber, you say General? You wanta tell the public all about it?" "Why sure." Perhaps it was fear of HUAC and Joe McCarthy, perhaps it was only the hysteria of the time, but in those years producers, directors, writers, and actors rushed to show which side they were on—only one cold war film had been released in 1947–1948, when the HUAC hearings began—then half a dozen in 1949, as many in 1950, a dozen in 1951, even more in 1952 (and I'm not counting the Korean War films, which put anti-communism on a firmer basis, cinematically).

But times change. The split between Hollywood and the Pentagon was evident early in the sixties. The unfavorable publicity and the congressional rancor that followed revelations that *The Longest Day* (1961) had used active duty troops in reenacting the Normandy Invasion had caused a tightening of controls at a crucial stage in the economic history of the American film: at a time when "our" film was becoming increasingly part of an international industry, with talents, money, and ideas flowing freely across borders, when it was becoming increasingly dependent on foreign audiences hostile to celebrations of American military might; when it was becoming less afraid of governmental control (simply because things couldn't be worse).

At just that point, the Pentagon began to dole out less gravy.* But in limiting the support it would give in terms of men,

---

*Hollywood's appetite for government assistance, however, remained healthy: in 1964, when Melville Shavelson wrote the treatment for *Cast a Giant Shadow*, the true story of Mickey Marcus, a West Pointer who died in the first Arab-

equipment, shooting locations, and technical advice, the Pentagon also limited the all-important control over scripts, the ability to stick in messages, to balance things.

Baruch tells me with nostalgic pride of some of the "plants" he was able to negotiate back in the fifties. In both *From Here to Eternity* and *The Young Lions,* Montgomery Clift was cruelly harassed. It was the Motion Picture Production Branch's duty to see that audiences were reassured that this harassment would not go unnoticed and unpunished by higher authority (as it had in the novel by James Jones, for instance). Almost overnight, at the same time Vietnam was getting out of hand, so were filmmakers. After such iconoclastic films as *Doctor Strangelove, Fail Safe,* and *Seven Days in May* (all released in 1964) depicted the military or its technology out of control, it was hard for the Pentagon to trust Hollywood again ("They have known my father for many years," Michael Wayne would say later in explaining why John Wayne got such speedy and elaborate assistance in making *The Green Berets*). Baruch is particularly bitter about *Seven Days in May*— not so much because the film depicted a military plot to overthrow a dovish President, but because one of John Frankenheimer's camera crews talked its way aboard a United States carrier to shoot exteriors for the scene in which Martin Balsam calls on an admiral involved in the plot. Military men are honorable men. They never do things they are not supposed to do, go places forbidden them, or tell lies.

Wanting to keep things friendly, I decide not to ask Baruch about Robin Moore's claim during a Mike Wallace interview that "the Pentagon threatened Wolper [the producer of a projected film based on Moore's *The Green Berets*] with reprisals which he could not live with if he went ahead and made it" (this was before John Wayne donned the Green Beret). Instead, I put the question in the most general terms: has the Pentagon in any way blocked films about the war in Vietnam? Baruch, an angelic man with a nimbus of white hair, assures me most candidly that DOD would have gladly assisted any producer who came forward with a suitable project.

Israeli war, he stressed that the friends Marcus had made at the Point "are still the friends of his memory today, right up to the Chief of Staff of the United States Army, General Maxwell D. Taylor." This name-dropping, Shavelson explained later, was "intended to provoke visions of endless free tanks, free heavy bombers, free aircraft carriers. Where to put them in a story about Israel was another question."

The catch, of course, is in the definition of "suitable." "Suitable" means in the best interests of the Armed Forces and the nation, and the Department of Defense would be the final judge of what did or did not serve those interests.*

Films critical of the conduct of the war would not have been suitable. What about films that showed both sides, I ask—would DOD have supported them? Yes, Baruch answers, as long as the military's position was shown fairly. What do you mean by fair, I ask—would your office support a film that showed the suffering on the ground in Hanoi as against the military necessity for bombing North Vietnam? It depends on how philosophical you get, Baruch shrugs, implying that philosophy might be a bad thing (he also used the word "philosophical" another time, when asked about DOD's willingness to assist a film on the bombing of Hiroshima).

I ask him if he can name a novel he thinks would make a good film from his office's point of view. Yes, James Gould Cozzens' *Guard of Honor.* I must look startled at the introduction of the 1948 novel, for he tells me that everything works out well in the end. No, I explain, I meant novels about *Vietnam.* He nods, goes back to *Guard of Honor,* tells me he's asked producers again and again why it doesn't get filmed. It's a good sound story and it has a happy ending.

The bombing of North Vietnam was controversial, I persist. Would DOD have given assistance on such a topic? Certainly, Baruch assures me, in the friendliest manner. Did Mark Robson come to you with such a project? No, Baruch answers, suddenly abrupt, his face closing down.† Did anyone try? Yes, one

---

*See Appendices II and III for DOD guidelines for support to commercial filmmakers and for a list of films receiving government assistance. It was clearly in the Pentagon's interest to encourage fictional films about the war, for such films can be controlled through the script—not until the script passes DOD inspection can a project get approval. As one producer wrote me, "News cameramen [who cannot be held to a script] simply do not get invited up in high-performance Navy jets. Our cameramen have been in them."

†True, Mark Robson did not come to Baruch, but Linda Gottlieb, who co-authored and produced Robson's *Limbo,* told me that the film's backers tried to get Department of Defense cooperation. *Limbo* deals with the wives of American airmen missing or captured in raids over North Vietnam. After the script was re-written to satisfy the Pentagon, assistance was denied on the grounds that the film, which depicts wives opposed to the war, would be shown to POW's by their captors and used as a propaganda weapon. The Pentagon, objecting also to the fact one of the wives is shown having an affair, claimed its own statistics showed less than one percent of the wives of MIA's or POW's were unfaithful. During the filming, the makers of *Limbo* were unable to obtain even technical information from the air force, and Mrs. Gottlieb sus-

producer did have Pentagon backing for a film about carrier pilots bombing North Vietnam from the U.S.S. *Enterprise.* It would have been a good story, Baruch says, but nothing ever happened.*

With the possible exception of *The Losers,* a motorcycle-gang exploitation picture, every American fiction film set in Vietnam has supported our involvement. None of these films oppose the war. There is, frankly, no evidence that this one-sided stand is a result of direct military pressure. External censorship was probably unnecessary, for a far more vicious form of proscription exists within the film industry itself—the "pre-censorship" that Murray Schumach calls "the infantile paralysis of Hollywood." Though Schumach described this process in *The Face on the Cutting Room Floor* a decade ago without mentioning Vietnam, his book is a primer for anyone who would understand the myriad pressures and neuroses that afflict the making of any film.

The basic cause of this pre-censorship is fairly obvious: a general disinclination to get involved in a brouhaha unless a significant opportunity for profit is involved. After all, the government is not weak, and the motion picture industry is a business subject, like any other, to controls, hassles, delays. William J. Lederer wrote me that Hollywood bidding on *Sarkhan,* the

---

pected that sudden difficulties during production—corporations that had agreed to cooperate on the filming by supplying locations or services reneging at the last minute, for instance—were a result of Department of Defense pressure.

*Though Baruch would not identify the producer who had gained assistance for the carrier pilot film or any other Vietnam project that did not reach the screen ("We are unable to provide you with their identification as a matter of courtesy as well as protecting the rights of the producer," he had written me earlier), I eventually traced the idea to Will Zens of Riviera Productions. Zens's story was one I heard from other producers, writers, and agents:

We are still working on attempting to finance the film about pilots flying off the USS *Enterprise.* . . .
Our working title was *Yankee Station,* but we also had other titles ready, such as one appealing to the women: *I'm in Your Arms Again.* . . .
Not one major distributor was interested in the project. It was as if they had all gotten together and come up with the identical answers: This is a television war, therefore no one will go to the theaters to see a film about it; or, since the audience in theaters is comprised of 75% who are under the age of 25 years and since this is the group who is totally against the war, no one will come to see the film; etc ad infinitum. *Of course, there have been no films released that can prove or disprove those statements* [my emphasis].

novel he co-authored with Eugene Burdick, "stopped abruptly when Washington hinted that if this novel were made into a motion picture, the industry might find it difficult to obtain export licenses." (*Sarkhan*, like Lederer and Burdick's *The Ugly American*, is set in a mythical Southeast Asian country that closely resembles Vietnam.) Veterans groups do make noises, and independent exhibitors who show films deemed unpatriotic by the Department of Defense do have to go on living in Dubuque.

Abroad, the situation is even more treacherous—a foreign government sympathetic to the vibrations coming from the local American Embassy might just ban an anti-Vietnam film, while a pro-Vietnam movie will only rile up the local students and make everyone else nervous.

So it all comes back to box-office, to money. Better to make a mediocre film that just might catch on or slip by than one doomed to the wrong kind of notoriety from the start. A merely stupid film can be sold to television. Hollywood can't take sides, Mel Shavelson says, because if it does it can't sell tickets to the other side. But, you say, *The Green Berets* took sides, supported the war, and made a fast profit. Yes, but it had John Wayne and was an oddity.

Others would probably argue that with the economy in lousy shape, partly because of Vietnam, films about the war were a doubly risky proposition because you must either go on location (and just try to insure a cast of big names in Vietnam) or pretend Vietnam looks like Southern California or Georgia. And faking it is not only expensive, but just doesn't work in the age of television.

Television. As it has for so many other Hollywood ills, television and its saturation coverage of the war gets the blame for the movie industry's relative silence on the war. *The Ugly American*, made during Kennedy's administration, had ended with a television viewer switching off a news program about troubles in Southeast Asia, but the public ignored the stereotype of itself and let the news run. It was Hollywood that switched off the war.

In Alain Resnais's section of *Far from Vietnam*, a character speaks of Vietnam as "the first war everyone can see, and yet do nothing about." This feeling of impotence, together with television's ability to present daily slices of a war in which the landscape, climate, and enemy never changed though the years sped by, made it difficult to give movie audiences the nicely shaped war drama of past years, the kind of film in which a single operation was an integral part of a discernible overall picture: if we can just capture *this* town, get gas to *those* tanks, make *that* plane go faster or the other rifle more accurate ... Earlier wars, with their clearly marked goals, seemed finite. But Vietnam and television changed all that.

Those who call Vietnam television's war, however, are speaking only of the factual coverage—of the evening news, the documentary specials, the debates and presidential addresses. Once we enter the realm of fiction a different story emerges. Again, as with the recent controversy over the television premiere of *Sticks and Bones,* there seems a failure of imagination, a failure of courage. To the best of my knowledge, the one attempt to round off the war in old-fashioned dramatic terms for television viewers was CBS's *The Final War of Olly Winter* back in 1967: Ivan Dixon played a professional soldier, a black veteran of World War II, Korea and the ghettoes who vows Vietnam will be his last war. It is. He is killed. Death is the only boundary, the only end in sight.*

Vietnam's disorienting effect on our society, the indeterminate nature of that war we couldn't seem to win or abandon, was reflected in our filmmakers' inability to find an appropriate format for presenting the war to a mass audience. Consider the difference between Vietnam and our past foreign wars, and you'll begin to see why it was and is hard to present in the fiction film. Before Vietnam, we always supported a recognizable ally against a clearly discernible enemy: the French and English against the Germans, for instance, or the Chinese against the Japanese. But in Vietnam there is no language or hereditary cultural difference between friend and foe. Fascism had been a hateful doctrine, but communism could be accommodated.

How Hollywood tells a war story, however, is conditioned by

---

*I have not made a formal study of the extent to which Vietnam was the subject of television drama—a casual poll of regular viewers turned up only one other title, *Some May Live* (1967), an espionage melodrama set in Saigon. Not only did networks and producers specifically avoid Vietnam, they also skirted issues that might conceivably apply to that war. A writer tells me of a script he did for *The Virginian* back in 1967 in which a Royal Canadian Mounted Policeman "deserted to help the Indians fight the rape of their land. No, said NBC. There is a desertion problem in Vietnam."

past films based on past wars. The war film is a very rigid and distinct genre, almost as formal as the Western. What is a war film? The obvious answer is "any film that deals with war." What, then, is a Western? Not any film that deals with the "West," but with certain activities in the American West during a fairly limited period of time. The war film would seem to lack such formal boundaries, but a survey of the successful and influential films of the last quarter century suggests that the war film is properly limited to "modern" war—specifically World War II—with its potential for mobility and mass killing.

Central to the war film is respect for action, for the machines and techniques of war. But Vietnam has made any action mere busy-work and turned the mechanics of war into monstrosities. Likewise, the moral justifications of a "good" war are missing. In countless World War II films, the enemy was shown destroying civilians and setting up puppet governments—now *we* were doing it ("Watching the Americans behave like the bad guys in Hollywood war movies," said Pauline Kael, "has undoubtedly helped turn the country against the war"). In countless earlier films, we first aided struggling nations, then were aided by native undergrounds—now we were interdicting aid to a struggling nation and fighting an underground. For lack of a formula, a way to "handle" the war, Hollywood turned elsewhere.

A few years ago I saw a television movie that made me think the complexities of Vietnam were forcing a re-examination of earlier war film clichés. But *Fireball Forward,* set in France after D-day and dealing with an American unit which seems to have a traitor in it, quickly developed its own chauvinistic bromides: suspicion falls on a series of Americans, but the real villain turns out to be a member of the French resistance whose wife is being held by the Germans. You can never trust the locals, you see; better by far to shoot them all at the outset.

Let those who doubt *Fireball Forward* has been shaped by Vietnam note that the division commander has a minority group aide-de-camp, one Captain Sanchez, who receives pacifist letters from his sister, causing the general to rip off lines like "you have to be a nut to *like* to kill." It's a wonderful story. Nobody likes killing, you see, but what choice do we have, so on with the violence. And the Americans, all drawn from diverse backgrounds and places of national origin, turn out to be united after all.

Other films ostensibly about World War II made positive

statements about American purpose and cohesiveness, statements seemingly unnecessary a quarter of a century after the
war in question. But where *Sergeant York* was obviously meant
to move an undecided nation toward commitment by looking
back to a period then considered safe, these films, few in number and weak in effect, kept a far lower profile.

For instance, when public resistance to the war in Vietnam
began to get out of hand in the mid-sixties, Warner Brothers
released *First to Fight,* a film about a Marine Corps hero who
wins the Medal of Honor on Guadalcanal, comes back to the
States for a war-bond tour, falls in love, gets married, and settles down to lead a "normal" life. Meanwhile, the war has been
going on in the Pacific, and the hero, beginning to fear he has
become a slacker, goes back to combat. After a brief period of
terror and a failure of the will to fight, he finds himself again
and leads his men into battle with new dedication.

If *First to Fight* was not intended as a metaphor for an entire
nation that had performed bravely in one conflict and was now
being aroused from sluggish normalcy for a new call to duty,
it certainly seemed that way to some critics. "There is every
good reason," wrote the *New York Times* reviewer, "why Warn-
ers, at a time when World War II seems remote and Vietnam
so very real, should have packaged a patriotic reminder of the
past. As a matter of fact, the picture is exactly the kind the
studios rolled out after Pearl Harbor."

Not only does *First to Fight* use a particularly old-fashioned
movie stereotype of war heroism in the year (1967) that *The
Dirty Dozen* was breaking new ground for anti-heroism,* but
it nostalgically compounds the cliché by evoking the magic of
another Warner Brothers film, *Casablanca.* The Marine hero
and his new bride go to see Humphrey Bogart sunk in his own
temporary selfishness, but rising to the occasion in time to commit himself to the universal struggle to save the resistance
leader and rouse the audience with "If it's December 1941 in
Casablanca, what time is it in New York? . . . I bet they're asleep

---

*Other filmmakers tried to recycle World War II to attack the mentality that
produced Vietnam. In *Castle Keep* (based on a novel by William Eastlake, who
also wrote a major novel about Vietnam, *The Bamboo Bed*) the central intellectual or moral conflict is whether or not an American unit, led by a one-eyed
general on a white horse, should hold a castle full of art treasures against the
Germans, thus forcing them to destroy it, or surrender it intact. Though the first
part of the film excoriates heroic posturing, the film eventually stops asking
questions and gives the audience what it probably wants—the violent destruction of the castle, its defenders and attackers. Vietnam is like that castle.

in New York. I bet they're asleep all over America"—and to command Sam to play it again, to play "As Time Goes By." Later, back in combat, the hero of *First to Fight* will be restored to himself by this tune played on a harmonica.

In the past few years, movie people have been raiding history for analogies with Vietnam. Understandably, they feel they must say something about it in their movies, but who knows what to say anymore? . . . the attempted historical parallels are never really parallel, and so the meanings are befuddled.
—Pauline Kael, *Deeper into Movies*

Vietnam went underground in the movies, tunneling into our subconscious, a true phantom of Hollywood, surfacing in strange places, taking off its mask only briefly. After I published a preliminary survey of films treating Vietnam, several people wrote to tell me I had missed *The Sand Pebbles.* That 1966 film had burrowed into their minds and left the impression it was set in contemporary Vietnam rather than China in the 1920s. Critical of our gunboat diplomacy (Candice Bergen asks Steve McQueen how he would feel about Chinese gunboats patrolling the Mississippi) but ending upon a regenerating shootout with the troublemaking natives, *The Sand Pebbles* had examined the uncomfortable position of Americans who find themselves involved in the civil affairs of a people whose language, culture, and aspirations they do not know (nor do they know that they should want to know).

Some reviewers immediately saw the connection. "Richard Crenna [as the *San Pablo*'s skipper] gives a reasonable approximation of what General Westmoreland might have been like in the '20's," wrote Andrew Sarris. Bosley Crowther called the film "metaphorically aligned with our current dilemma in the Far East":

In the ire and resentment of his crewmen as they have to take on the task of fetching American citizens out of the bristling hinterland, we feel the tightening muscles and the quivering nerves of American men in Vietnam. And in the open suspicion and frank withdrawal of [Steve McQueen], we catch the current vibrations of antagonism towards our present jam.

The Sand Pebbles is an obvious example of a film shaped by the war—if not consciously through the skills of the artists who made it, then through the attitudes brought to it by the audience as Vietnam impinged on the national conscience. Other films were similarly affected. Not just military stories, but Westerns, police dramas, and a broad range of films about individuals in conflict with American society itself.

First, a sampling of films that, in their popularity with the young audiences who were most closely touched by the war, seem to reflect changing perceptions of America. I apologize for not putting them into neat categories, but they are best seen as the scraps of a crazy quilt, as heaps of broken images.

The biggest, most obvious patch in the quilt is *The French Connection,* about the war on narcotics that Andrew Sarris, reviewing the film, called "our domestic version of Vietnam, and our continuing proof that we learned nothing as a nation and as a people from the moral disaster of prohibition." Robin Moore, best known as the author of *The Green Berets* and most recently for two other Vietnam novels, *Court Martial* and *The Khaki Mafia,* opened the book on which the film is based with the claim that "The account that follows is a case history of what must qualify as one of the finest police investigations in the annals of United States law enforcement" and "the most crucial single *victory* to date in the ceaseless, frustrating *war* against the import of vicious narcotics into our country." Substitute "army" for "police" and "communist subversion" for "narcotics," and you are right back in Vietnam. Other cheap ironies abound: the executive producer for the film, G. David Schine, is none other than Joe McCarthy's old aide, and the French Connection himself is a cold-blooded representative of that nation which left us holding the bag in Indochina and would now leave us holding other bags of the nickel and dime variety.

As in *The Green Berets,* in which the murder of a little girl militarizes the pacifist reporter with whom doves in the audience are meant to identify, violence on "our" side is justified in *The French Connection* by the death of innocent civilians. Thus, when Frog One's henchman snipes at Popeye and hits a young mother pushing a baby-buggy, of *course* Popeye is justified in endangering other civilians in that car-train chase. And of course the bad guy escalates the violence, causing more innocents to die. In New York as in Vietnam, in the war on narcotics as in the war on communism, we are going to save you even if we have to kill you in the process.

Here is *Joe,* ending with the massacre of a commune and propelling its unlikely hero into the pantheon of beloved American grotesques, a film that commented on the temptation to exterminate those who threaten us or don't wish to live the way we do (which is threatening enough). Over there is *M*A*S*H,* not so much about Korea (*or* Vietnam) as about their common denominator, what the man who wrote the film, Ring Lardner, Jr., called "a special kind of war, an American one on the Asian mainland, and our habit of taking our culture along with us and ignoring the local variety." And here comes *Downhill Racer:* the American (Robert Redford) finally wins the international championship and with it the knowledge that he will probably lose it next time around to the younger German competitor who bettered his time at each mark but fell before finishing the course.

A British critic, writing in 1953: "The stubborn and successful American resistance in the murderous Battle of the Bulge and in the Korean encirclement were partly the end result of a conviction nourished by cowboy films, that the good hero always wins if he holds out long enough."
                    —Jacobson, "Cowboy, Pioneer and American Soldier"

Two Swedish critics: "The Western, too, has often proved itself particularly well able to symbolize current nationalism on an allegorical level. Strong, silent, lonely men ride in from the prairie, conquer their aversion to the use of weapons and, without profit to themselves, defend freedom-loving farmers against gangs bent on grabbing land and power—this national myth fitted the United States to perfection when the Truman doctrine against communist expansion was proclaimed. . . . Some years later . . . the Western plot offers the perfect filter through which to look at the Vietnam war."
                    —Furhammar and Isaksson, *Politics and Film*

Pentagon blurb on *Shotgun Rider,* a segment in the Army's *Big Picture* series: "The shotgun rider, protecting the stagecoach, blasted a colorful trail through the pages of American history. Today, he still plays a colorful role, for the war in Vietnam has put the shotgun rider back in business. Not aboard a stagecoach, but in a helicopter. His weapon is no longer a shotgun, but a machine gun. His mission, however, is the same—to protect the interests of a free people as he stretches from his helicopter firing at enemy targets."
                    —Quoted by Shearer in "The Brass Image"

Pauline Kael on *Little Big Man:* "The picture is about genocide—about the Indians and about Vietnam . . . the massacres of the helpless Indians on the screen are, of course, like the massacres of Vietnamese villagers."
                    —*Deeper into Movies*

A campaign worker for James L. Buckley, explaining why he thinks

Chisum is an allegory for the war in Vietnam: "Both sides were wrong and John Wayne came in as the third force."

—*New York Times*

That night at Nam Luong the Americans showed an epic western for the Vietnamese strike force, projecting it against the side of a white-washed building. It was a Cinemascope production, but the camp's 16-mm. movie projector was not equipped with a Cinemascope lens so the cowboys, Indians and horses all were long and thin. However, the strikers loved the action and identified themselves with it. When the Indians appeared the strikers screamed "VC," and when the soldiers or cowboys came to the rescue the Nam Luong irregulars vied with each other in shouting out the number of their own strike-force companies.

—Robin Moore, *The Green Berets*

William Calley to John Sack: "We were just playing games here, and we were being laughed at. Cowboys, the Vietnamese called us."

—*Lieutenant Calley: His Own Story*

A news item informs me that exiled Vietnamese have found employment in France as Indians in Spaghetti Westerns. A Vietnamese acquaintance tells me that General Ky and other gung-ho types are referred to by their countrymen as "cowboys" because they ostentatiously pack firearms on their hips, a custom most un-Asian. The Saigonese, according to the *New York Times,* like Westerns. I imagine they liked *A Yank in Vietnam,* which employs the standard Western chase, complete with the air cavalry arriving just in time to save the good guys from the VC redskins.

I wonder, however, what moviegoers in Saigon make of some recent changes in the Western. Quite abruptly the old gaiety of the Western began to evaporate. *Butch Cassidy and the Sundance Kid* opens with the endearing optimism of the genre. Listen to our heroes in the brothel scene:

Madame: "I'm losing my piano player—he's enlisted to go fight the war."
Sundance: "What war is that?"
Madame: "What war? *The* war. Against the Spanish."
Butch: "Remember the *Maine.*"
Sundance: "I could never forget it."

Butch: "Hey—let's enlist and go fight the Spanish—you and me in the war—listen, we got a lot going for us: experience, maturity, leadership. Hell, I bet we'd end up officers."

But they go to a losing war, end up down in Bolivia surrounded by hundreds of brown-skinned militia, out-numbered, out-gunned. They make one last dash, certain that other gay adventures lie ahead. The image freezes on that final mythic posture of defiance, looks away from their annihilation, but on the soundtrack we hear the truth—volley after volley of massed gunfire.

Quite abruptly, too, the enthusiastic celluloid sacrifice of Indians ended and Hollywood entered a period when, as in *Little Big Man,* the Indian wars were presented as something shameful and Custer a mad fool. That our mistakes in Vietnam helped cause this reassessment is clear in *Soldier Blue* (1970). Candice Bergen lectures Blue: "Brave lads, coming out here to kill themselves a real live Indian . . . putting up their forts in a country they got no claim to. What the hell do you expect the Indians to do? Sit on their butts?" By the end of the movie she has won over Soldier Blue, and after the slaughter of a tribe's women and children in a sequence consciously intended by the director to evoke Mylai, we see him in chains for criticizing the leader of the massacre.

The classic settler–Indian conflict of so many Westerns provides a natural metaphor for the war in Vietnam. Early proponents of our Vietnam policy in the State Department, the Pentagon, and (once upon a time) the press used the same techniques for justifying our action there as the Puritans and other colonials did for exterminating the Indian: the red enemy is a godless heathen (that is, not Christian) who attacks undefended communities, burning, raping, pillaging, disrupting family life and simple agricultural pursuits. As late as 1965, Sam Peckinpah was able to pit whites against Indians in *Major Dundee* in order to unite old Civil War enemies in a common cause ("Fall in behind the Major! Fall in against the losers! Fall in behind the Major! And we'll all get home again" goes the title song). But that kind of movie can't be made anymore. Instead we get blacks and Indians against whites in *Buck and the Preacher* or bloodthirsty Apaches presented sympathetically in Robert Aldrich's recent *Ulzana's Raid.*

Whom do you kill when you can't kill Indians? Where do you go when you can't go to Vietnam? Sam Peckinpah seems to have found two cinematically viable answers. In *The Wild Bunch,* he sends the good guys (first seen disguised as American soldiers) down to Mexico and has them die destroying a nasty Mexican general and his army. The general is named

Mapache (rhymes with Apache), oppresses innocent villagers, gratuitously cuts the throat of a nice guy named Angel, and has a *German* military adviser. And in *Straw Dogs,* Peckinpah transplants the Vietnamese Western lock, stock, and gunbarrel to England where he has a bookish American professor (Dustin Hoffman) protect his "homestead" against five local marauders who cavort about in the dark like so many drunken savages.

That *Straw Dogs* is covertly concerned with Vietnam and is a closet Western are both suggested by Peckinpah's source, Gordon Williams's *The Siege of Trencher's Farm.* The novel opens with the puzzling and contradictory words, "In the same year that Man first flew to the Moon and the last American soldier left Vietnam. . . ."* The central character is an American college professor, an inveterate Western buff who feels that "given the choice, wouldn't any man prefer to know he could defend his land and log cabin against Shawnee war parties?" At crucial moments, he remembers bits and pieces of old Westerns— of women helping their men fight off Indians, of how to act when a man has a gun on you ("Don't watch his face, watch his finger").

The film drops the novel's overt allusions to Vietnam and the Western, transforms the American from a mere professor of English studying an obscure eighteenth-century diarist into an unwilling representative of American power, an "astro-mathematician" who has used a government grant to escape his responsibilities in America. His wife accuses him of hiding from America in England, of having left the States because he did not want to take a stand or commit himself. In the novel, the marauders are a fairly generalized collection of English louts, but Peckinpah turns them into rapists and neo-Fascists. One even wears four pieces of Nazi insignia on his work clothes and shows up for the siege adorned with a fake toothbrush moustache—given such an enemy, what red-blooded American liberal could fail to employ whatever violence was called for?

In *Straw Dogs,* made in an era in which America was faced with its first major military setback, if not outright defeat, the beleaguered settler survives and prevails in exactly the manner approved by hundreds of cowboy sagas. Of course he was justified, of course: the attackers quite intolerantly wanted to lynch a local simpleton—the good American can no more turn the village idiot over to a raging mob than, say, betray President Thieu.

---

*These events did not happen the same year—the novelist is establishing a fairy-tale setting.

The war itself, as fought in Vietnam, stubbornly refused to render up an iconography, to present a target (to cite Stanley Kramer again) on which one could "draw a bead." The war produced no heroes or places that one could exploit in a title, no *Back to Bataan* or *Sands of Iwo Jima. Tet?* Their initiative. *Mylai?* Our mistake. *Calley?* Forget it. So we settled for a Green Beret. Even poor little Korea first came to us wearing a Steel Helmet.

What *didn't* Vietnam give us? It gave no movies about aircraft carriers in the South China Sea. No comedies about boys on furlough in Japan or Hawaii or Australia. No spies or saboteurs. No bomber crews sweating out a run on Hanoi or Haiphong. No prisoners of war holding out against fiendish captors. No generals making command decisions. No hapless GI's suffering for those decisions. No front-line hospitals (unless we count *M*A*S*H,* which won't admit to being about Vietnam). No dramatizations of the differences between communism and democracy (blame the dozens of cold war films for exhausting this topic) or the transformation of civilians into soldiers (instead, we would get stories of soldiers who couldn't make it back to civilian life). No sagas of the indomitable spirit of simple but photogenic peasants in the face of the vile occupiers (like as not, we were the invaders). No affirmation of eventual American solidarity in spite of initial hostility (for hostility begat fragging, not fraternity). No indictments of overweening military ambition (Hollywood was just getting around to Patton, and MacArthur is still waiting in line). No true-life stories of individual heroism, eccentricity, or determination (only Rusty Calley—all else is silence).

What films we got were void of prayers, of the crusading spirit, of miraculous interventions. God seems to have forsaken America. It's enough to make one cry out, with apologies to Joel McCrea in *Foreign Correspondent,* "Ring yourself around with steel, World. The lights are going out all over America."

EPILOG

Back to Sergeant York

Home! Buford Pusser's come home. After eight years soldiering and wrestling, he's come home to settle down. On the side of his house trailer is the legend, BUFORD THE BULL, but he's tired of fighting—against other men, against the system. "I'm not gonna fight with nobody any more." So he's come home to Ser-

geant York country, the hills of Tennessee, home to Mom and
Dad. (Dad is Noah Beery, Jr., one of Gary Cooper's sidekicks in
Sergeant York.)

He goes with his parents and wife and children to see a farm
down the road. Good bottom land, two catfish ponds, a nice little
house. It's the same reward Sergeant York came back to. In the
next scene he's coming out of the courthouse between Mom and
his wife. The women decide to go shopping while Buford re-
lives old times with a buddy from high school. "There's just one
thing, Buford," says Mom. "If you look around town you might
see some changes. But, er, pay them no mind. They've got no-
thin' to do with you."

The old friend, one Rudy McVey, takes Buford to the Lucky
Spot, a new roadhouse. "You can lay a bet or a broad or the base
for a three day drunk," Rudy cackles. But Buford doesn't approve of what he sees in the Lucky Spot—the half-naked girls,
the drinking and gambling. His eyes narrow like Gary Cooper's.
He spots cheating at the crap table. A fight starts. It's a good
old-fashioned saloon brawl. Buford the Bull is finally over-
whelmed. The gang that runs the Lucky Spot pin him down on
a gambling table, rip his shirt open, begin to carve him up.

"I didn't know it was going to be like this," a girl in back of
me weeps.

Walking Tall is a Bing Crosby Production, a picture for the
whole family. It's been making a lot of money all over the
country during the months I've been writing this book. A sequel
is being planned. Like *Sergeant York,* it's a true story, even
opens with a dedication to Buford Pusser, "a Living Legend."

The Lucky Spotters, not knowing they have a Living Legend
on their hands, dump Buford (Joe Don Baker) in a ravine to
bleed to death. He manages to crawl to a highway. Many cars
pass him by. No one wants to get involved. Finally, a truck
stops. Cut to Buford's living room. A doctor comes out of the
bedroom, speaks of two hundred stitches. Buford's wife (Eliza-
beth Hartman) emerges bearing a pile of bloody towels. She
speaks: "Three years in the Marine Corps. Five years in the
ring. He has to come home to get half killed."

Buford gets well, whittles himself a big stick, goes back to the
Lucky Spot, wrecks the place, breaks arms, legs, heads. Arrested and tried, he bares his seamed torso to a jury of local
folks, gets acquitted.

Seeing his courtroom victory as a sign and swearing to rid the county of the Lucky Spot and all it stands for, he runs for sheriff against the corrupt incumbent (Gene Evans, whom we will meet as Sergeant Zack in the next chapter). The old sheriff tries to run him down, dies in a fiery crash. Buford, the Living Legend, is elected, learns himself some law to get around the corrupt judge, begins to crack down on the Lucky Spot gang. They try to kill him. He survives two bullets point blank. "We've all had a nice vacation with pay," he tells his men when he's recovered. "Now back to the war."

Back to the war. But the war comes to him. First they kill his dog, then they murder his wife (the most realistic battle wound I've ever seen, shards of white bone sticking out the mess in the top of her head), shoot his lower face away. He goes to his wife's funeral wearing a plaster cast from the eyes down. After the services, he gets into his official car by himself and drives over to the Lucky Spot. The last two members of the gang are just preparing to leave town. They see Buford a-comin', grab their weapons. But he drives right into the Lucky Spot, kills them both with his big car.

Now that the entire gang is dead or gone for good, dozens of townspeople suddenly awake to the need for community action, rush into the Lucky Spot, begin to burn the furniture and gaming tables. Cut to a close up of Buford Pusser. A trickle of blood runs out the air hole in the center of the plaster mask, and from one eye rolls a tear.

On the sound track, Johnny Mathis sings, tells America it's not too late to start Walking Tall.

TWO

IT'S THE ONLY WAR WE'VE GOT—HOLLYWOOD AND KOREA

May Britt: "Do you like the war?"

Robert Mitchum: "It's the only war I've got."

—*The Hunters*

Farley Granger doesn't want to go to the war, to Korea. If the war really needs to be fought, he whines, why not send atom bombs instead of boys. His tenderhearted sister-in-law, Dorothy McGuire, who can see the Big Picture, tears into his selfishness for wishing a holocaust upon the world. She cares enough to send the very best: "I don't like wars and I'm not crazy about armies and I'm sorry that we're such barbarians that the men we love have to go out and settle things with guns, but I'd be a lot sorrier if they hadn't gone. Now you get out of here."

"I'd say the same thing to you," the beautiful woman sitting next to me in the dark whispers.

"I'm too young, Mother," I reply, but I'm secretly proud. War is a serious business.

It's early 1952 in Santa Fé, and we're watching Sam Goldwyn's *I Want You.* We've come a long way from Covington, a longer way from my fourth birthday at *Sergeant York* back in 1941. Yet neither distance is all that great. My grandfather, the head of the draft board, is dead, but Ray Collins runs the draft board on the screen; Farley Granger, like my father, eventually enlists, goes through basic training, and comes home to marry the girl from Covington, Peggy Dow.

I

Mickey Rooney: "How'd you get out here in a smelly ditch in Korea?"
William Holden: "That's just what I'm asking myself."
        —The Bridges at Toko-Ri

Chuck Connors: "I didn't have to join up. I had a good job. . . . My girl and I decided there was a future for me in the Marines."
        —Hold Back the Night

Dana Andrews, on learning Jim Backus has volunteered: "What did you do that for?"
Jim Backus: "Oh, I don't know. Maybe I'm a Boy Scout at heart."

Dana Andrews, explaining why he has finally decided to volunteer: "I want to be able to face my children when they ask 'What were you doing when the world was shaking, Daddy?' "
        —I Want You

Alan Ladd: "This is a testing ground for the Reds, and if we don't stop him here, he'll use his arms somewhere else."
        —The McConnell Story

First Airman: "How'd you get into this? You didn't have to. . . ."
Second Airman: "Eh—for all the corny reasons. I've got an eight-year-old kid that's growing up in a sick world. And if it takes this kind of surgery to cure it, then I want to help."

—*Hell's Horizons*

Humphrey Bogart: "What's a girl like you doing in Korea, anyway?"
June Allyson: "Getting in the war like everybody else."

—*Battle Circus*

All those films. All those reasons for going. The Korean War hit me at just the right time—it was my war. I was twelve when it started, fifteen when it ended (No, not yet! I'll be too old for the next one). My high school ROTC instructors were men who had just returned from combat to give us the benefit of their experience. One had even met Master Sergeant Tony Herbert, Korea's most decorated soldier. When we went to the range with our M–1's, carbines, and BAR's, we half-hoped we might soon be firing at targets that could shoot back.

When I went to see *Fixed Bayonets, Retreat, Hell!*, and *Battle Circus,* the war was hot and immediate. Today, Korea seems cold and somehow irrelevant, at best a suitably anachronistic backdrop for *The Last Picture Show* or a safe setting for a television comedy. Korea, the good gray war, so unprepossessing that the recent film celebration of the era, *Let the Good Times Roll,* forgets to mention it.

Several years ago I taught a course called "War and the Popular Arts in America." As we began the section dealing with Korea, I asked the class to list popular slogans and films inspired by that war. Hardly anyone remembered MacArthur's "Old Soldiers Never Die, They Just Fade Away," though a few had him saying he would return—a nice mixture of wars. No one knew any novels, but almost everyone could cite *Pork Chop Hill, The Bridges at Toko-Ri,* and *M*A*S*H.*

For my students and most of the generation born after Panmunjom, the Korean War is known only through a disparate handful of movies, saved from oblivion by television reruns. No total image emerges, only bits and pieces: Woody Strode turning his rifle against Gregory Peck on Pork Chop, green-hatted Mickey Rooney pulling Bill Holden out of the cold sea, Sally Kellerman clutching the last shreds of dignity.

Korea occasioned over fifty films, but only one copped an

Oscar (*M*A*S*H*, Best Screenplay) and that did not happen until nearly twenty years after the hostilities erupted.

In spite of the filmmakers' brave efforts to give American involvement in Korea the same patriotic and inspirational treatment afforded World War II (*Hold Back the Night*, for instance, tries to slide home on nostalgic flashbacks to Hollywood's favorite war), not one of these films can work the magic of a *Casablanca* or a *Mrs. Miniver*. Hollywood tried to treat Korea as a sequel to that earlier war, but it was, in fact, the military and cinematic proving ground for a later conflict. Like Vietnam, Korea was a limited war fought in Asia during peace time to demonstrate the United States' resolve to hold back Communist agression. Everything that happened in Vietnam happened first in Korea: fratricidal strife and the often indiscriminate slaughter of civilians, the American military out of control, or nearly so, and peace talks that dragged on to an ambiguous conclusion.

In the absence of a body of films depicting combat in Vietnam, the Korean War supplies a kind of shadow history. It was Korea that forced Hollywood to confront such issues as the morality of killing inconvenient prisoners of war or refugees and civilians who knowingly or innocently harbor enemy guerrillas, the difficulty of motivating men to fight when the home country is not directly threatened or totally committed to the war effort (this, combined with the curious effect of fighting for political rather than military goals, results in many incidents in which tired men challenge their superiors), and a vague suspicion that something is not right, that our boys are not doing their best—or that indeed there is no best to do. But the unique meaning of the Korean War was never translated to the screen, nor did it enter popular literature or legend. I refer to the disparity between the terrific expenditure of power and the negligible military gains thus achieved.

Robert Mitchum: "The only trouble is, [Korea] came along too soon after the real big one. It's hard to sell anyone on it."
May Britt: "You are not sold on it?"
Mitchum: "I'm regular Air Force. I don't have to be sold."
—*The Hunters*

The American film industry had several years to prepare for our involvement in World War II, time to get a feel for the war, time to develop stereotypes for our allies and our enemies, time to decide which issues to stress, which to avoid. Korea surprised us in the summer of 1950, a year when Hollywood was just beginning a new cycle of films about World War II and its aftermath: *Breakthrough* (Frank Lovejoy hits the Normandy beach), *An American Guerrilla in the Philippines* (Tyrone Power stays behind to welcome MacArthur back), *Twelve O'Clock High* (Gregory Peck cracks under the strain of daylight bombing). Mainly we were still coming home: *Home of the Brave* (James Edwards in a veterans hospital), *When Willie Comes Marching Home* (Dan Dailey in comic hot water), and *The Men* (Marlon Brando in a wheelchair).

Before the filmmakers could come to terms with World War II, they were suddenly swept up in another one to be sold to the public. There was much confusion: would the public go to see films about an old war now that a fresh one was in the news? What was the new one about? Into the fray leapt Howard Hughes, who dispatched a producer to Washington to arrange Department of Defense assistance for a project dramatizing cooperation between ground and air forces. Bouncing ideas off the Pentagon, the Hughes people took two years to bring the war to the screen in *One Minute to Zero.*

Meanwhile, working with a cast of unknowns and without government assistance, Samuel Fuller wrote, directed, and produced *The Steel Helmet.* "Shot in 12 days," Fuller wrote me. "Cost, $104,000. Locations: Griffith Park. . . . a cardboard tank was painted, a pole slammed into its face for a gun. . . . Twice the Goddam cardboard tank fell on its face." Completed before 1950 was over, this widely admired cult film was not only the first to show the Korean War but a classic example of the combat genre in its own right.

The basic plot (a small unit besieged by superior enemy forces and beset by an internal conflict between a tough, pragmatic sergeant and a by-the-book officer) could have come from any war, but Fuller worked out a series of incidents that got to the heart of the new war. For instance, he dramatized the confusing quality of the war through the ignorance of the new allies about one another. Take this early exchange between Sergeant Zack (Gene Evans) and the little Korean boy who saves his life:

Zack: "You talk more like a dog-face than a gook."
Boy: "I am no *gook!* I am *Korean!*"
Zack: "All right, all right, all right—so you're not a gook."

Later, a chaplain's assistant plays "Auld Lang Syne" on a portable organ while the Korean boy sings along in his own language. The GI is surprised that the boy can sing this "foreign" song at all: the boy is amazed that the American knows how to play the South Korean National Anthem.

The film opens with the image of Sergeant Zack prostrate in a field of corpses, his hands tied behind his back and a bullet hole in his steel helmet where he has been shot and left for dead. The little Korean boy cuts his bonds and a few minutes later saves him from being killed by a North Korean disguised as a woman. It is a war of total betrayal—booby-trapped American corpses, an enemy major hiding behind a statue of Buddha, women who turn out to be men, captors (on both sides) who shoot their helpless prisoners.

To cut through this complexity, to get out of Korea without turning his back and having "some old lady shoot my head off," Zack comes up with a simple rule for distinguishing between friend and foe: South Koreans run with you, North Koreans run after you. There is no room in Zack's world for neutrality, no room for those who stand still. Zack's automatic slanging of the Korean boy as a gook and his transformation of the boy into a little American (new name, uniform, and imitation dog tags) smells today of cultural imperialism, but in 1950 American filmmakers and audiences could not think of a higher compliment than asking others to "run with us."

Fuller's vision is of a multi-racial America, all running in the same direction. After Zack, the film's two most sympathetic characters are GI's meant to affirm American solidarity in the face of a captured North Korean's charge that America exploits its minority groups: the competent Nisei sergeant Zack affectionately calls Buddha-head and a dignified medic played by James Edwards, Korea's token black soldier (in *Men in War* he was a mechanic, he got to fly combat missions in *Battle Hymn* and to fight on *Pork Chop Hill,* and finally came home, like everyone else, to have bad dreams in *The Manchurian Candidate*).

The Steel Helmet created a furor. The Pentagon turned down a request for combat footage, explaining the film was anti-American because it depicted Sergeant Zack killing an unarmed prisoner. "Hell, I could only stare," Fuller wrote me. "It was evident that these men had no conception of what a human, with a weapon, will do. ... Victor Reisel, the labor columnist ... called me a Fellow Traveler for showing the US in such a bad light. At the same time the *Daily Worker* ran an editorial branding me a goddam war-monger who was financed by Douglas MacArthur. . . . I look back now and laugh . . . since the Army (after the film was a hit) utilized several sequences in their Infantry School to teach wetnoses how to smell out and destroy unseen snipers."

With the firing of MacArthur and his famous farewell speech, Korea produced its first major motto. Twentieth Century–Fox and MGM both registered the title *Old Soldiers Never Die,* but before either studio could build a film around the phrase, a World War II British film was reissued under that title. The major studios were looking for an angle, for a big picture that would set the standard for this war.

Meanwhile, a flock of minor efforts trundled off the assembly line throughout early and mid-1951. The next film to reach distribution after *The Steel Helmet* was Columbia's *A Yank in Korea,* a perfect example of the old in-and-out routine: at the outbreak of the war, Andy Smith sees his duty clear, gets married, enlists, is trained, goes to Korea, proves himself in battle, and comes back to the States with an inspirational letter his late sergeant entrusted to him for delivery to his children.

Then RKO tried to give us back our old World War II enemies —in *Tokyo File 212* the hero investigates Japanese Reds interfering with the war in Korea. Warner Brothers tried the old Hollywood Canteen gimmick in *Starlift,* a flimsy story (about stars shuttling between Hollywood and San Francisco to entertain Korea-bound troops) held together by a romance between a flier and a starlet.

Late in 1951, a year and a half after the invasion of South Korea, came the first two major films about the war. *Fixed Bayonets,* written and directed by Samuel Fuller for Twentieth Century–Fox, had a bigger budget and cast than *The Steel Helmet,* but a smaller impact. Where Fuller's earlier effort was very specifically a reflection of the new war, *Fixed Bayonets* is standard combat fare with no relevance to Korea. The enemy is faceless, the main set (a cave) is clearly a plaster and canvas affair, and the men have melting pot names like Borcellino, Vogl, Bulcheck, Ramirez, Walowicz, and Zablocki.

Opening all across the country in time for Christmas 1951 was Samuel Goldwyn's *I Want You,* "the story," as Bosley Crowther put it, "of average Americans resisting the necessity of facing up to another war and then finally standing still for it because it is the patriotic thing to do." Directed by Mark

Robson, written by Irwin Shaw, starring Dana Andrews, Dorothy McGuire, and a half dozen other big names, *I Want You* was Goldwyn's attempt to recapture the honors and profits that befell him and MGM for *The Best Years of Our Lives* (1946), that wonderfully schmaltzy story of three veterans (including Dana Andrews) returning to their hometown at the end of World War II.

I Want You begins in the classic propaganda style that marked another Goldwyn last-moment-of-peace film, *The North Star* (1943). Instead of a family of simple Russian villagers around the breakfast table, here we have a typical small-town midwestern family around the dinner table. As in *The North Star*, Dana Andrews and Farley Granger are brothers. Not until the second reel is the war itself mentioned and even then at several removes from the family. After all, the Greers are tired of war: the head of the family (Robert Keith) had been in the Great War, son Dana had done his duty in World War II, and another son had died in that one. Now there's a third generation of Greers to rear in peace.

Beyond the dining room is the kind of little town where all the men went to war together. Dana Andrews's old colonel, Jim Backus, wanders in and out, and Andrews is called "Lieutenant" by the local bartender. Slowly the war insinuates itself: a young man in the family construction firm is called up, ex-Colonel Backus puts on his uniform again, and a draft notice comes for Farley Granger, the kid brother. When the boy's mother hides the telegram so his Christmas holidays won't be spoiled, Dana Andrews muses: "maybe that's the way we all are —we think we're on a holiday, but somewhere, somebody knows that the holiday is over." War is normal, peace but a brief vacation.

In the last reel, after his kid brother has accepted the call to duty, Dana Andrews decides to go back to the army. Though he is only three years away from his last war and has just settled down in his first house, he gets wife Dorothy McGuire's blessing. After all, she implies, if he doesn't go over *there,* they might come over here. Besides, it's for the children—not only does he want to protect them from bloodthirsty beasts like the ones who ravished his village in *The North Star,* but he wants to be able to face them when they ask "what were you doing when the world was shaking, Daddy?" So off he goes with Jim Backus to build airstrips in Europe, to make the enemy "think twice or three times or a dozen times before hitting us. And maybe they'll never do it. And I know we won't start anything. It isn't peace exactly . . . but whatever it is, I must say I prefer it to war."

There was surely some nostalgia in Goldwyn's vision of undeclared universal war. Hollywood had blossomed in the war years, and *I Want You* tried to rekindle the romance by making the cold war as warm and appealing as the war that had given us the best years of our lives.

Nineteen fifty-two brought a diverse sampling of conventional stories exploiting the war. In Paramount's *Submarine Command,* William Holden mastered guilt feelings left over from World War II in time for a Korean shootout. Allied Artists' *Battle Zone* tore two Marine photographers away from nurse Linda Christian long enough for them to snap pictures behind enemy lines. King Vidor had a veteran bring Shirley Yamaguchi home in Twentieth Century–Fox's *Japanese War Bride.* And Warner Brothers, having frittered away its energies on *Starlift,* finally got into combat with *Retreat, Hell!,* taking a Marine unit from Stateside training to the Inchon Beachhead, the battle around the Chosin Reservoir, and the withdrawal to the evacuation fleet, at which point the title was finally explained in Frank Lovejoy's lines as a Marine colonel: "Retreat, hell! We're just attacking in another direction."

Not until late 1952 did a major studio present a film reflecting the unique quality of this particular war. In RKO's *One Minute to Zero,* America's relation to the United Nations is explored in terms that can only be called allegorical: a United Nations functionary (Ann Blythe) comes to love and trust an American colonel (Robert Mitchum). Naturally, the romance is not an easy one, but as in other films of this genre the audience is not kept in suspense, for Ann Blythe introduces herself as an off-camera narrator at the start of the film in terms that telegraph the conclusion: "My name doesn't matter. I'm any wife, any daughter, any sister, mother, or sweetheart." To tell the truth, her name is Linda and his is Steve.

The film then takes us back to Linda's first meeting with Colonel Steve, the kind of lovable diamond in the rough who started as a private and will end as a general without losing the Hollywood enlisted man's no-nonsense way of speech. Note this exchange on the eve of the invasion of South Korea:

Steve: "The Communist armies are already mobilizing."
Linda: "Yes, so we've heard. But you can't honestly believe they're planning war."
Steve: "The plans are made in Moscow."
Linda: "They wouldn't dare! They'd be taking on the whole world."
Steve: "That stop Hitler?"

When the war starts right on schedule to prove the tough army pragmatist right and the naive United Nations spokesperson wrong, Steve forcefully evacuates her from Korea—war is no place for civilians, women, or the UN. Like all Hollywood women, Linda secretly likes being manhandled and soon a romance blooms when she nurses Steve after he is wounded. Steve wants to marry her, but having already lost one husband in World War II, she doesn't want to go through the waiting and the bad news and the Medal of Honor ceremony at the White House.

The crisis comes when Steve, whose radio code name, appropriately enough, is "Butcher Control," orders an air strike on a column of refugees because he knows Communist guerrillas are using the civilians in order to infiltrate Republic of Korea defenses (cf. Fuller's Sergeant Zack in *The Steel Helmet:* "some of these guys . . . hide behind them white pajamas and them women's clothes . . . make their kids play near bombing targets. They're smart"). Linda witnesses the slaughter of the innocents, and gets very uptight even though there's a United Nations doctor handy to legitimize Steve's act with a neat little metaphor: "Linda, war is the most malignant disease of the human race. It is an infection. It is contagious. When we doctors amputate, we sometimes cut good tissue along with the bad because we cannot take the chance."

Linda begins to understand why Colonel Steve had to trash the refugee column when she sees the bodies of American soldiers who have been shot with their hands tied behind their backs. After musing, "you just don't believe it until you've seen it," Linda finds Steve and announces "I want to be your wife." So Steve wins through on his own terms, is promoted to general, and goes on with the war while Linda, the "any wife, any daughter, any sister, mother, or sweetheart" of the introduction, prays in a voice-over as we watch men and material moving down a road: "Oh, please, dear God, watch over them . . . protect and guide them. Lead them to Victory. Spare them to know a lasting peace. And in thy infinite mercy, dear God, bring them safely back to us."

The following year, Twentieth Century–Fox examined the trials of working with our United Nations allies in *The Glory Brigade.* "All right," barks Victor Mature, "you guys have been yammering that if this is a UN war, where are our allies? Well, tonight . . . we'll be under Greek command." Though Mature is happy to have other countries share in the glory ("Some of my closest friends are Greeks, including my father"), friction soon rages between his combat engineers and the Greek infantry they are supporting. The experience is not a happy one in military or cinematic terms, and from that point forward Hollywood decided to let Americans fight alone without interference. (An ominous side note: only rarely is it even hinted in these films that we had the assistance of the ROK army, much less that we were assisting them. Korea, on the screen, is America's war.)

The last film to appear before the war ended in mid-1953 was MGM's *Battle Circus,* a witty and sardonic romance between Humphrey Bogart and June Allyson, as front-line surgeon and nurse. Opening with a shot of a sign reading "MASH 8666—Mobile Army Surgical Hospital," *Battle Circus* is a clear source for 1970's *M*A*S*H:* shower-tent humor, helicopter-borne casualties, emergency operations on children, officers who mock authority, and the peculiar quality of life under canvas. But where *M*A*S*H* opens with the song "Suicide Is Painless," the mood for *Battle Circus* is set by the legend "This is a story about the indomitable human spirit." Between these two beginnings, both involving shots of drifting helicopters, lie seventeen years and a major revision of how Hollywood looked at Korea.

II

A GATHERING OF LAMBS

So the war ended, but the films dragged on in a dreary succession enlightened only by occasional bursts of patriotism or unintentional silliness. Still in production at the time of the cease-fire were a number of tributes to various branches of the service: *Mission Over Korea* (two conflicting generations of American warriors in a low-budget salute to unarmed spotter planes), *Sabre Jet* (not so much about Robert Stack and his brother pilots as about their wives waiting back in Japan), *Take the High Ground* (the training camp—in come the green recruits from all over America and out go combat-ready troops), and *Flight Nurse.*

Over the next decade, Korea would be the setting for another two dozen films. There would be a string of those strange stories that manage to interject beautiful women into combat situations: a blonde in a tight sweater mixed up with Richard Conte and Charles Bronson in *Target Zero* (1955); four GI's trapped behind enemy lines with nurses and a beautiful Eurasian girl in *Tank Battalion;* Audrey Totter as a beautiful Russian nurse traveling around the countryside in *Jet Attack;* and a gaggle of USO girls trapped behind enemy lines who join forces with a GI patrol in *Operation Dames* (the last three all released by AIP in 1958–59). This madness finally peaked in *The Nun and the Sergeant* (1962) with a whole busload of convent girls.

The most revealing films were those that continued to call for unremitting struggle or offered up sacrificial lambs. Let me start with the cycle of POW films. Korea was the first war in which the conduct of American prisoners became a national issue. Nearly a third of our POW's collaborated with the enemy in some way, and not a single American escaped from a permanent camp in North Korea. William Bendix, Rory Calhoun, and Richard Jaeckel made it back to our lines with the help of a little Korean boy and his dog in *The Young and the Brave* (1963), but that was only a movie.

The POW genre began in 1954 with a bit of wishful thinking called (naturally enough) *Prisoner of War.* Ronald Reagan plays an officer who is asked to become a POW in order to report on conditions within the camps. Of course, he will not be helpless in this captivity, says a general: "in the next few days we're going to teach you all we can about communism. . . . It may come in handy." Once behind barbed wire, Reagan finds that the Communists are using POW's to study American strengths and weaknesses (will Pavlovian conditioning work on Americans, a naive North Korean asks his suave Russian counterpart) and that most of the Americans are holding up bravely, flaunting film-generated flippancy in the face of cynical interrogators.

Russian Colonel: "Where were you trained?"

American named Joe: "In the White House, where my family lived."

Russian: "Where does your family live now?"

Joe: "In Hollywood with my brothers, Clark Gable and Spen-

cer Tracy, and my sisters, Esther Williams and Janie Powell."
Russian: "What is your father's occupation?"
Joe: "He's a capitalist, a monopolist, and an imperialist war-
monger. And every morning he gets up and takes an autographed picture of Joe Stalin and spits it in the eye."
The film sets up a GI named Jesse as a despicable collabora-
tor, a model of how not to act. But at the end, we learn Jesse is
really *another* army plant meant to penetrate into Russia (he
breaks security to let Ronald Reagan in on the happy secret).
So the horrible example does not discredit the United States or
imperil our happy self-image after all, and at fade out Reagan's
Heroes are singing a gay ditty expressing their indomitable
spirit: "But here's a little thought/ That will get you on the go
—/ Your Uncle Sam is a better man/ Than their old Uncle Joe."

Though *Prisoner of War* was made with government assistance (after MGM complied with a four-page list of script
changes, a former POW was assigned as technical advisor), the
Department of Defense withdrew support. The Adjutant General's office was preparing to courtmartial collaborators and
wanted a harder line, wanted the message that to yield once is
to yield forever. Joe's wise-guy replies to the Russian colonel
were bad enough, but the playfulness had gone too far when
Reagan seemed to collaborate with the enemy by broadcasting
a false confession containing hidden messages.

Allen Rivkin, the scenarist, objected to the Pentagon's sudden
backpedaling, but MGM did not challenge the decision lest it
endanger cooperation on future projects. A few years later,
MGM gave the military the kind of POW story it wanted. In *The
Rack* (1956), Paul Newman played a former POW accused of
collaborating with the enemy. As the military had come out the
villain in the public eye for prosecuting collaborators, Rod Serling's script made it clear that the Newman character was not
a hapless draftee who had been thrust into combat ignorant of
the enemy and of what was expected of him. Instead, the central figure is trebly representative of the professional army: an
officer, the son of a colonel, and the brother of another officer
who died in Korea.

The Rack is an uncomfortable, unsettling film because we
keep looking for a sudden reversal in the damning evidence
produced in court against Newman. After all, every other film
about POW's in Korea had or would have such reversals: the
perfidious Jesse in *Prisoner of War* turns out to be a double
agent; the supposedly cowardly major played by Richard Base-
hart in *Time Limit* (1957) is finally and sympathetically re-

vealed to have collaborated to save his later accusers from death; the Communist scheme to turn Laurence Harvey into a Medal of Honor winner in *The Manchurian Candidate* (1962) ultimately backfires; and we finally learn that Lee Marvin was probably a great hero and not a traitor in *Sergeant Ryker* (made for television in 1963 and released as a film in 1968).

But *The Rack* is a dramatization of the army's "findings" that those who gave in once to the enemy were continually harassed, while those who resisted from the first moment were soon left alone. So Newman must be sacrificed. In the last scene, after he has been found guilty of collaboration, the camera slowly moves in on him as he delivers this speech directly to the cinema audience: "Every man has a moment in his life when he has to choose. If he chooses right, then it's a moment of magnificence. If he chooses wrong, then it's a moment of regret that will stay with him for the rest of his life. I wish that every soldier . . . could feel the way I feel now, because if they did they'd know what it's like to be a man who sold himself short, and who lost his moment of magnificence. I pray to God that they find theirs."

Prosecutor: "Amen." The lamb had been chosen.

And then there were the bio-pics spanning World War II and Korea, about real men who had given their all in one war and were back for more—Sterling Hayden as a one-legged admiral in *The Eternal Sea,* Alan Ladd as a jet ace in *The McConnell Story* (both 1955), and Rock Hudson as a flying, fighting preacher in *Battle Hymn* (1957), the most spectacular of the species. Produced by Ross Hunter and directed by Douglas Sirk in that slick period when both were bouncing stories off Rock Hudson's vinyl facade, *Battle Hymn* is a breathlessly religious homage to the Reverend Colonel Dean Hess, the Ohio minister who collected orphans when he wasn't busy training the ROK Air Force or shooting up the countryside. More than a simple homage to Hess, it is a film that paints what is supposed to be a heartwarming portrait of the American military, the kind of portrait the Pentagon was always ready to back with men, hardware, and authenticating prologues (in this case, General Earle C. Partridge, Commander of the Fifth Air Force in Korea, told the audience that they were to see a true story, and the air force assigned Colonel Hess to the film not only as a technical consultant but as commander of the operational aircraft and active duty pilots on loan to the studio for the many aerial combat scenes).

So there is Rock Hudson, the sincere man of God who goes off to Korea to renew himself because his heart is no longer in his sermons. Once there, he is assisted by Dan Duryea as a laughable, loveable, cigar-chewing topkick with a heart of gold and James Edwards as a soulful black pilot who croons children to sleep with "Swing Low, Sweet Chariot." The Koreans are just as loveable—a sweet-tempered, Bible-quoting old gentleman, and the kind of adolescent-fantasy Oriental girl who wears long white robes, does a lot of bowing, and dies in our hero's arms (as Martha Hyer is waiting back in Ohio this is the only way to work in an excuse for a romantic closeup).

An emotionally and morally inflated film, *Battle Hymn* is as overweight as the supposedly starving Korean waifs saved by Hess (two dozen were airlifted from Korea as set dressing). Hess's story fairly screamed for an intimate, realistic black-and-white film; instead, it got the full-blown Hollywood treatment of wide screen, brilliant color, thundering music, and a dreadfully stereotyped reworking of reality in a landscape (locations in Southern Arizona) in which it never snows or freezes.

The grandiose style of the film balances the effort it expends doing a job of moral bookkeeping in relation to the slaughter of children. Flying over Germany during World War II, Hess had accidentally destroyed an apartment building being used as a day school. The film slicks up this irony of war, turning the pedestrian apartment building into a little orphanage next to the very same little church in which Hess's grandmother was baptized. What follows in the film is the personal redemption of Dean Hess via his founding of an orphanage for Korean children.

The characters around Hess are constantly delivering little sermonettes to the strains of the "Battle Hymn of the Republic." Hess takes these as trail-marks out of his moral wilderness. For instance, when the black pilot accidentally strafes refugee children, he turns Hess's attempt at consolation aside with a greater consolation: "Sir, it's the way of things, I guess I figure it's all God's making and will. Doesn't the Book say no sparrow shall fall to the earth unless He first gives His nod? Well, He must have given His nod to what happened out there today."

The oily solemnity of this scene is broken by the shooting of a Korean woman who was discovered about to throw a grenade into the ammunition dump. "Chung had suspected her ever since the day you let her onto the post with those kids," says Hess's hard-boiled sidekick in a reminder that it is not possible to tell which refugees are harmless innocents, after all. Another step down the long road to enlightenment. Hess blurts out the Moral of the Scene: "She picked up those poor, starving kids to make her look good."

Naturally enough, the greatest enlightenment and the chief justification for a course of action that often destroys the innocent must come from a wise *old* Korean. Again, the "Battle Hymn of the Republic" swells in counterpoint as Philip Ahn, an old Hollywood hand, gives America carte blanche: "In times like these, can a man of good conscience ask others, 'protect me, kill for me, but do not ask me to stain my hands'? What must one do when a choice between two evils is all that is offered? . . . In order to save, at times we must destroy." Hudson, soulfully: "Is that the answer?" Old Korean Gentleman: "The true answer . . . is in the Book: 'Oh Lord, Thou hast seen my wrong —judge Thou my cause.' " Words, Rusty Calley, to live by.

Make way for the sacrificial lambs.

Battle Hymn is a covert guide to national policy: Americans must make hard choices between evils, must trust that disastrous choices are part of a benevolent Deity's Master Plan, must be willing to stain their hands in righteous causes. Other films of the era didn't bother to hide these messages, but delivered them directly. A prime example is Paramount's *The Bridges at Toko-Ri* (1955), based on the novella that James A. Michener wrote at the behest of *Life*'s editors.

Rarely did filmmakers analyze the reason for United States involvement in Korea, and never with any sense of the complexity of our policies and aims. The typical response was pragmatic—I don't know why I'm here, but let's get it over with and go home. *The Bridges at Toko-Ri* is probably the fullest statement of the conventional explanation for the war: If we don't stop Communist agression here, *where* will we stop it? In those years following the House Un-American Activities Committee exorcism of the film industry's Red devils (one of the Hollywood Ten who went to prison was Ring Lardner, Jr., who wrote *M*A*S*H*, perhaps in revenge), no one bothered to ask whether we should take it upon ourselves to stop communism in the first place.

Thus, Fredric March, as the crusty old admiral commanding a carrier task force off Korea, has a clear hand in explaining to William Holden, a reluctant retread from Denver, why he must again interrupt his law career and marriage to Grace Kelly in order to fight yet another war. The fact that the film did not reach the screen until a year and a half after the war ended adds to the suspicion that the issues involved have not as much to do with Korea as with a posture that the backers of this film seem to think the United States must maintain.

And who was responsible for *Toko-Ri* and its message? First, there was James A. Michener, a writer who made his fortune with sentimental tales of American warriors in the Pacific and based his novella about the bridges at Toko-Ri on first-hand observation aboard an aircraft carrier (six months before Paramount released *Toko-Ri,* MGM brought out *Men of the Fighting Lady,* with Louis Calhern impersonating Michener and delivering that film's message: "A man must do what he must do"). Then there was the Department of Defense, always glad in those years of declining budgets to help a producer with a project that stressed the need for constant vigilance, sacrifice, and expenditure. (Prominently displayed over the Pentagon desk of Donald E. Baruch, chief of the Motion Picture Production Branch, is a signed portrait of *Toko-Ri*'s producer, George Seaton, flanking a framed cartoon, captioned "Roll 'Em, Baby," showing a Hollywood type shouting directions at a beached aircraft carrier labeled "Defense Department Assistance to 'Friendly' Movies.") Finally, there was the multitude of talents headed by director Mark Robson, who had seen Dana Andrews through his back-to-war paces in *I Want You.* The result was an epic piece of affirmation suitable for the whole family, and the film opened at Radio City Music Hall the year the last levy of boys to die in Vietnam was being born.

The film's inspirational message is worked out in several scenes between Lieutenant Brubaker (Holden) and the childless Admiral Tarrant (March) who allows the retread the luxury of doubt because the younger man reminds him of the son he lost during World War II. The old admiral is the voice of calm wisdom, the bitter young pilot is on the verge of self-pity (though not quite the would-be slacker Holden would portray several years later in *The Bridge on the River Kwai*). The debate always goes the way the admiral wants it to, as though the script forbids Brubaker the courtesy of examining the admiral's assumptions. Listen to the old man explaining why the young man must fight:

Admiral Tarrant: "Son, whatever progress this world has made has been because of the efforts of the few."

Brubaker: "I was one of the few, Admiral—New Guinea, Leyte, Okinawa. Why does it have to be me again? . . . I think we ought to pull out."

Tarrant: "That's rubbish, son, and you know it. If we did, they'd take Japan, Indo-China, the Philippines. . . ."

No, the admiral persists, America must draw the line somewhere, and Brubaker's mission is to draw it (roll of drums) at the bridges at Toko-Ri. Knock those bridges out, says the old man, gripped by a vision of a world made sane again by American stick-to-it-iveness, and the Communists may finally be convinced that "we'll never weaken in our purpose. And that's the day they'll quit." After some other business to flesh out this simple story line (chiefly a holiday in Japan with Grace Kelly), Brubaker helps knock out the bridges. Shot down, he ends up dying in an irrigation ditch alongside Mickey Rooney. As the image of Brubaker's body fades out, the carrier fades in and we witness the admiral's reaction to his protégé's death—the music swells and Fredric March wonders aloud why America is lucky enough to have men willing to fly into combat from a speck lost on the cold sea. "Where do we get such men?" he repeats in awe at the marvel of a country that can produce a ready supply of citizen-soldiers. And in a thousand moviehouses across the land, from the grand Radio City Music Hall to the humble Star, mommies and daddies squirm in their seats, hot to breed such men should America ever need them again.

The emotional burden of the Tarrant-Brubaker confrontation is in the tradition of those key films of World War II celebrating the transformation of ordinary citizens into heroes. It is a strategy for making American audiences think well of themselves, for making them less resistant to the demands of a potentially man-hungry military. Perhaps the opposition to Vietnam and the draft would have reached an effective strength much earlier had Hollywood ever shown William Holden or Dana Andrews walking away from the war *and* getting the girl. But there was neither profit nor honor in such a course when even the *Saturday Review* could applaud *Toko-Ri*'s central notion "that an accident of history required a small group of men to do a dirty job on behalf of a nation, and that out of the necessity of the moment and their own tradition and training they found the means to fight magnificently."

The success of Paramount's *The Bridges at Toko-Ri* (it is on *Variety*'s list of "All-Time Box Office Champs") inspired several imitations. The following year (1956), John Ireland bombed a bridge on the Yalu in *Hell's Horizons,* billed as the "blasting story of the most dangerous mission since Toko-Ri." In spite of a crash landing, he survived for a happy fade out. And in 1958 Paramount tried to convert the dialectic of *Toko-Ri* into pure action: *The Hunters* had Robert Mitchum lead a cowardly young pilot toward courage and upped the stakes with *three* jets crashing behind enemy lines (everybody made it back this time). But these films did not approach the critical, financial, or lasting popular success of *The Bridges at Toko-Ri,* the first film in which the central character dies in Korea.

America had tasted of the sacrificial lamb and would not settle for less.

III

Captain: "Come back. The war is over."
Private Endore: "Which war?"

—*War Hunt*

Bogart: "Maybe the war's catching up with me. Its ugliness, its stupidity, futility."
Colonel: "It's a job, that's all."
Bogart: "Yeah, but other jobs get done."

—*Battle Circus*

Robert Ryan: "I was wrong—this war's gonna last a long time."

—*Men in War*

Norman Fell: "I thought this war was all over with."

—*Pork Chop Hill*

Chuck Connors: "This thing could go on forever."

—*Hold Back the Night*

Kirk Douglas to Robert Walker, Jr.: "Kid, any day a war ends is a nice day."

—*The Hook*

Captain: "The war is over."
Private Endore: "There'll be another."

—*War Hunt*

The first film about the Korean War ended with a prophetic coda: "There is no end to this story." In a week of viewing films about Korea, I began to have the feeling that *The Steel Helmet*'s tag line applied directly to me. As I worked through the stacks of reels for the late fifties and early sixties, I grew weary of the same bit players dragging their way to dusty deaths ("Willie and Walter Soo Hoo, who portray Chinese Red soldiers . . . fight the Korean War for the 15th time. . . . So far, Willie has survived twice and Walter but once"—pressbook for *Time Limit*). But again and again I would witness a last-minute reprieve, an upbeat ending that would give me the strength to thread yet another reel and start the cycle once more.

Example: in Anthony Mann's *Men in War* (1957), a decimated platoon led by Robert Ryan is surrounded by the enemy and burdened with a rebellious sergeant (Aldo Ray) dragging a shell-shocked colonel around with him. The time is the bleak September of 1950, on the eve of MacArthur's counteroffensive, and hope is mighty low:

Aldo Ray: "We're licked, the war is over. The colonel and me are going home."

Robert Ryan: "My wife and three kids might agree with you —but not yet, sergeant, not yet." Late in the film, a very tired Robert Ryan says, almost despairingly, "I was wrong—this war's gonna last a long time." Immediately, someone runs up to announce that the Yanks are coming through, and Ryan suddenly changes character to read out a list of Silver Star winners. Abruptly, the dark and pessimistic mood is swept away in time for an inspiring musical finale over the credits: a hearty song with the refrain "I'll remember men I knew, men in war."

We're all tired of war, these films of the late Eisenhower era and early New Frontier whisper. But only hang in there a bit longer and we'll make it through. The classic in this line is *Pork Chop Hill* (1959), the first of the cycle of five celluloid nightmares about tired, confused men who must go on fighting and dying though the cease-fire is at hand.*

Based on General S. L. A. Marshall's factual account, *Pork Chop Hill* opens with a statement of deep gratitude to the army for its cooperation—cooperation that extended to the assignment as technical adviser of Captain Joseph G. Clemons, Jr., who actually led the attack on Pork Chop and who is played by Gregory Peck in the film. The producer, Sy Bartlett, we will meet in Chapter Four; suffice it to say that former Colonel Bartlett built a reputation for writing and producing films in which

---

*I do not count Hal Wallis's 1953 *Cease Fire!* in this category, for it is not a fiction film but a 3–D "documentary" edited to represent the activities of an infantry platoon on the day of the armistice.

Americans are called upon to exert maximum effort. The director, Lewis Milestone, famous for the most downbeat and futile of all war films, *All Quiet on the Western Front,* is said to have tried to emphasize the absurdity of the attack on Pork Chop through ironic contrasts and counterpointing, but the final product was straightforward cold war heroics affirming the same never-say-die posture promoted by *The Bridges at Toko-Ri.*

The story-line is simplicity itself. Lieutenant Joe Clemons (Peck) must take his company (Harry Guardino, Rip Torn, George Peppard, James Edwards, Woody Strode, Norman Fell, Robert Blake, Martin Landau, etc.) up a hill held by the Chinese. His colonel warns him that he may experience a spot of difficulty: "You've got a hundred and thirty-five men, all of them thinking about the peace talks at Panmunjom—and it's a cinch they don't want to die in what may be the last battle of the war." Beyond that, Peck finds that understanding and explaining why the hill must be taken is almost as difficult as the actual battle.

Unlike Peck, however, the audience knows that the battle is not to be fought for tactical advantage but to convince the enemy that the United States is determined to go on fighting regardless of the cost until it gets the truce settlement it wants. For the audience has been privy to a high-level cigarette break in the Panmunjom negotiations in which an admiral played by the grandfatherly Carl Benton Reid ponders aloud that the North Koreans on the other side of the table "aren't just Orientals—they're Communists!" All else logically follows from that, for Communists deal in abstractions: "I'm beginning to think that they picked [Pork Chop] because it's worth nothing. Its value is that it has no value. . . . They're willing to spend lives for nothing, or next to nothing. [*Pauses, has insight, turns*] That's what they want to know—are we as willing to do that as they are?"

Slowly, ever so carefully, Peck puzzles his way through the whys and wherefores, refining the basic Gary Cooper resolution-of-doubt that Peck does so well. To his second-in-command he explains that "Pork Chop is just a chip in the game at Panmunjom—everytime the Reds win a chip here, they raise the ante there. So I guess we gotta convince them we're not going to give up any more chips." Peck's explanation gets through to his brother-in-law, another lieutenant played by Rip Torn ("You say that nothing's got a value except the value that men put on it, and I don't know how men can put a higher value on something than by dying for it"). But Woody Strode, as the black private who threatens to kill Peck, isn't buying: "I don't want to die for Korea. What do I care for this stinking hill? You wanta see where I live back home—I sure am sure I ain't gonna die for that." Peck's answer is not a conventional patriotic or selfless speech, but a flatly pragmatic warning that Strode will surely die on Pork Chop if he doesn't start fighting back against the Communists.

Finally, Peck lectures the audience directly in a voice-over: "Pork Chop Hill was held—bought and paid for at the same price we commemorate in monuments at Bunker Hill and Gettysburg. Yet you will find no monuments on Pork Chop. Victory is a fragile thing and history does not linger long in our century. Pork Chop is in North Korea now—but those who fought there know what they did, and the meaning of it. Millions live in freedom today because of what they did."

This last speech is delivered in the same insanely calm tone of the true-believer that Peck used a few years before for Captain Ahab's harangues of the doomed *Pequod*'s crew. Indeed, Peck's Lieutenant Joe Clemons often resembles Ahab, especially in his reliance on raw exertion and sheer will. One moment he tells his executive officer that he is too weak to win and too strong to quit, then he gathers all his strength to order a bayonet charge, "right," as the exec puts it, "out of the Stone Age." *Pork Chop Hill* may not be in the same league as *Moby Dick,* but note that this monomaniac film was made by Peck's *Melville* Productions.

Signs and portents notwithstanding, *Pork Chop Hill* represents the kind of thinking that has been reinforced by films if not inspired by them in the first place. To again cite what Herbert Jacobson said twenty years ago, "the stubborn and successful American resistance in the murderous Battle of the Bulge and in the Korean encirclement were partly the end result of a conviction, nourished by cowboy films, that the good hero always wins if he holds out long enough."

Sergeant: "How can I hold with one squad against all those Chinese?"

Peck: "Do it—ask me later."

Of the five films dealing with men waiting for the cease-fire, *Pork Chop Hill* is the only one to receive Pentagon support or to treat affirmatively the need to keep on fighting until negotiating teams can jockey into acceptable positions. The other films in this category were all bleak and depressing sagas. Perhaps it was the purely political nature of the cease-fire itself that disillusioned filmmakers and audiences who had spent the years from Pearl Harbor on making or watching movies that stressed there could be no peace until the enemy and all he stood for was completely annihilated. Perhaps it was the deadlocked, immobile nature of the endwar fought along a no-man's land. The war film thrives on action and mobility, on meaningful physical goals rather than the abstract whims of truce negotiators.

I cannot think of a more appropriate example of the difference between the conventional war film and that about men under the tensions of an approaching armistice than two features released by Twentieth Century–Fox in mid-August 1961: *Marines, Let's Go!* and *Sniper's Ridge*. The first is standard formula—an opening section showing a diverse group of All-American Marines in combat in Korea, a comic middle section following them on leave in Japan, and a final combat sequence to work out tensions, give the "coward" a chance to prove himself, and provide the exciting last-minute rescue of a Marine and his Korean girlfriend. Directed by that master of the action film, Raoul Walsh, *Marines, Let's Go!* is the kind of cheerful martial adventure that has always been welcome in the trade.* The *Variety* reviewer, writing the week the Berlin Wall went up, felt the film "could not be hitting the market at a more opportune peace time juncture, what with the current drive to hike the U. S. Military force. This burst of nationalism and the renewed interest spurred in military life and times, especially among young men eligible for duty, is sure to exert a favorable influence on the film's box office."

Not surprisingly, *Marines, Let's Go!* received DOD assistance. *Sniper's Ridge*, the other Fox release, didn't. Had the seers at the Pentagon been capable of reading the entrails of Grade B films, they might have divined what was ahead for America, might have found some hint that the nation was tired of wars that go nowhere. *Sniper's Ridge* opens at the front lines on 25 July 1953, the day before the fighting stopped, yet it could have been set in Vietnam in early 1973. The central character is a private who is almost eligible for rotation Stateside. He

---

*Pierre Salinger reports (in *With Kennedy*) that when Jack Warner suggested Raoul Walsh as the director of *PT–109*, a showing of *Marines, Let's Go!* was arranged at the White House—"The President slid into the . . . showing and came to the conclusion that it was not his kind of picture."

demands to be transferred to the rear before his luck runs out. He even threatens to shoot his commanding officer rather than risk his neck patroling Sniper's Ridge. Peck had been threatened on Pork Chop, but that was by a sullen, fear-crazed, craven slacker—what makes *Sniper's Ridge* ominous is that the incipient fragger is the best fighter in the unit.

For a while, the film seems to be headed for a genuine confrontation between the private who wants so badly not to be the last man killed in Korea and his make-work, vindictive company commander. Then the captain steps on one of those cunning land-mines that go off when the victim steps away.

Captain: "A mine! I'm on a mine!"

First soldier: "Good!"

Second soldier: "That's the way it goes." At this point, we know *Sniper's Ridge* is going to back away from the brink of rebellion—the reluctant warrior saves the captain by knocking him off the mine and is gravely wounded in the process, thus earning a medal and a trip to the safety of the rear.

The following August came a cease-fire drama that pulled no punches. *War Hunt* was directed by Denis and Terry Sanders, who won an Academy Award in the mid-fifties for *A Time Out of War,* a little allegory about two soldiers—one Confederate, one Union—who become friends during a lull in the Civil War. *War Hunt* introduced Robert Redford to the screen as a "good" soldier who struggles with a psychopathic war lover (John Saxon) for the soul of a little Korean boy. Possibly the first half-conscious criticism of what was beginning to happen in Vietnam, this cautionary tale is unprecedented among American films in its ability to suggest the disorientating effects of an unwinnable war fought against an unseen and culturally alien foe.

War Hunt opens in the grand style of contemporary "antiwar" films with lyrical shots of spring grasses and wildflowers accompanied by an off-camera choir of Korean children. After the credits and a title proclaiming "Korea, May 1953," we see Robert Redford in the back of a truck and hear his off-camera voice describe the feelings of an infantryman in the pipeline toward his first combat. Arrived at the forward area, Redford is briefed by his new company commander: "We've got a funny kind of war here—a war we can't really win because it's gotta be settled around a conference table." The captain rationalizes that the continued fighting and dying is to teach the enemy that every day he stalls at Panmunjom will cost him men. Then Redford is led to his squad by a little Korean boy, Charlie, orphaned when his parents were napalmed by our side ("Gee, I'm sorry," says Redford; "OK—it mistake," replies Charlie). Along the way, Charlie tries to stab another little boy, whose mother comments indirectly on the incident with an ironic salutation to Redford: "Welcome to Korea. I hope you don't die."

Continuing his initiation, Redford meets members of his squad, which includes *M*A*S*H*'s Tom Skerritt as a jesting corporal and a private who has been in the army since 1937 and bitches that "we haven't lost a war yet, but we sure are pussy-footing our way through this one." Night comes, and Redford gets his first glimpse of Raymond Endore (John Saxon), a shadowy figure who sleeps during the day, talks little, and hides an impassive face behind black camouflage. As Endore vanishes into the night, a young Korean girl comes out of the gloom to announce she loves Redford and will fix his troubles. "Sweetheart," he replies, "You know what my trouble is? I can't believe I'm here." Thus ends the new man's first day.

Redford soon becomes an experienced trooper, going into shock during his first enemy barrage, but managing to kill a Chinese soldier in hand-to-hand combat to save his own life. No amount of acclimation to the war, however, accustoms him to Endore lounging around the squad bunker during the day wearing sunglasses, whistling, and resting up for his next nocturnal ramble. By chance, Redford witnesses Endore dancing his rondo, silently and joylessly jigging around the body of a Chinese sentry he has knifed. Redford complains to the captain that Endore is crazy, but the captain is willing to harbor an obvious psychopath who hunts by night for the sake of the intelligence concerning enemy positions and strength Endore gathers.

Redford tries to divert the little boy Charlie to wholesome interests by playing catch with him. But Endore, a proponent of pre-adolescent Koreanization, has promised to teach the boy how to kill, and tells Redford to butt-out or else. Before this confrontation can go any further, the long-awaited cease-fire is announced, and Endore, no future before him Stateside, escapes with the boy into No Man's Land. Pretending to be a graves registration party, Redford and the captain go after Endore before he can violate the truce terms. When Endore refuses to come back, the captain shoots him. As little

Charlie, orphaned once more, runs off into the wilderness of the demilitarized zone, the children's choir is heard again.*

Nineteen sixty-three brought another sardonic black-and-white film about men waiting for the war to end. But where *Sniper's Ridge* and *War Hunt* had been made by and with relative unknowns, *The Hook* was made for MGM by the team of George Seaton and William Perlberg (who had produced *The Bridges at Toko-Ri*) and starred Kirk Douglas as a master sergeant who receives an order from an ROK major to kill a North Korean prisoner of war.

The order comes by radio because the sergeant, his two men, and their prisoner are aboard a Finnish freighter (conveniently loaded down with an explosive cargo) off the coast of Korea. The ship, with its philosophical but uninvolved captain, makes for a neat little universe in which the conflicts generated by the death sentence can be worked out. An order has been given—never mind that it is a hasty and offhanded command, or that the authority is Korean and not American. The sergeant has spent nineteen years in the army. He knows the rules, stands by the law (not because of its majesty or humanity, but because an infraction might spoil his record and endanger his pension). He passes the order down the chain of command to the two privates, but it only boils back up to him. The first private (Nick Adams) gets drunk to avoid his duty; the second (Robert Walker, Jr.) insists that "killing a man out of combat is murder. . . . Orders or no orders."

Sergeant Douglas: "I gave you an order."

Private Walker: "But he's a prisoner."

Douglas: "If it was the other way around, he'd kill you."

Walker: "Well, if we're going to be like that . . ."

Douglas (anticipating answer): ". . . then what are we fighting for?"

---

*"You will be the first to know that *War Hunt* was based on a newspaper account of a Marine in Korea called The Candy Bar Kid," Stanford Whitmore, the scenarist, informed me. "He would load up with candy and disappear for days, killing, and was much admired by those who knew. But the Marine Corps is a discipline that doesn't tolerate freelance killing, so when the word got back to HQ the CBK was privately whisked away from the war and into a Vet hospital where he may still reside. My original aim in *War Hunt* was direct and uncompromising, and it was a sell-out that Endore was portrayed as ever bringing back *any* information. He was meant as pure killer, curried and encouraged by a Captain who would have to kill his monster when the rules changed."

Finally, the sergeant decides to do it himself. As he moves toward the "gook" to slit his throat, he recites the excuses one clings to at such times: they-do-it-to-our-prisoners and "if there's any stink later, it's the ROK major's fault. He gave the order. I'm just the poor little sergeant that had to carry it out." (Are you out there in the dark, Rusty? Are you listening?)

When the sergeant finds he can't kill in cold blood, it looks as though the prisoner will survive. The armistice comes, the prisoner escapes down into the hold full of gasoline drums. Robert Walker crawls down after him to explain that they mean him no harm though they have tried to kill him three times. But the government-issue Korean-English phrase book doesn't cover such unlikely abstractions as peace, truce, armistice: "A word for damn near everything except that."

As the prisoner has matches and the hold is full of fumes, the survival of the ship depends on his surrender or destruction. The tough sergeant goes down to tell him the war's over, but the prisoner keeps waving a razor and shouting, in Korean, "I can't, I can't." Interpreting this cry of impotence as a banzai scream, the sergeant kills him.

The film ends with the members of this little universe assembled to mourn a single death. Kirk Douglas gets the last word: "Kid, any day a war ends is a nice day." But what has ended? Only the war in the microcosm of the ship, and only because one man finally killed another.

The war in Korea (at least as far as Hollywood is concerned), is over. There has not been a combat film set in Korea since Burt Topper's *War Is Hell* was released in 1963–64 (I'm not forgetting 1970's *M*A*S*H,* but that was not a combat film nor were the long-haired, pot-smoking Vietnam-era rebels at home in the Korean setting). Like *Sniper's Ridge* before it, *War Is Hell* seems to exemplify how the growth of the conflict in Indo-China invited a faltering, hesitant revision of the meaning of the American experience in Korea. Remember Woody Strode and the protagonist of *Sniper's Ridge* threatening to kill their officers? In *War Is Hell,* long before the Vietnam fraggings became common knowledge, it finally happened. A cowardly, lying, medal-happy sergeant kills his officer so a citation for heroism will not be revoked. He then goes on fighting, withholding from his men the fact that the war is over. The glory hunter and his men are wiped out by the enemy in Hollywood's first visitation of mass retribution upon an American unit.

War Is Hell is quite obviously not a standard Hollywood prod-

THREE

GROWING OLD AT THE MOVIES

William Calley to John Sack: "We thought, we will go to Vietnam and be Audie Murphys. Kick in the door, run in the hooch, give it a good burst—kill. And get a big kill ratio in Vietnam. Get a big kill count."
—*Lieutenant Calley: His Own Story*

Gregory Peck to young Robert Blake, who has not returned to the rear to be treated for wounds sus-tained in wiping out a

North Korean machinegun
nest: "Who do you think you
are? Audie Murphy?"
—*Pork Chop Hill*

PART ONE: AUDIE MURPHY DIED FOR OUR SINS

November 11, 1955. With two or three other officers, I am marching at the head of a battalion of fine young Americans. It is Armistice Day (I've never liked the new name, Veterans Day).

I am wearing the basic uniform of the United States Army since World War II: the short Ike Jacket and matching olive drab trousers. Beyond that, all is changed, magical. On top, a chrome-plated helmet, carefully stored in tissue paper except when taken out for ceremonial occasions; below, spit-shined paratrooper boots. In between, a gleaming Sam Browne belt, huge brass buckle, silver-plated scabbard, stainless steel cavalry sabre, insignia of rank and regimental badge (two of each), shoulder patches, service stripes, and crossed rifles of the infantry on each lapel, white silk scarf, rope-like fourragères (one blue, one red, one white, one yellow) with brilliant brass pips, medals (just gobs of them), marksmanship badges, and (closest to my heart) four rows of ribbons (red, white, blue, yellow, green, orange, purple, brown, and combinations thereof) absolutely spotted and clotted with stars, bars, and oak leaf clusters.

The truly marvelous thing about all this is that I'm only seventeen years old, a cadet major in the Junior ROTC battalion at West Phoenix High School, and I am marching down the main drag of Phoenix, a captive city. This parade means a lot to me and to almost everyone else in Phoenix, a city that takes pride in the military competence of its children. My mother, one of many mothers, wives, daughters, sweethearts, waves from the crowd on Central Avenue. Old men, liver-spotted, paunchy, and balding, their duty done, take our salute from the reviewing stand.

Taa-Rah-Rah, Boomp!-Ti-Ay.

No one scoffs at the ROTC in Phoenix. Is it not democracy in action? Is not the battalion commander at Camelback an Afro-American (or, as they said in those days, a fine, upstanding colored boy)? At Phoenix Union he's a Polish-American. My own West Phoenix, the city champion in last spring's military competition, is the most ethnic conglomerate of all: I'm just a WASP from the South, pure American, but one of the company commanders, my good friend Danny DeLeon, is a Mexican-American, another company commander is a compact little Japanese-American, and the cadet colonel, Herbie Dreiseszum, is a fine Hebrew-American, just like the owner of Goldwater's department store downtown who is both a United States Senator and a brigadier general in the Arizona National Guard.

I'm in the National Guard too, and so are Danny and a lot of the other cadet officers, but as we're only privates and corporals in the guard, bare of brass and real campaign ribbons, we prefer to march with our Rotcy units.

The parade reaches its end. We've marched four or five miles, and army trucks are waiting to take us back to our local assembly areas. With another cadet major, I decide not to ride back to West Phoenix. Instead, we walk back past Goldwater's to the central downtown area, clanking under the weight of our medals and paraphernalia, through the admiring crowds of postparade shoppers and sightseers. We're going to a movie, to see Audie Murphy in his own life story (if you can credit a life ending with the hero only a few years our senior). For three years, my friend and I have tried to out-do each other in winning medals and badges and fourragères. Audie, the most decorated soldier of World War II, is our hero.

November 11, 1969. My son Joshua is being baptized in the Sage Chapel at Cornell University. The priest is Dan Berrigan, and the infant, a symbol of innocence, is the focus of an act both religious and political. Dan prays that the child will grow into a man of peace, that the old significance of Armistice Day will not be lost. It's a long way from Phoenix.

It is not to brag that I have played back the home movie of me at seventeen, at half-life, for the image I summon up embarrasses me and would puzzle those who know me today.

No, I want you to know I am speaking as one who once admired what Audie Murphy stood for (and who may still, in a strange way), as one who has traveled a long road from the days when he stood at the top of his class at NCO school at Fort Hood, Texas (the general shook my hand)—as one who still can't bear to throw away his awards from the American Legion, the Sons of the American Revolution, and the National Rifle Association, but hides them away with his old stamp collection, another relic of a happy middle-American childhood and adolescence.

I want you to understand that this investigation into the ironies of Audie is, for me, a journey back into time, a journey in which I see, with old eyes but a new vision, what I saw in movies and magazines half a life and more ago.

Finally, I want you to understand that Audie Murphy's death a few years back struck me as a reminder of both personal and national mortality. I had forgotten him, had seen none of his films since 1958, had left him as an all-American boy-faced hero. And there he was, splashed on the front page of a local paper, middle-aged, jowly, heavy-eyed, wearing the face of an outwardly successful auto dealer who might, any day now, be indicted for fraud.

Audie. The image he makes. Our very own Dorian Grey. In death, the jowls drop away, the fat melts, the movie runs backward, and suddenly we see the timeless youth once more, an image frozen in the mold set by this twenty-year-old *Saturday Evening Post* head:

HE DOESN'T WANT TO BE A STAR

He ran away to war at 17, won 23 decorations and the Medal of Honor by personally killing 240 Germans. A semidisabled veteran at 21, Audie Murphy reluctantly became a big-money Hollywood star, but he's still just a sharecropper's kid—lonely and sometimes afraid of his own dreams.

Afraid of his own dreams . . . the real world was safe, but the world of dreams full of snares and delusions. "I had nightmares about the war—men running and shooting and hollering, and then my gun would fall apart when I tried to pull the trigger." So at first he slept with a loaded pistol under his pillow, with a gun that wouldn't fall apart—if he couldn't pull the trigger in the dream world, at least he could in the real. One night, awaking to find a luminous switch glaring at him in the dark, he blasted away, startling out of her own dreams the starlet sleeping at his side.

The Great Audie Murphy Dream and Time Machine
Reel One: Ceremonies and Celebrations

When the lieutenant general pinned the Medal of Honor and the Legion of Merit on Audie, nine United States senators on a jaunt to Berchtesgaden stood in line to shake his hand.

He came back from the war, stood on a reviewing stand on Fifth Avenue next to another general. "Where do you plan on going, Murphy, now that the war is over?" the general is supposed to have asked under his breath. "Home, General. Is there any other place to go, Sir?"

Home, of course, was Farmersville, Texas, and we know he went back, for *Life* went with him and the *Saturday Evening*

Post proclaimed the homecoming too. He didn't stay long. Whether Farmersville had changed, or Audie had changed, makes no difference. Everything seemed changed, even the old battle fields when he went back to France in 1948 as the guest of M. le President Auriol: "He traveled 1,500 miles visiting battlefields where he fought but even after they were pointed out to him by former members of the Maquis he had difficulty in recognizing the localities." General de Lattre de Tassigny, the chief of staff, pinned the Legion of Honor and the Croix de Guerre on Audie, and home he came, to Hollywood.

Whatever happened to Farmersville?

When a girl wanted his autograph in Dallas in 1948, Audie signed himself a "fugitive from the law of averages." He meant that he had escaped death when so many had not. But one law of averages he was never able to escape: that by winning more medals than anyone else, he marked himself for life. Few writers, no matter how brief the space provided nor the reason for writing, were able to avoid some version of the magic formula: "The Most Decorated American Soldier of World War II."

To his dying day, Audie carried not one but a whole flock of albatrosses, and the biggest hung around his neck on a star-spangled blue ribbon.

He tried to give them away in 1950. The Medal of Honor went to his eight-year-old nephew back in Farmersville, the Distinguished Service Cross to a girl in Tennessee as a high school graduation present. But there was no escaping the medals, the awards dead men couldn't collect ("I feel," he once said, "as if they handed their medals to me and said: 'Here, Murph, hold these,' "—Murph, the patsy), for the army quickly replaced them, gratis.

He was like a man who had broken the law of averages in a crazy crap game played for symbols, and though the symbols could be exchanged for money (and were—as *Life* put it in commercial metaphors, "He got the big one for a *day's work* near Holtswihr. . . . His medals got Murphy a *contract* in Hollywood"), they carried with them a doom.

The Great Audie Murphy Dream and Time Machine
Reel Two: Real Life

My country. America! That is it. We have been so intent on death that we have forgotten life. And now suddenly life faces us. I swear to myself that I will measure up to it. I may be branded by war, but I will not be defeated by it.

Gradually it becomes clear. I will go back. I will find the kind of girl of whom I once dreamed. I will learn to look at life through uncynical eyes, to have faith, to know love. I will learn to work in peace as in war. And finally—finally, like countless others, I will learn to live again.

—To Hell and Back

As the last words of his autobiography suggest, Audie Murphy was the kind of childlike man who knew too much about death before he knew about life. Trouble was, *Life* knew about *him*. As Citizen Kane is seen through the Lucean newsreel, so with Audie through *Life,* the picture magazine.

He burst forth upon America on the cover of *Life* for 16 July 1945. There he is, in all our libraries today, smiling down at the camera as though at a younger brother. (Perhaps I'm that younger brother, for I first saw him there myself.) Strong, even, white teeth, hundreds of freckles, and for caption the inevitable formula: "MOST DECORATED SOLDIER." There he is, full blown, the all-American boy that press agents would blather about for another generation. James Cagney saw his picture, called his brother, a producer, and, the story goes, a star was born. Well, almost.

The four-page spread inside ended with a picture of Audie, back home in Farmersville, getting his tie straightened by his "special girl," nineteen-year-old Mary Lee: "Audie hopes she is his own girl but he isn't quite sure yet because he usually blushes when he gets within ten feet of any girl."

Life just couldn't leave him alone. As long as he kept his boyish looks, he was good for yet another four-page spread. So two years later he is seen showing his medals to yet another nineteen-year-old girlfriend, Wanda Hendrix, an aspiring (as they used to say) starlet he had first seen on the cover of another magazine: "At present, Wanda and Audie consider each other more important than any career. They are reportedly engaged and the love affair, unlike so many others in moviedom, is said to be the real thing. . . . Audie has simply given Wanda his medals—'just for safekeeping.' "

Life was right: it was the real thing, though they didn't do a spread on the end of the affair two years later when Wanda was granted a divorce on uncontested grounds of mental cruelty (that shootout with the lightswitch didn't help things).

The bloom was off the Texas rose, but *Life* was still game for yet another four-page spread when Audie starred in his own life story based on his own autobiography. The combination of art and life was just too much, so there in the 1955 Fourth of July issue, was Audie manning the machine gun on a burning tank under the head "A War Hero Turned Actor Acts Himself as Hero."

Sixteen years passed before Audie returned to *Life.* It took his death to do it. No more the four-page spread, but half a page by his old colleague-in-arms and fellow actor, Bill Mauldin, who rendered the immortal eulogy: "Long before his plane flew into a mountain he was nibbled to death by ducks."

No more the front cover, but now the "Parting Shots." *Life* had given Audie fame twenty-six years before, and Audie had blown it. The final irony, surely unconscious, was that the last of the Parting Shots for that issue was the full page photograph of a baby-faced South Vietnamese general, absolutely dripping with medals, ribbons, fourragères, badges, and gew-gaws, receiving his thirty-first decoration. The caption reads "It has been a very long war in Vietnam."

The Great Audie Murphy Dream and Time Machine Reel Three: The Movie Begins

To examine Audie Murphy's life as a work of art is like reading a novel by a deranged disciple of Kurt Vonnegut. Audie was (is?) just as much the unwilling traveler as that other victim of wartime excess, Billy Pilgrim. Where Billy came unstuck in time, Audie came unglued in reality. Actors, you say, don't really live their parts—but Audie was no actor and made no pretensions along that line. As he once told a director, he had a "hell of a handicap: No talent."

The people who first put Audie Murphy in front of a camera were interested in what he was, not in what he could pretend to be. He was, simply, a war hero on a scale as spectacularly wholesome as anything Hollywood could dream of.

His movies, then, are not so much roles as an alternative life. Quick, let's examine that life before you suspend belief. His first bit part was a simple extension of the life he had begun to dream of while in the army: he had wanted to go to West Point after the war, but a battle injury kept him out—Hollywood sent him there as a cadet in *Beyond Glory* (1948), a film about the problems of a veteran (played by Alan Ladd) still recovering from the effects of combat.

Then Audie began reliving the possibilities of his old life

before the war: in *Bad Boy* (1949), his first top billing, the orphan from Texas played another Texas orphan, a teenager afoul of the law (but basically a good kid, the kind a stint in the army or Marines would soon straighten out). The story continues in his very next movie, *The Kid from Texas* (1950), but instead of joining the army and becoming the Audie Murphy we know, the bad boy from Texas becomes Billy the Kid, the Billy of myth, not history—a misunderstood boy who kills a score of men to avenge the murder of a friend and benefactor.

Traveling back in time, see. First a contemporary boy, then a youth of the 1870s, then all the way back to the Civil War in 1951, a vintage year for Audie, the year in which he played a nameless Union soldier in *The Red Badge of Courage,* then acquired a name (Jesse James) and joined Quantrill's *Kansas Raiders* to take revenge on the Yankees. A pretty good trick for a boy who began the Civil War in the Union camp.

Once he came unstuck in reality, it was hard for him to get back to his starting point—so the peak of his acting career came when he attempted the impossible for a boy without talent: to be himself, to play Lieutenant Audie Murphy in an adaptation of the book by Audie Murphy about Audie Murphy (he was the first actor to star in his own life story on the screen, Arlo Guthrie was the second, and therein lies one difference between two generations).

"I didn't think I was the type myself," he told a *New York Times* interviewer. Maybe he wasn't: when he delivered in the reel world lines he had first spoken in the real, it was with the embarrassed self-consciousness of the little boy repeating for Mommy the cute thing he once said spontaneously and had now lost.

Loss. When Audie acted himself, he left something behind on the screen, as if fulfilling that fear anthropologists have found among some primitive peoples: the camera can steal the soul.

"War is like a giant pack rat," Audie said at the time of the autobiographical *To Hell and Back.* "It takes something from you, and it leaves something behind in its stead." Movies too. "We changed the part where Brandon died in my arms. That was the way it had really happened, but it looked too corny, they said. I guess it did."

Audie seems to have been programed for loss, like the hero of Hemingway's "Soldier's Home," a cruel little story about a boy who comes home from the war to find that he can't talk honestly about his experiences: "All of the times that had been able to make him feel cool and clear inside himself when he thought of them; the times so long back when he had done the one thing, the only thing for a man to do, easily and naturally, when he might have done something else, now lost their cool, valuable quality and were lost themselves. . . . Krebs acquired the nausea in regard to experience that is the result of untruth or exaggeration. . . . In this way he lost everything."

Not that Audie lied or exaggerated, God forbid. But, like Hemingway, he lived for decades on the dividends of a small amount of experience, he transmuted a brief portion of his life into art, he cashed in his medals.

No, not that he lied, though one suspects that much of what he said to interviewers or published under his own by-line in the popular press had been combed and cared for by press agents. Thus with the piece he wrote for *Colliers* on the strange position of "a man who has fought an honest war, then come back and played himself doing it": "Twelve years stood between . . . this powder-puff battle and the real war, between the lucky and the dead. And time, I'd learned, can be a good thing. It stretches quietly between the present and the past, like a membrane. But I was beginning to discover that the membrane can be broken, and suddenly you are back at the beginning, in the real war. The charges going off in the make-believe battle are blanks, but the shrapnel goes off in your mind."

The automatic reaction of the sophisticate is that Audie Murphy couldn't have written this, but then, are Hollywood press agents any more given to existential paradox and irony than simple Texas farmboys caught up in the "strange jerking back and forth between make-believe and reality, between fighting for your life and the discovery that it's only a game and you have to do a retake because a tourist's dog ran across the field in the middle of the battle"?

The Great Audie Murphy Dream and Time Machine Reel Four: Previews of Coming Attractions

In 1957, when Audie, taking advantage of contract clauses that gave him story approval, began asking for vehicles such as *Peer Gynt* and Dostoevski's *The Idiot,* his producer sued him for a million dollars, claiming Audie was trying to break his contract by proposing unsuitable parts. But think! What if he was serious? What if Audie *was* beginning to see himself as Prince Myshkin? It's not impossible, after all—get your mind straight, clean out your prejudices, and you too can see that Audie might have made a native American Myshkin, an innocent, trusting, childlike, and misunderstood figure too good for the world around him.

In fact, that's just the role he played in his very next film, *The Quiet American*. From the opening montage of happy smiling Vietnamese faces (and how long has it been since you've seen a smiling Vietnamese?) to the closing dedication to the people of the Republic of Vietnam, the film evokes a lost innocence and springs back upon us a holy idiocy in which Audie plays a Yankee Myshkin, an idealistic young entrepreneur who wants to bring democracy and plastics to Southeast Asia. Ah, but wicked men doubt his motives, and have him betrayed and murdered.

As it is fit and proper for our heroes to set examples for the young, it is worth noting that Audie was perhaps the first American to die in Vietnam, if only on the screen.

And Now, a Word From Our Sponsor

Audie's involvement in the cold war did not end with *The Quiet American*. In his next film, *The Gunrunners* (also 1958), he was a fishing boat captain forced to smuggle arms to Cuban revolutionaries. He killed the smugglers and did his part to prevent the Communist overthrow of a dependable ally in the bastion of freedom. The producers of the film were trying to exploit popular interest in Castro and to refine Audie's image by having him repeat the role of Hemingway's Harry Morgan as played by Bogart in *To Have and Have Not* and John Garfield in *The Breaking Point*. And in *Trunk to Cairo* (1966) he was an American agent in conflict with a former Nazi scientist helping the Egyptians plot the ruin of Israel.

In retrospect, the casting of Audie Murphy in certain specific roles—as the democratic spokesman in Vietnam, as the defender of Israel, as a boy learning to bite the bullet in four or five different wars—becomes a political act. Go back over his career and you'll find he was an unwitting salesman for grass roots militarism in the days when the movies were a perpetual public service announcement. In his very first minor role he played a West Point cadet in a film about a villainous (and, of course, unjust) attack on the principles of the United States Military Academy. The film ended with General Eisenhower delivering a graduation speech about the traditions of the Academy—with fine boys like Audie preparing to be career officers, how could anyone doubt the essential rectitude of the Academy, the army, and the pentagon for which it stands?

The Great Audie Murphy Dream and Time Machine
Part Five: Apotheosis

Ask the man in the street about heroes, and, if he isn't demonstrating, he'll probably respond along these lines: the greatest American hero of World War I was Sergeant Alvin York, a quiet, humble boy from the South who killed and captured more enemy soldiers singlehanded than just about anyone else (Hollywood turned him into Gary Cooper, and all was well); the greatest American hero of World War II was another quiet humble boy from the South who won more medals and killed more enemy than anyone else (and Hollywood turned him into Audie Murphy).

And then came Vietnam and a time when some said The Greatest was an unquiet, unhumble, and unwhite boy (though you better not call him *boy* to his face) from the South—and he wasn't even in the army and hadn't even killed any one, though he did make a mess of Sonny Liston.

The times were confused, the landscape unclear, so when a genuwine old-fashioned quiet humble boy from the South saw his opportunity and took it, suddenly the magic didn't work anymore.

But lo, the very season that Lieutenant Calley was convicted rather than rewarded for doing what he thought the movies and the history books had all told him to do, George C. Scott (though unquiet and unhumble and definitely no boy) got the Academy Award for *Patton.* Hollywood protects its own.

And Lieutenant Murphy (Retired) traveled about speaking in behalf of Lieutenant Calley ("I'm not so sure that in those days, having been indoctrinated to a fever pitch, I might not have committed the same error—and I prefer to call it an error—that Lieutenant Calley did"), but he lost his bearings and found, like the title of his last movie, *A Time for Dying.* Searchers found his body on Memorial Day, but the younger generation was protesting too loudly to take much heed.

General Westmoreland came to the funeral, and President Nixon sent his aide across the tumid Potomac to represent him at Arlington. The President released a statement:

As America's most decorated hero of World War II,
Audie Murphy not only won the admiration of millions for his own brave exploits,
He also came to epitomize the gallantry in action of America's fighting men.
The nation stands in his debt
And mourns at his death.

PART TWO: OLD ACTORS NEVER DIE

From the Hairbreath Harry of his P. T. boat exploits through the political campaigns with their exceptional chances . . . through the . . . decision to run for President . . . the adventure in Cuba, the atomic poker game with Khrushchev . . . when the biggest bluff in the history of the world was called—yes, each is a panel of scenes in the greatest movie ever made.

—Mailer, *The Presidential Papers*

Lieutenant Kennedy (Cliff Robertson) to a sailor afraid of dying: "It could happen, Andy. You could die. That's war. Whenever I think about that, I try to remember the odds are on our side."

—PT–109

Sign on the marquee of a Georgia moviehouse showing *PT–109:* "See how the Japs almost got Kennedy."

Lieutenant Kennedy: "The odds are on our side."
Lieutenant Ross (Robert Culp): "Boy, you kill me, you really do. Here we are, beat and burned and given up for dead, living on green coconuts and no water in the middle of fifteen thousand Japanese soldiers, and you decide the odds are with us?"
Kennedy: "It's a flaw in my character."

—PT–109

News item on *PT–109:* "Its first mass booking since President Kennedy was assassinated will be on March 19 in neighborhood theaters in Dallas."

—New York Times, 19 February 1964

December 1973. Driving across Memorial Bridge toward Arlington, I pass the spot where I stood ten years before when John Kennedy was borne past toward his grave, and think of the movie I saw a few weeks earlier, *Executive Action.* "He is going to pull out of Vietnam," a character complained of Kennedy. Others spoke of the need to kill President Kennedy before he could sell Saigon down the river, and the rich old conservative played by Will Geer did not make up his mind to throw his fortune behind Executive Action until he watched a newscast juxtaposing a riot in Saigon with JFK's announcement that more troops would be pulled out of Vietnam.

Could it be that John Kennedy really did die because of Vietnam? His death, coming so close to that of Ngo Dinh Diem, had seemed ominously poetic, as though some force larger than coincidence was saying America had gone too far this time in trying to rewrite the script, to recast the movie.

And driving on through the morning rush-hour traffic toward

Arlington and the Pentagon beyond, I have time to reflect that
Audie Murphy is buried up there too. Suddenly disparate piles
of notes for this book fall into place. Audie Murphy and John
F. Kennedy, the foremost Americans to die for Vietnam—one
on the screen and the other by sacrifice through association.
The people who made *Executive Action* were relying not on
any historically observable cause and effect relationship, but
on nothing more substantial (or less seductive) than the legend-
monger's desire to turn chaotic and aimless reality into neatly
structured and motivated fairy tales.

　　To even mention JFK and Audie Murphy in the same context,
much less put them back to back in the same chapter, may
seem to fall from the sublime to the ridiculous, yet the connections are worth exploring and extend far beyond the simple
irony that one started in Texas, the other ended there, and both
came to share a common place of burial, far beyond the more
complex and prophetic irony of the transmutation of Graham
Greene's Kennedy-Bundy quiet Harvard man into the quiet
Texan played by Audie.

　　Both Kennedy and Murphy had come of age during World
War II—Murphy to the early maturity of the adolescent forced
into bloom by circumstances, Kennedy to the delayed manhood
of the princeling operating, for the first time in his life, inde-
pendently of his family's name and wealth. The war gave each
the opportunity to break out of the prison of birth: Murphy to
rise above the sharecropper's station, Kennedy to dip down into
the broader fraternity of mass culture.

　　Both returned from this initiation as heroes in an era of
heroes—Murphy distinct by virtue of the sheer numerical bulk
of his citations, Kennedy by virtue of his survival under conditions that made a good yarn for national magazines (*The New
Yorker, Reader's Digest*), even at the end of a war that glutted
the press with true-life tales of heroism.

　　And both found themselves acting out scripts other men had
written. As early as 1960 Norman Mailer was trying to get at the
elusive detachment of Kennedy: "he was like an actor who had
been cast as the candidate, a good actor, but not a great one—
you were aware all the time that the role was one thing and the
man another." Chance (the fact of his continual survival
against odds) had made Murphy a national figure and thence
an actor, and chance (the war-time death of the older brother
who wanted to be President) thrust John Kennedy from the
understudy's role and cast him as the leading man. But leading

men do not long retain their box-office appeal unless their personal images fit the roles—and chance again dealt John Kennedy a winning hand: the beautiful head of hair, the endearing smile, and the nagging back trouble (the hero's stigma) that set up subconscious national associations with FDR and gave him the enforced leisure in which to write *Profiles in Courage* and win his first surrogate Oscar, the Pulitzer Prize. And then there was *Life*.

That summer, when Jackie paid her first visit to Hyannis Port, looking forward to a weekend of sailing with Jack, she found a third sailor in the boat, a photographer from *Life* who was doing a picture story on their courtship.

—*Johnny, We Hardly Knew Ye*

In the most eerie photograph ever to come out of the White House, we have seen the President, darkly through a terrace window, the troubled lord and monarch of us all, utterly alone with the Cuban crisis, his conscience, and a *Life* photographer.

—Alistair Cooke, *Show*, April 1963

When Henry Luce, the inventor of *Time, Life,* and *Fortune,* proclaimed in the foreword to a book by a twenty-three year old Harvard graduate that "If John Kennedy is characteristic of the younger generation—and I believe he is—many of us would be happy to have the destinies of this Republic handed over to this generation at once," he was setting in motion an infernal machine. Henry Luce did not make predictions lightly, nor lightly did he extend the destinies of the Republic. So it is not too surprising that *Life* and *Time* gave particular attention to the growing career of young Kennedy in the early fifties. Just as Audie Murphy came into many living rooms on the cover of *Life,* so did a spray-drenched Jack and Jackie the week the Korean War ended. *"Life* Goes Courting with a U. S. Senator" ran the cover story title, a title to sweeten the dread impact of the week's editorial on "the first war U. S. did not win." *Life* went to the wedding a few months later, followed his career with mounting enthusiasm, and when the sole photographic record of the bursting of his head went up for sale, *Life* was there with the highest bid.

The summer of 1962. I've just finished graduate school and have my first teaching job lined up. I'm spending the holidays

in Washington with my mother, who is now married to a
retired government official. From her shaded side porch we can
watch Bill and Mary Bundy entertaining their New Frontier
friends and relations next door (he's McGeorge's older brother,
she's Dean Acheson's daughter). The big tree in Mother's garden overhangs George Ball's back yard, and mother makes
jokes about soaking its roots in anticipation of stray hurricanes.
Later William Manchester will move in on the other side to
write *The Death of a President* and Bundy will move from
Defense to State, build a patio, and give bigger parties. Mother
will die—the same day as Henry Luce—and her coffin will rest
in St. Matthew's over a plaque announcing that John Kennedy's
had rested on the very same spot.

But that's still in the future. For the time being, all is well,
and we're all having a gay time, though mother is periodically
enraged by the incessant attention to the young President
("Young? He was born the same year I was!") in the magazines
she likes to read. She is particularly disturbed by a *Life* Picture
of the Week late in the summer—a full-page shot of a dripping
wet JFK emerging from the sea off Santa Monica and being
mobbed by admirers, many of whom have waded into the ocean
fully clothed. A beefy middle-aged woman is reaching out to get
her hand on the broadly smiling, handsome-as-an-actor figure
trapped between the pressing flesh and the men with cameras.

"You see what's happening?" demands Mother, who always
credited me with more insight into her thought processes than
I ever possessed. "Hmmmm," I nod, not wishing to start another
interminable argument and have to stop drinking her bourbon.
"They are deifying him," she throws the magazine down, starts
into the house to get another toddy. "Oh, cool off, Winnie," says
my stepfather, who was born in Washington during Grover Cleve-
land's first administration. He's seen 'em come and he's seen
'em go, he's always willing to tell you. "Let me tell you, it's not as
bad as it's been." He's about to launch into his number on FDR.

"You listen to me, both of you," Mother snorts, "it's going to
be worse. Much worse. Do you know, they're even making a
movie about the man?" She comes back to us so the New Frontiersmen pressing in on every side can't hear. "Before this is
over, you will see this country in ruins. Ruins!"

"Christ, what a touchy woman," says my stepfather when
she's gone. "It's just a goddamned movie."

So I went right to the top after we bought the Donovan book. President Kennedy assured me that I had his permission to make the pic-

ture, and the moment the script was finished I sent a copy to the White House. I recall listening to radio reports on Col. John Glenn's progress the night he was in orbit around the world, and I heard some newsman ask Pierre Salinger: "What is the President doing while Glenn spins around the world?"

"He is reading the script of *PT–109*," Salinger replied.
 —Jack Warner, *My First Hundred Years in Hollywood*

It was like something out of *The Godfather*. Picture the man of dignity (the good Catholic family man and capo of what the press delighted in referring to as the Irish Mafia) sitting behind his desk on the East Coast. He tells his adviser to go out to the West Coast and take care of a casting problem. But it's not Marlon Brando, of course, but JFK dispatching Pierre Salinger to persuade a reluctant Warren Beatty to play the lead in *PT–109*. The casting of this film was given more care and thought than is customarily given to the casting of the vice-presidency. "We checked out every one of the people in the cast," said Bryan Foy, the producer, "to be sure we didn't have any Communists, or some guy who had his mother in the poor house." It pays to be careful.

Though Salinger explained the delicacy of casting the Kennedy role in *PT–109* in broad terms of national security ("Since the picture would be shown overseas and could disseminate an image that might be very bad for the United States if it were not handled with dignity"), the real reason is obvious: Kennedy would be coming up for re-election not long after the film premiered, and a good film that presented the right image could go a long way toward helping the voters forget any little flaws that might have surfaced during the first term. After all, the film itself, over which JFK would have final script approval, would be an all-purpose metaphor for his first administration: Lieutenant (jg) John F. Kennedy came aboard the PT–109 in the same way he came aboard the ship of state—eager but untested. True, the *PT–109* sank, but JFK had led the survivors to safety. So, no matter how desperate things might look in 1964, Kennedy's supporters could count on a nation that had celluloid proof of the skipper's track record. If he could snatch victory from defeat once, could he not again? The odds are on our side.

Kennedy himself, the legend goes, had not capitalized on his war record, but he could not stop his supporters from circulating (as they did during his first congressional race in 1946) reprints of the *Reader's Digest* version of John Hersey's 1944 account of the PT–109 saga. And during the crucial 1960 West

Virginia primary some eager-beavers in the Kennedy camp not only trotted out the old *Reader's Digest* piece, but saw to it that the *Navy Log* sequence on PT–109 was re-run for the benefit of voters who didn't already know which candidate was the only combat hero in the running. And the idea for the Hollywood film came not from JFK but from Joseph Kennedy, Sr. Who could deny a proud father the right to call his old crony Jack Warner and suggest a movie?

So the casting was a delicate matter. "When we learned that Warner Brothers was making *PT–109*," Salinger told a *Saturday Evening Post* reporter, "we asked for the normal courtesy that the President be allowed to approve the man chosen to portray him." (As no film had ever been made about a living President, it is hard to see what was normal about this particular courtesy, but let it pass.) Alvin Cluster, who had been Lieutenant Kennedy's immediate superior in the Pacific and was then marketing manager for a California firm making aerospace components, served as liaison during the casting, shuttling between Hollywood and the White House with screen tests. The President rejected the likes of Jeffrey Hunter (who had just played Jesus in *The King of Kings*), Kookie Byrnes, Peter Fonda, and other pretty faces, asking instead for Warren Beatty. But Bryan Foy argued, according to Salinger, that Beatty was "a mixed up actor and said if he played Kennedy, the President would also emerge as 'mixed up.'" For his part, Beatty (who would later become a chief supporter of George McGovern) turned down the Kennedy draft because he thought the film would be a disaster in the hands of Bryan Foy.

Then lightning struck Cliff Robertson, who was, at thirty-eight, twelve years older than the character he would be playing.* "But why did the President choose me?" he asked Cluster. "Not only because you're a fine actor, but because you're young-looking, and yet mature enough so that the world won't get the idea that he's being played by a parking lot attendant." *The world.*

The timing of the film made it a deranged echo of John Kennedy's brief tenure. First announced shortly after his inauguration, and released shortly before his assassination, *PT–109* was

---

*Public recognition came to Cliff Robertson for this part, but the Oscar would have to wait until he played another son of Boston, the simple-minded Charly whose biggest race is not with another PT boat but against a mouse named Algernon.

an embarrassment from start to finish. Item: the preproduction activity in the Florida Keys, where Warner Brothers closed off several islands, built a World War II navy base, dredged channels, and assembled a flotilla, spurred rumors of a new invasion of Cuba to follow up on the Bay of Pigs. Item: the Coast Guard kept mistaking the scruffy Hollywood navy for a Cuban invasion fleet attacking Florida.

The making of the film was a bit like a mis-managed war, with the older general (director Lewis Milestone) fired because the politicians back home (the studio chiefs) claimed he was not advancing fast enough against those implacable foes, boredom and the budget (Jack Warner told Salinger that Milestone was "directing the picture at too slow a pace. This was an action picture . . . and needed an action director"). Meanwhile, the experienced campaigner, Milestone, the director of some of the most famous war films ever made—*All Quiet on the Western Front, A Walk in the Sun, The Purple Heart, Pork Chop Hill*— was telling reporters the war was unwinnable because the plan of battle, the script, stank. Replacing Milestone with an obedient refugee from television only compounded the disaster.* Perhaps if Milestone had been given his way, he could have pulled it off, just as he made a success of *All Quiet on the Western Front* without benefit of a happy ending (let the Germans win, he is reputed to have suggested by way of crushing the studio's wishful thinking).

Why is it that *PT-109* is such a dreadful film? Is it just that it is a long-winded, self-conscious version of *McHale's Navy* full of pointless comic relief and cute plays on the audience's knowledge of what the modest hero would become? Is it that it turns the vitally *human* John Kennedy into a smug, pious, priggish, and pompous model for the young, the kind of jerk who turns down a goldbricker's suggestion that he use his high connections to get them both transferred out of the combat zone with "Rogers—I'm surprised at you—where's your spirit?" or who dispels his second-in-command's doubts about a new crew ("Do you think they can do a good job for us?") with "Sure, if we do a good job for them" or answers a frightened man's plea ("What can a man do, Mr. Kennedy, except pray?") with "You can do your job, like all of us."

Or is it that the film unconsciously strips away the dignity

---

*Les Martinson, the new director, would follow up the fiasco of *PT-109* with *F.B.I. Code 98;* producer Bryan Foy also produced *I Was a Communist for the F.B.I.;* Richard Breen, who wrote the script, also did *The F.B.I. Story.* Do we detect a conspiracy?

and seriousness of John Kennedy and makes one momentarily suspect that, like the titles of his books, what we admired was the sugar coating over a strychnine marshmallow—that *Why England Slept* was a presumptuous exercise for a callow young Ivy Leaguer, that *Profiles in Courage* was a sermon meant to make us dig deeper into our psychic pockets in order to finance the Indo-Chinese and Caribbean annexes to the cathedral, that *To Turn the Tide* was the prerogative of the moon, not man?

Or is it because one detects a fatal optimism, the first step into big muddy, in exchanges like those that follow the collision of PT–109 with a Japanese cruiser. Kennedy and his surviving crew huddle on the slowly sinking wreckage. Democratically, the leader asks his men what they think should be done, but when they begin to squabble, he shuts them up and organizes a four-mile swim. "Sir," says the kid played by Robert Blake, "some of these men don't swim too well—how far did you say that island was?" "Don't worry, Bucky," replies the college swimmer, "we'll make it." As they begin their long swim, Bucky reaches out for encouragement again: "You think we're gonna make it, don't you?" "Take a bet on it, Bucky," says the gambling man. "Either you win or you don't pay off." And after they have paddled a short distance, Bucky weighs in again: "Four miles—a long way." "It's only three inches on the chart, Bucky." And Kennedy swims on in the lead, pulling a wounded man by a strap clenched in his teeth, a veritable profile in courage.

Once on the tiny barren island, Kennedy must struggle against even greater challenges to his leadership and confidence. Without the immediate danger of drowning or discovery by the enemy, the men grow weaker, less resistant to confusion, doubt, and despair. After several days he canvasses his men, learns they all doubt they will be rescued (or, worse, no longer care), announces they *will* survive. "The odds are on our side," he intones, to loud objections from Robert Culp. Fortunately, help arrives almost immediately, so the audience sees it can trust Kennedy's judgment.

Afterwards, as JFK and his men are heading back to their home base, one of the cowards comes forward to apologize for popping off and throwing tantrums. Kennedy, savoring his coffee and the fullness of the moment, demonstrates what is probably meant to be his ability to value criticism and opposition: "Howard," he says beneficently, "if I ever get in a jam like this again, I hope I have plenty of men like you aboard—men who aren't afraid to say what they believe, even though the odds are against them. Stay available, okay?" But wait, the odds were not against Howard being right in his suspicion he was doomed, and Howard did speak out and have fits because he was afraid, not because he was espousing a carefully thought-out position.

"If I ever get in a jam like this again." Even as Cliff Robertson was delivering this and other lines in the final stages of studio shooting, the real JFK had gotten into another such jam: the Cuban missile crisis. The leading man's unfinished first administration was beginning to assume the shape of the film. We had seen the young patriot eager for glory, walking through Tulagi base for the first time with a big grin betokening how much he appreciated the good spirits of the men he was joining (analogously, remember JFK dashing from one inaugural gala to another in 1961, then riding up Constitution toward the Capitol with that huge smile?). Then we saw him take command of the boat no one wanted rather than settle for a staff or maintenance job. The key to the movie, as well as to all that followed in the real world, is in Lieutenant Cluster's line as he contemplates the young fire-eater's delight over PT–109, a run-down reject: "Mr. Kennedy—if you'll try this, you'll try anything."

Yes, he will try anything, and the movie presents the trait admiringly. He mounts an anti-tank gun on his new toy ("he'd mount a tank if he could get one"), he makes a practice torpedo run on an American warship, and, racing another skipper, rams *PT–109* into a dock when he can't reverse his engines. The assumption of powers beyond his authority, the romantic brinksmanship, the gay rush toward catastrophe, all contribute to the formation of the energetic, confident, inspirational, and domineering leader who keeps his crew together and moving.

The Cuban missile crisis was just a bigger kick than the time he ran his PT boat in under the Japanese destroyer—in the blockade of Cuba, he ran the nation itself in under a far more crushing prow. After the Cuban crisis, Kennedy presented each of his closest advisers—his crew—with a silver memento in the shape of a calendar for the month of October 1962. The thirteen crucial days were more deeply engraved than the others—there was no inscription, just the skipper's initials in the upper right-hand corner, the recipient's in the left. It was, like the famous PT–109 tie clip, a talisman.

October 1962. With only two more months to go before my eight year reserve obligation is up, I have just heard the rumor of alerts and call ups. Like the cowardly professor of English in *The Steagle* who freaks out in film-generated fantasies in reaction to President Kennedy's announcement of the blockade, I, a cowardly instructor of English, flee my apartment and the phone that might call me into uniform, and go to a movie that was just then beginning its first run: *The Manchurian Candidate*. I went into the theater not because I then knew the reputation of John Frankenheimer as a director, or enjoyed the acting skills of Frank Sinatra, or even liked the bold Queen of Diamonds poster, but because the moviehouse was there. No other reason why.

From my sullen gloom, this picture lifted me as no other has done, before or since. When Raymond Shaw—the Medal of Honor winner programed by the Russians and Chinese to assassinate the Republican presidential candidate so his right-wing stepfather, the vice-presidential nominee, will be swept into office, there to do the bidding of his Communist masters—when Raymond Shaw swung his sniper's rifle from the presidential candidate at the Republican National Convention in Madison Square Garden and shot the Manchurian Candidate through the head, then blasted his mother, I went into a state of glee that held me through a second showing and drew me back the next night, and yet the next—not to watch real-life presidential pal Frank Sinatra unravel the conspiracy and save the nation, but to feast on the rubber-faced James Gregory's bellowing, whining, sneering protrayal of that silly fool, the McCarthyish Manchurian Candidate.

Summer 1963. I'm back in Washington again, about to start teaching at Georgetown. Mother has become a confirmed Kennedy watcher, gone from ranting against this flashy upstart to collecting everything she can find on him, building a case to show he is an agent of the conspiracy that will bring about the mongrelization of the races and one-worldism. In her harmless mania, she has even read Donovan's *PT-109*, which she now passes on to me. I explain this to set the stage for a small epiphany—for having read *PT-109* I then went to see the film later in the summer, curious to learn how much reshaping would be necessary to force that small and not very exciting bit of heroism into a wide-screen epic. What leapt out at me was the casting of James Gregory, the Manchurian Candidate himself, as Kennedy's fictional nemesis. In the film, this character, a gruff maintenance officer, stands for the older generation's

doubts about the cocky young sportsman from Cape Cod.
Though the James Gregory character comes around to a grudg-
ing admiration of Kennedy, I felt a peculiar sense of threat in
the coincidence that brought back my many viewings of *The
Manchurian Candidate*. Beyond interpretation or analysis,
this very free association would irrevocably link Frankenheimer's film with the death of Kennedy in my mind.

But this is all so much ephemeral vapor, you object. Perhaps,
perhaps. It embarrasses me to mention such tenuous interfaces
between movies and the times, yet bear with me. Is there not
something odd about the rash of films that treated presidential
politics in the few short Kennedy years, films that all placed
presidents and presidential candidates in the dramatic context
of betrayal and disaster—Fonda as the rich young President in
Fail Safe, who destroys New York City; Cliff Robertson, right
out of *PT-109*, as Fonda's ruthless opponent in *The Best Man;*
Peter Sellers as the pitiably weak President Muffly in *Doctor
Strangelove*. And then there was *Seven Days in May*, Frankenheimer's first film after *The Manchurian Candidate*.

I read the galleys and hired Rod Serling to do the script. I loved the
anti-MacArthur, anti-McCarthy theme. It was at a time when the military was very strong in this country and, God knows, they're strong
now, too, but this was just after Kennedy got in, after eight years of
General Eisenhower, which was pretty tough to take. Those were the
days of General Walker and so on. I think that, even though we are
involved in this ridiculous thing in Vietnam, the temper of the country
has swung the other way; but then things were bad. President Kennedy
wanted *Seven Days in May* made. Pierre Salinger conveyed this to us.
The Pentagon didn't want it done. Kennedy said that when we wanted
to shoot at the White House he would conveniently go to Hyannis Port
that weekend.

—John Frankenheimer, in *The Celluloid Muse*

Go to your library and get the *New York Times* microfilm for
late November 1963. The last frame of the November 22 issue
is a full-page add for *Seven Days in May*. At the top of the page
is a picture of Burt Lancaster as General Scott, the right-wing
chief-of-staff who unsuccessfully plots the military overthrow
of the President. Advance the reel one frame and the fatal
headline leaps out at you. Go see *Executive Action* and there is
Burt Lancaster plotting the events of November 22.

These coincidences mean nothing, but they suggest a terrific interplay between fantasy and reality. It was as though the "presidential" films in the early sixties were classical portents of what lay ahead for presidents, the presidency, and the nation. After the politically and militarily dull Eisenhower years, Kennedy had restored a sense of adventure, an excitement that penetrated into the film industry. And the industry's response had been to start documenting how many things could go wrong.

Old Joe Kennedy to Young Jimmy Roosevelt: "There are only two pursuits that get into your blood—politics and the motion-picture business."

—*Time*, 12 August 1940

Whereas a generation earlier the fantastic-minded might have gone to Hollywood to seek their fortunes in writing movies, in the early sixties many from California—and particularly the RAND Corporation—came to the Department of Defense. There they hawked their studies, created war games, and wrote scenarios.

—Marcus Raskin, *The Pentagon Watchers*

Jack Kennedy understood that the most important, probably the only dynamic culture in America, the only culture to enlist the imagination and change the character of Americans, was the one we had been given by the movies. Therefore a void existed at the center of American life. No movie star had the mind, courage or force to be a national leader, and no national leader had the epic adventurous resonance of a movie star.

—Mailer, *The Presidential Papers*

Was it just happenstance that the 1960 Democratic National Convention was held at the Los Angeles Sports Arena, or was the setting a hint that it was Hollywood's turn to cast the Big Role? John Kennedy fit the role, not just because he was a consummate politician but because he could move easily among actors. "He enjoyed the game of pleasing others, which is the actor's part," Gore Vidal would say later; "he was droll, particularly about himself, in a splendid sort of W. C. Fields way." Nixon, the man who rose out of the West to take his seat on the HUAC Hollywood witch-hunt, was clumsy in the actor's part, as when he tried the Pat O'Brien role at the 1968 Convention: "Let us win this one for Ike." It didn't come off as he intended (and had he forgotten, or never known, that the original exhortation, "Let's win this one for the Gipper," referred to Ronald Reagan?).

Movie people played a special role in the festivities of the Kennedy administration. In *Johnny, We Hardly Knew Ye,* Ken O'Donnell and Dave Powers tell fondly of the President, only hours after his inauguration, sneaking away from his wife and the Lyndon Johnsons to drop in on a private party Frank Sinatra was giving for the stars who had appeared in the pre-inaugural gala ("When he finally returned . . . looking rather sheepish and carrying a *Washington Post* under his arm, as if he had just gone outside to pick up the newspaper, his knowing wife gave him a rather chilly look"). Kennedy's friendship with Frank Sinatra inspired only slightly less gossip than the rumored link between JFK and the second most famous set of initials in the land, MM (after all, Monroe had captured or been captured by two great cultural heroes, Joe DiMaggio and Arthur Miller—where does one go from there?).

On the day he was murdered, the *New York Times* carried a story on Kennedy's plans for an unprecedented tribute to the film industry: a White House luncheon to be held on December 10 honoring a broad range of Hollywood's top people—studio heads, producers, stars. Even as he was dying in Dallas, the rush was on to call in favors and nail down an invitation. It is hard to imagine an invitation from the Johnson or Nixon White House having the power to indicate one's status within the industry. Kennedy was a pacesetter in a way that other presidents had never been. When Marlon Brando appeared on the set of *The Ugly American* in cutaway and striped trousers, someone whispered excitedly, "This will be the first time Brando will be so dressed up in a movie. The outfit he is wearing was bought from the same place that made President Kennedy's."*

Kennedy liked movies, he liked to have Paul Fay, the old friend he made Assistant Secretary of the Navy, sing "Hooray for Hollywood," he liked movie people, and they liked him. "There was something special about the movie industry's grief," Murray Schumach observed the week after the assassination. "In President Kennedy, the men and women of the cinema and video factories thought they had a partisan, even a friend. He seemed, by his youth and temperament, to have a particular fondness for show business and a special sympathy for the problems of those who try to make a living by entertaining others."

---

*The context of this sartorial gossip will be found in the middle of the next chapter.

Those were the years when Hollywood and the District of Columbia were seeing they were not, after all, a continent apart. Peter Lawford was married to the President's sister, Jack Valenti would soon go west, Shirley Temple and George Murphy would soon come east, and Ronald Reagan would step up to the office Nixon failed to win in 1962. Arthur Schlesinger, Jr., was reviewing movies—and John Wayne was reviewing Schlesinger and the New Frontier.

Local promoter, apologizing for size of town: "I admit it's a small town. Local paper has only eighty-two subscribers."
John Wayne: "Well, eighty-two people could take over the whole goddam country."
Local promoter: "How's that?"
Wayne: "Well, they've got Schlesinger . . . Rostow . . . Rusk."

Wayne, on the characterization of Mexico's Santa Anna in *The Alamo:* "He wasn't all bad, although he's always been made out to look that way. We studied him from every angle. You know, he was quite a boy. He got a charter of freedom for the Mexican people that was a lot like ours. But then, when he took over, he pulled a Kennedy and started grabbing the power."

—Esquire, May 1963

Magazine writer, sitting next to Wayne in a plane flying over Southeast Asia: "Duke, when you were a kid did you ever think that when you grew up you'd be the number one movie star in the world?"
Wayne: "Hell, no. I thought I'd be President of the United States. I didn't see how I could miss."

—George Carpozi, The John Wayne Story

Hollywood press agent: "That Duke—he draws crowds like the President."

—Esquire, May 1963

As John Kennedy moved toward the White House in the summer of 1960, John Wayne bought the inside cover of *Life*'s Special Fourth of July Issue on American politics. On the reverse of the foldout cover depicting a political rally was a painting of the Alamo, and facing this a full-page Statement of Principle:

THERE WERE NO GHOST WRITERS AT THE ALAMO

Very soon the two great political parties of the United States will nominate their candidates for President. One of these men, by a vote of the people, will be assigned the awesome duties of the White House: civilian leader of the nation, commander-in-chief of all its armed forces and keeper and director of its nuclear weaponry. . . .

Do we know him? Have we ever known him? Will we ever know him?

Who has written his speeches? Who—or what board of ghostwriting strategists—has fashioned the phrases, molded the thoughts, designed the delivery, authored the image, staged the presentation, put the political show on the road to win the larger number of votes?

Who is the actor reading the script?

The Statement of Principle was not specifically an attack on Kennedy, the Democratic frontrunner, or an endorsement of Nixon. It was merely a gratuitous call for a fearless leader "who will put America back on the high road of security and accomplishment, without fear of favor or compromise." But in the light of the staunchly conservative Wayne's later attacks on Kennedy and his administration, the "actor" in question was clearly the man about to steamroll through the Democratic Convention in Los Angeles, a convention at which the delegates had been treated to free tours of the Hollywood studios and surrounded as never before by politically enraptured stars (a few weeks later, *Life* would show JFK standing in prayer next to Judy Garland).

Why did John Wayne feel animosity? Was it because he thought the New Frontier stole its name from the title of a 1935 John Wayne movie? Was it because, like the cowboys he played, Wayne wanted absolute distinction between good and evil while Kennedy prized ambiguity? Was it because when he was finally nominated for an Oscar as the tough sergeant in *The Sands of Iwo Jima,* the award went to Broderick Crawford for playing a mere politician in *All the King's Men?* Was it because the first movie JFK saw in public as President was not *The Alamo* (Wayne's epic recreation of a patriotic mass sacrifice) but *Spartacus* (Kubrick's celebration of an abortive slave rebellion)?

Was it that he heard the story later recounted by Jim Bishop in *The Day Kennedy Was Shot:* "In 1960, when [JFK] was in California fighting Richard Nixon for the Presidency, he was aroused by motion picture star John Wayne's efforts for the Republican party. On a note pad he scribbled: 'How do we cut John Wayne's balls off?' "

Or was it simply that he didn't like politicians acting like actors, playing at reality in the same way he had, but for bigger stakes?

And yet John Wayne and John Kennedy were not so terribly far apart. Both were trying to awaken their countrymen from lethargy, to inspire them with tales of courage, to make them feel better, more energetic. Where do we draw the distinction between the inaugural promise to "pay any price, bear any burden, support any friend, oppose any foe, to assure the survival and success of liberty" and the better-dead-than-Mexican message of *The Alamo,* a message reflecting what the editor of *Films in Review* approvingly called Wayne's transfiguration "by a desire to use . . . an historical event which has the emotional and dramatic power to strengthen men and women as human beings, to unite them as Americans."

Kennedy and the people around him *did* try to be the tough men that John Wayne had called for in his Statement of Principle. Halberstam has documented the fear of the Kennedy people lest they appear soft; Ward Just explains JFK's attraction for Maxwell Taylor, the actor-handsome general who left the army to head Lincoln Center for the Performing Arts (well, war *is* a performing art) through a line in a book Taylor wrote: "There is no substitute for the personal sharing of the danger." Kennedy's selection of Arlington as his gravesite, his continued sponsorship of the Special Forces and his restoration of their distinctive headgear when conventional army generals tried to outlaw the Green Beret emblem—by these signs did Kennedy and his circle demonstrate they were worthy of the Alamo's memory.

We become what we pretend to be, says Kurt Vonnegut in one of his books. No better example exists than John Wayne, the midwesterner who became a frontiersman by dint of repetition, the son of a druggist who became a cattle rancher after punching all those studio cows, the twentieth-century man who built a full-scale replica of the Alamo and the village around it, the life-long civilian whose idea of a pleasure boat is a 136-foot converted minesweeper, whose admirers and detractors alike began to believe the legends or pretend they did. James L. Buckley, treating his young campaign workers to a showing of *Chisum,* reminds them that "John Wayne won World War II— he's a kind of folk hero"; Joan Bartell, less kindly, calls him "the man who, from 'Fort Apache' to Bataan, has never lost a war."

Where Audie Murphy moved from real-life war hero to celluloid cowboy, John Wayne reversed the process, starting as a cowboy, becoming a film soldier, then entering a state of permanent war against America's enemies—not so much the physical enemies outside the gates as the psychic enemies within. Wayne's war was against doubt and doubters, against those Americans who wished to step outside the straight and narrow. It was a war he waged on and off the screen. In *The Searchers* (1956) he tried to shoot his niece (Natalie Wood) when she announced she wished to stay with her Indian captors; a decade later, speaking of peace demonstrators who carry Vietcong flags, his prescription for apostacy was the same: "I think they oughta shoot 'em. . . . As far as I'm concerned, it wouldn't bother me a bit to pull the trigger on one of them." While other Hollywood figures were committing professional suicide before the House Un-American Activities Committee, Wayne, one of the founders of the ultra-patriotic Motion Picture Alliance for the Preservation of American Ideals, played a HUAC investigator in *Big Jim McLain,* the kinda guy who was never too busy chasin' commies to stop a minute 'n' visit a war monument.

He could not prevent communism from spreading, but he could lead Chiang's Children out of Mao's Land across the newly Red sea to the promised land of Formosa in *Blood Alley* (1955). He could honor those who fought the good fight in the media battles, as when he played Spig Wead in *The Wings of Eagles* (1957), the story of the early proponent of air power who became a Hollywood writer after being crippled.*

In every way he could, John Wayne did his part. When Mel Shavelson was putting together the package for *Cast a Giant Shadow,* a risky project about an American Jew who went to the aid of Israel, he knew that he could find no backing unless he could snare a major WASP. With some trepidation, he asked John Wayne to play a Pattonesque American general who would establish the Jewish protagonist's "credentials" as a brave American. To Shavelson's surprise, Wayne agreed immediately, explaining "Everybody's knockin' the United States today. . . . claiming we're sendin' troops all over the world to knock over some little country where we've got no right to be. They've forgotten how we are and what we've done. At a time like this, we *need* to remind them of how we helped the littlest country of all to get its independence."

That was in the mid-sixties when the American adventure in

---

*The story is true. Frank (Spig) Wead wrote many service dramas, particularly about military aviation and the navy. He also wrote one of Wayne's best war movies, *They Were Expendable.*

Vietnam was beginning to make our allies nervous. Wayne was about to go to Vietnam to see what he could do to turn the propaganda war around. John Wayne was doing his part.

It is impossible to go through a shelf of recent books on American politics without encountering John Wayne. Accounts of the 1968 election have Wayne sending weekly checks of ten thousand dollars each to George Wallace, Wayne being considered as Wallace's running mate (both probably apocryphal, as Wayne, who stumped Texas in 1956 for Eisenhower, was a Nixon man), Wayne doing an inspirational reading on the topic "Why I am Proud to be an American" at the opening of the Miami convention. He turns up in Lady Bird Johnson's White House diary ("In came Lynda, fresh from Acapulco. . . . she told me about being the houseguest of Merle Oberon. . . . John Wayne had been there too—Lynda liked him so much. She says he is very conservative, but that he had spoken kindly of her father") and in a Bobby Kennedy joke about a proposed Vietnam study committee ("The problem was that [President Johnson] and I couldn't agree who should be on the commission. I wanted Senator Mansfield, Senator Fulbright, and Senator Morse. . . . And the President, in his own inimitable style, wanted to appoint General Westmoreland, John Wayne, and Martha Raye.").

Consult the *New York Times* and it's Wayne the political figure as much as Wayne the actor. Wayne donating his talent as narrator for a USIA film on Spiro Agnew, putting together a ninety minute TV special in honor of great American heroes and events, mixing patriotism and slapstick (Bob Hope doing a USO turn at Valley Forge, Rowan and Martin inventing the airplane); dropping in to Dallas to pick up the Veterans of Foreign Wars Gold Medal for Americanism; heading the Golden Circle Club, an organization financing Republican candidates in California; slamming press coverage of Watergate on his way to a White House Banquet for POW's; dismissing Watergate as a "damned panty raid by underlings"; proclaiming that Senators who voted to cut off funds for Vietnam "would have been tarred and feathered in the old days"; being honored by a New Year's call from President Nixon, growing bigger and bigger, sleeker, easier, more relaxed, powerful, potent, and . . . alive.

Washington News Item: "President Nixon last week named Mrs. John Wayne to the advisory committee of the John F. Kennedy Center for the Performing Arts."

Variety, 22 March 1972

The best revenge, some say, is living longer than your enemies. Wayne had begun the Kennedy years recommending the Alamo as a model for Americans but had survived to a time when survival itself began to seem a more valuable trait than heroic sacrifice. JFK was dead in Big D in '63, but Wayne had licked the Big C in '64. Others fell off life's horse, but Big Duke gritted his teeth and climbed back into the saddle.

John Wayne came back from Vietnam, made a movie, and students booed; Robert Kennedy came back from Vietnam, made a John Wayne joke, and they cheered—but soon enough RFK was in his grave, shot down in the movie capital of the world, the city where his brother had begun his journey to the White House.

And that same summer of 1968, on the Fourth of July, John Wayne went to Atlanta to present a memorial honoring the Green Berets to the Commander of the John F. Kennedy Center for Special Warfare. (Today the memorial, a large stone, stands near the Kennedy Chapel at Fort Bragg.) That summer, too, Wayne's *The Green Berets* opened across the land, recouping for Warner Brothers the money it lost on *PT-109*. Like *The Alamo*, the first film he directed, it was entirely a reflection of his will, containing no image he did not expressly desire or permit.

(The film begins. Monochromatic still images flicker across the screen during the credits. Then one image suddenly turns from monochrome to full color, from still to moving. It is a bright red sign: John F. Kennedy Center for Special Warfare, Fort Bragg, North Carolina.)

Time heals, brings reconciliation. In the summer of 1973, flying over the Grand Canyon in the President's own plane, Leonid Brezhnev, the chief card-carrying Communist of them all (on his way to a mock shootout with Chuck Connors in San Clemente) turns to Richard Nixon and says he has seen the desert before—in cowboy movies. "Yes," says the President, saying it all. "John Wayne."

January 15, 1974. John Wayne, having accepted the *Harvard Lampoon*'s challenge to invade "the most intellectual, the most traditionally radical, in short the most hostile territory on earth," crosses the frigid Charles, comes to Cambridge, the citadel of the Kennedys, the Bundys, the Schlesingers, rides into enemy country, clanks through Harvard Square on an Armored Personnel Carrier manned by troops in black berets. He is here to receive a pair of matched brass balls signifying (Taa-Rah-Rah, Boomp! -Ti-Ay) something.

He is an old man, liver-spotted, paunchy, his baldness neatly wigged, his duty never done, and the APC, a tank-like vehicle, is both the center of the parade and reviewing stand. The carrier crew scan the points of the compass, wary lest a surviving Vietcong or Nazi or Apache should appear. But the conquering hero rides tall, takes the cheers of the crowd, bats away random snowballs. The French tri-color unfolds from a shell-pocked balcony, and Wayne straightens his helmet, stands up in the jeep, slowly raises his arm in salute. A little girl comes out from among the grateful settlers, holds up a desert flower, and he pushes back his sweat-stained campaign hat, leans from the saddle, takes the tribute. A flight of war planes—some with two wings and struts, then gull-winged Corsairs, now sleek jets—arc above the carrier, and on the bridge, up in flag country—timeless, timeless—he tilts his gold-braided cap, squints into the sun, and smiles.

FOUR

WHAT GAY ADVENTURES LIE AHEAD— HOLLYWOOD GOES TO VIETNAM

James Lee Barrett, a talented young Hollywood screenwriter, went to Vietnam to gather material for writing a screen treatment of the John Wayne *Green Berets* movie, and among the many things that impressed him over there was the attitude expressed by one officer who told him that "These people don't want to be free, but by God we're going to *make* them free!"

"To me," Barrett said, "that's a new and exciting concept."

While he was in Vietnam Barrett was in areas of combat, and he found something else exciting which also seemed involved in the very reason for the war being fought. . . . "I tell you," Barrett said, "being over there in that kind of danger where a grenade might get you while you're sleeping because there's usually some Vee Cee in every outfit, and the fighting and getting shot at, it's *exhilarating.* I really believe that men don't want peace. If they did, they'd have it. Men want war."

—Dan Wakefield,
Supernation at Peace and War

Viva: "I knew a boy once who said, 'I wish'—this was before the Vietnam thing got so big, years ago—he said, 'I wish we'd have another war so that I could

feel like I'm *doing* some-
thing.' "
　　—Andy Warhol's *Blue
　　　　Movie*

　　Jim Hutton, shouting over
the roar of the helicopter
carrying him into the combat zone: "With joyous
memories we leave the
mystical city of Da Nang.
What gay adventures lie
ahead? Brother, this trip is
going to make LSD feel like
aspirin."
　　—*The Green Berets*

The little Vietnamese boy had first lost his puppy to the Vietcong, then his GI buddy Jim Hutton got impaled on bamboo stakes. Now, as the movie ends, he is all alone in a cruel world, standing on the shore of the South China Sea as the sun sinks slowly in the east.

Hamchunk (for that is his name): "What will, wh-what will happen to me now?"

John Wayne: "You let me worry about that, Green Beret. You're what this is all about."

Don't say that, Big John, I want to yell. Don't make any promises I won't keep. Besides, that little boy may not be as guileless as he looks—the first time we saw him, wasn't he stringing a wire to trip Jim Hutton? What separates him from the bigger boys who sprung the practical joke that left Hutton hanging, upside down with six inches of bamboo sticking out of his chest?

I'm scrunched down in a seat up front in the Strand Theater in Dover, New Hampshire, making the first notes for this book. I'm feeling mighty mean, little knowing that I will see this film many times in the next five years—on television, in a film archive, in classrooms, even p: ojected against my very own living room wall. I don't know I'm going to write a book—I'm simply in the habit of jotting down reactions to things that impress me for good or ill.

When I disinter these early notes nearly six years later, I find they make almost no sense, but that's all right, for the material I've gathered on *The Green Berets* now spills out of a twelve-by-twelve file box in a room littered with twenty more boxes. As near as I can tell, what bothered me my first time through the first and only major combat film set in Vietnam was the grotesque cheerfulness of the thing, the jokes that popped up even as people died.

There was another summer, only six years before, when Vietnam was a joke, or at least the occasion for bawdiness. Still a bachelor, I had met a young woman at a cocktail party in Washington. She was bored. Her husband was in Vietnam with the Army Band. It was all very ludicrous and unlikely, and the idea that there were enough troops in Vietnam to justify sending the Band was drowned out in the novelty of having broken yet another of the Ten Commandments.

The summer of 1968 was no time for jokes—Bobby Kennedy in an early grave, the Democrats in a shambles after Chicago, Nixon about to be nominated in Miami. So absorbed am I in my jottings that I am still seated when the "Ballad of the Green

102

Beret" ends and the Star Spangled Banner—which I have not heard in a movie house for years—begins. Suddenly I realize everyone else is standing up. I hunch even lower in my seat, my eyes down. I will not stand, I will not be forced into a false solidarity. But before the first stanza is done, I have panicked and risen in shame and dread.

Vietnam snuck up on us. I know where I was the day of Pearl Harbor. I can vividly remember the first summer of the Korean War. But Vietnam's impact was slow and cumulative. In not one of my college ROTC courses in the late fifties did I hear of even so much as our advisory role (yes, I was listening). There were no clear lines of departure, no Pearl Harbors, no sudden dramatic jumps from peace to war. Oh, efforts were made, ex post facto, to give the on-going war some legitimacy, to rewrite the script. But who can remember where he was during the Gulf of Tonkin incident? Who cares? Vietnam was like a movie that had gotten out of hand: gigantic cost overruns, a shooting schedule run amuck, squabbles on the set and back in the studio, the first *auteur* dying with most of the script still in his head, the second quitting in disgust, and the last swearing it was finally in the can, but still sneaking back to shoot some extra scenes.

First Soldier: "There's a new war shaping up in Vietnam—do you think you'll be in it?"
Second Soldier: "No, I don't like the director."
—How I Won the War

Just as the beginnings of the war are lost in the swirl of trivia that occupied us through the fifties and early sixties, its cinematic manifestations are equally forgotten or ignored. Writing in early 1968, three different observers found little or nothing of the war reflected on the screen: "There haven't been any movies about the war in Vietnam," wrote Dan Wakefield in *Supernation at Peace and War;* "the only Vietnam war picture thus far," proclaimed Axel Madsen in a brief article, "is John Wayne's forthcoming *The Green Berets*"; and Peter A. Soderbergh found only one other film, *A Yank in Viet-Nam.* But there is more: in the twenty years before *The Green Berets* brought what Renata Adler was to call "The Absolute End of the Romance of War," at least a dozen American films dealing with the struggle against Communist agression were set in Vietnam or mythical Indo-Chinese nations.

Let's look at the incunabula.

THE ADVENTURE BEGINS

It all began back in 1948 with Alan Ladd and Veronica Lake in *Saigon.* Not much of a start: three air force veterans, footloose after the Big War, fly to Saigon on a job and stumble into a money smuggling plot, which they duly expose. The issues of the brand-new civil war were only dimly evident. The important thing was that Saigon was a trouble spot into which American characters could blunder to right wrongs.

Later in 1948, Dick Powell went to Indo-China to join the *Rogues' Regiment.* About the only simple thing in this baroque Eastern was the vision of the teeming Saigon waterfront as a picturesque study in bamboo and wickerwork with rolling California hills in the background. A secret service agent, Powell enlists in the French Foreign Legion to track down Martin Bruner (read Martin Bormann, the name by which the early press releases identified this character), an escaped Nazi who was once Hitler's top aide. After hearing a French colonel explain why the rebels have no chance in their war against the French, Powell survives what one reviewer called "a brief but lurid skirmish with native guerrillas," escapes guerrilla captivity, and uncovers all kinds of sordidness, including another ex-Nazi (Vincent Price) who is now an agent of the Russians supporting the guerrillas. At the end, Powell sees Martin Bruner hanged at Nuremberg, then goes back home to settle down on a Nebraska hay farm with the beautiful French spy he met in Saigon.

Four years later, Hollywood went back for *A Yank in Indo China.* Now the American role is clearly more humanitarian —and more military in the bargain. Two Americans* are flying food to French and Vietnamese fighting Communist guerrillas. Captured by the Vietminh, they escape; recaptured, they escape once more and end up leading the French and their native allies in a successful paratroop attack on the guerrillas. Holly-

---

*One was played by Douglas Dick, who was also with Alan Ladd in *Saigon.*

wood couldn't seem to wait to get involved. Well, why not? "Harmless for the family trade," pronounced one industry reviewer.* That was 1952, and many of the men to die in Vietnam were still in diapers, and little Rusty Calley was not yet ten.

The real film combat, the nitty-gritty stuff, complete with obsessive ideological hatred of communism, did not appear until 1957 when Samuel Fuller wrote, directed, and produced *China Gate*. Just as Fuller had rushed into celluloid with the first film about the Korean War, he scooped Vietnam with a newsreel-style prolog outlining the history of the conflict up to 1954 and introducing American film audiences to Ho Chi Minh.

The political issues are crystal clear: Vietnam is torn between godless communism and a wonderful Christian tradition that has brought spiritual and material fulfillment. Though that simple dichotomy is worked out dramatically, Fuller makes sure everyone gets the point by opening with a scene of peasants working in rice paddies while a narrator delivers the pitch: "This motion picture is dedicated to France. More than three hundred years ago French missionaries were sent to China to teach love of God, and love of fellow-man. Gradually French influence took shape in the Vietnamese land. Despite many hardships, they advanced their way of living and the thriving nation became the rice bowl of Asia."

And though what follows is the story of how a group of Foreign Legionaires blow up a huge Communist ammunition dump at the outpost known as China Gate in 1954, the action is led by "Americans" and the ultimate reward an American dream. Not only are the Legionaires guided to China Gate by Lucky Legs (Angie Dickinson), a beautiful Eurasian saloon keeper who has agreed to undertake this mission in exchange for the guarantee that her little boy will be sent to America, but the patrol is commanded by Lucky Legs's estranged husband and the father of her little boy, a tough American sergeant named Brock (Gene Barry) who never made it home from Korea. Under Brock are Nat King Cole and a collection of mercenaries from around the world—Asians, a German, a Frenchman, a Hungarian—constituting a simple extension of the melting pot American units of earlier wars. "For Fuller," says Phil Hardy of this film, "the whole world is America and

---

A Yank in Indo China was not reviewed in the *New York Times* and is not listed as having been reviewed by the sources indexed in standard bibliographies. Perhaps national security was involved.

its divisions are but metaphors of America's internal divisions."

American involvement in Vietnam begins with *China Gate. Saigon* and *A Yank in Indo China* were about Americans who got swept up because they were there. Here it is emotional. To be sure, Brock talks like a cynic, but so did Bogart in *Casablanca* (a comparison is useful: both films are set in exotic French colonies; Lucky Legs, the neutral saloon keeper, and the expatriate Brock share traits of Bogart's Rick Blaine; Lucky Legs, like Ingrid Bergman, is out of the American's past and must make a choice between two lovers; Nat King Cole, who sings the title song, fills the Dooley Wilson part; and both films revolve around a safe conduct out of the war zone).

Lucky Legs: "Why'd you join the French?"

Brock: "Soldiering's my business. Korea got cold—Indo-China got hot."

Lucky Legs: "Are you really that interested in fighting for the French?"

Brock: "Sure. I don't particularly like the Commies, and France was left holding the bag." Nat King Cole is less shy about his motives for leaving his own army to fight for the French: "What I started out to do in Korea I didn't finish. There are still a lot of live Commies around." At the end of the film, Cole is seen cleaning his rifle, preparing for the next installment of the war.

These and the other characters on the patrol seem sufficiently committed to the defense of Western culture against barbarianism to inspire a puzzled compliment from the *New York Times* reviewer who called them "strangely unconvincing types even though they are dedicated to a just and honorable cause." Note the assumption: people who are dedicated to just and honorable causes should be convincing by virtue of their causes. By such small tokens was it made manifest that Something was Wrong. Perhaps the *Times* reviewer should have questioned the reason if his gut told him that Gene Barry and Angie Dickinson just didn't seem to be the saviors the script said they were.

There were other false notes in this outwardly idealistic film. By calling Vietnam the "barrier between Communism and the Free World," Fuller was unconsciously signing a death warrant for that unhappy land. Then, too, the chief American character, Brock, is good with weapons, at fighting, but lousy in the personal realm, and his eventual reconciliation to the fact his son looks like an Oriental is not quite the cause for rejoicing that Fuller intends it to be. That a racist shall take the hand of one slant-eyed little boy at the fade-out because it is *his* slant-eyed little boy is no millennium.

Having inexplicably chosen the half-French, half-Chinese Lucky Legs as the sole representative of the Vietnamese people in the film, Fuller then proceeded to make her neutral toward the war until she saw cooperation with the French as a ticket to America for her son. This may be meant to tell us how much the Vietnamese admire and respect the United States, but it says damn little for their commitment to their own land. I admit I should not belabor Fuller with his own allegory, for he is working in a favorite Hollywood groove: the American soldier as the guardian of future generations, the protector of future generations of Oriental cast-offs in *Battle Hymn* and *Cry for Happy, Battle Circus* and *War Hunt.* We'll even see it in *The Green Berets.*

To assure the little boy's passage to America, where he will be safe from the horrors of Vietnam, Lucky Legs blows herself up with her Communist lover, not suspecting that as the boy was born in 1949 he will be just the right age to come back to Vietnam with other young Americans in time for the Tet offensive.

China Gate turned France's struggles in Indo-China into America's. That transformation was no less startling than what it did to the face of the enemy. Fuller cast the perennial Western villain Lee Van Cleef as the love-sick Major Cham, a Communist "war lord" who rules from what looks for all the world like a Norman castle. By a weird perversion of all that we came to know about Vietnam, it is the Communist who has a stationary nineteenth-century power base and the "Americans" who operate as guerrillas. Moreover, Major Cham sounds less like a follower of General Giap than one of the Joint Chiefs of Staff selling a new escalation to the President. "The war will soon be over," he assures Lucky Legs. "A dozen more bombings and they're all finished." And listen to the fine public relations job he does for the so-called colonial oppressors in explaining why he has not exterminated the local Buddhist monks: "It's smarter to let them wander around the temple grounds. It looks more peaceful from the air, and those French pilots are as stupid as the Americans were in the other war. They don't bomb temples or churches. That's why we will win all of Asia. We bomb everything."

THE ADVENTURE GROWS SERIOUS

When Rocky Cline and George Schlicker, experienced Hollywood special effects men, detonated explosives to re-create Saigon during the Indochinese war, the city's population became noticeably jumpy, Saigon's mayor was even summoned to President Diem's office to explain what the shooting was about. The country, after all, has been at complete peace for only a little more than a year, and nerves are still a trifle frayed.

—New York Times account of the filming of *The Quiet American*

Major Cham's vision of Americans as naive fools who will not bomb civilians to save their world was not a view shared by Graham Greene in his 1956 novel, *The Quiet American.* Opening with a tag from Byron,

> This is the patent age of new inventions
> For killing bodies, and for saving souls,
> All propagated with the best intentions,

Greene depicted an idealistic young American "economic aide" as behind a series of terrorist bombings in Saigon. American reviewers were outraged at the book's criticism of our initial involvement in Vietnam in the early Eisenhower years, but Joseph L. Mankiewicz plunked down sixty-five thousand dollars for the privilege of correcting Greene's calumnies on the screen.

Where Greene's Quiet American was responsible for the murder of innocents, Mankiewicz's totally innocent character is simply framed by the Communists. In Greene's novel, the Quiet American has exported explosives in cannisters labled "plastics" (*now* you know why that fellow in *The Graduate* took Dustin Hoffman aside and whispered the magic word in his ear, "plastics"—he was recruiting for the CIA); in the film the plastic *is* plastic, not *plastique,* and the Quiet American just a selfless entrepreneur who wants to give the citizens of Southeast Asia cheaper masks and horns for their festivities through the miracle of chemistry (but when his body is found floating in a Saigon canal at the height of the Chinese New Year celebration, the festivities end, everyone screams and runs away—how long has it been, can you guess, since the Vietnamese have screamed at the sight of anonymous bodies in their waterways?).

Where Greene's American works for the government, Mankiewicz's is a private citizen employed by a group called "Friends of Free Asia" (don't laugh—the film premiered in Washington in January 1958 as a benefit for the American Friends of Vietnam). And where Greene's Fowler, a cynical British reporter, walks off with the beautiful Vietnamese girl after betraying the Quiet American to his murderers, in the film the girl walks away while another Englishman points out that Fowler (Michael Redgrave) is "middle-aged . . . unshaven, unwashed, unwanted." In Mankiewicz's cold war rule-book, there can be no happiness, to say nothing of dignity, for anyone who forsakes or betrays America.

And where Greene peopled his novel with numerous pompous or foolish Americans, Mankiewicz focused on the title character played by Audie Murphy and on Granger, a battle-savvy correspondent played by Bruce Cabot (who would later brief John Wayne on Vietnam in *The Green Berets*). In the novel, Granger is encountered only as a noisy or maudlin drunk in the setting of Saigon cafés and hotel bars. In the film, he is seen only at the front, where he soberly analyzes the war, much to the British correspondent's annoyance:

Fowler: "Let them run their own war, Granger; it's the French who are dying."

Granger: "Too many French are dying who don't have to die. They are my friends. I can't be unconcerned about friends who die unnecessary deaths."

French Officer: "Unnecessary? What do you mean?"

Granger: "I mean a defense of this country that was conceived in the nineteenth century and fought in the twentieth." The burden of this speech and others like it is two-fold: America does not abandon its friends; only America knows the way out, only those whose spirits have been untouched by the taint of colonialism, who have themselves struggled to throw off that yoke, can see the light at the end of the tunnel.

The novel had been an incredibly prescient warning about what would happen should Americans thrust themselves into Vietnam with their boundless energy, optimism, and cash, a warning based on Greene's years of experience in Southeast Asia. Mankiewicz rushed in to slap Greene's wrist with a movie that said "you've got it all wrong—Americans don't louse things up; the spoilers are those who doubt America's good-will and obstruct her destiny."

Set in 1952, before the partition of Vietnam, *The Quiet American* is a film about destiny—America's and Vietnam's. Within two minutes of his first appearance in the film, Audie Murphy has switched from discoursing learnedly on the relative merit of milkshakes at the Continental versus those at the milkbar across the square to proclaiming the desirability of a "Third Force" somewhere between colonialism and communism: "Twenty-two million Vietnamese deciding for themselves how they want to live." This simple message of self-determination is stretched through the film. Drop in on the Quiet American and Fowler as they take cover in a watchtower manned by two young Vietnamese sentries. Fowler predicts that the sentries will run off into the rice fields should the Vietminh attack:

Fowler: "They don't believe in anything. . . . They just want enough rice. They want one day to be much the same as another. They don't want our white skins around telling them what they want."

The Quiet American: "You're telling them what they don't want, which is the same thing. The skins in Russia are still white." To keep the argument from remaining academic, the Vietminh attack and the Quiet American has the pleasure of observing pointedly that the sentries didn't run: they stayed to get killed. Vietnamization *will* work.

But turning the struggle for non-Communist independence over to the Vietnamese people is to be defined in American terms. The Quiet American exudes an almost saintly confidence as he contemplates what the future holds for Vietnam. How does he know? Well, when he was a graduate student at Princeton, he met a "prominent Vietnamese living in exile in New Jersey." Fowler should know who this person is, says Pyle, "because if all goes well, if Vietnam becomes an independent republic, this man will be its leader." *If all goes well.* The qualification is not explained, nor is it explained why a man in American exile should be the leader.* The reasons are all implied, buried somewhere in the assumption that America shall now save the world: "I'm from a country that's been in existence for less than two hundred years. . . . fifty years ago we were barely taken seriously as a nation, much less a great force

---

*If this man is to lead his country, what is he doing in New Jersey? The Quiet American's speech neatly documents a flaw in American thinking that would have major repercussions. Cf. David Halberstam: "The men who formed the government in the South were men whom Westerners would deal with, men who were safe precisely because they had done nothing for their country during the war; they had either fought side by side with the French or profiteered on the war, or, as in the case of Ngo Dinh Diem, stayed outside the country, unable to choose between the two sides" *(The Best and the Brightest).*

for wisdom and decision. But suddenly, now, a watch-tick of history later, the world waits angrily for us to find answers it hasn't been able to provide in fifty centuries."

When Joseph Mankiewicz arrived in Saigon in 1957 to begin shooting, the script was in its final form. According to Vinh Noan, the former South Vietnamese official who is listed on the film's credits as "production associate," President Diem approved the project, though neither he nor Vinh Noan appreciated the fact that the only important Vietnamese character starts as the mistress of an Englishman then switches to an American, and can't wait to escape the country. Outside of the many backgrounds filmed in and around Saigon to lend a suitable air of the Mysterious and Teeming Orient, *The Quiet American* does little to suggest the quality and character of Vietnamese life. Vietnamese extras were good enough for crowd scenes, but when the camera moves in close, we get Hollywood faces—an Italian starlet as the Vietnamese love interest, and Richard Loo, a Chinese-American character actor known for villainous Japanese roles, as the sinister *Chinese* agent of the Communist assassination committee that does in the Quiet American.

There were other such slips; the American regrets that he can't speak French with the Vietnamese girl—it didn't occur to Mankiewicz that the character should regret not speaking Annamese, just as in *The Green Berets* the sole example of local culture is a girl in "Le Club Sportif de Da Nang" singing (in French and English) about finding her lost lover on the banks of the River Seine. Vietnam, then, is full of people who take their identity from the West. These slips seem *de rigueur:* from *Saigon* to *The Green Berets,* American films set in Vietnam always emphasized American characters and did not create a single important Vietnamese who is not defined through his or her relationship to Americans or (in the case of the heavies) by a scriptwriter's notion of how a confirmed Marxist sounds. Almost as an after-thought, the film ends with a dedication to "the people of the Republic of Vietnam—to their chosen President and administration—our appreciation for their help and kindness."

Greene's analysis of dangerous American naïveté had been subverted by Mankiewicz's screenplay; ironically, the advertis-

ing campaign undid the writer-producer-director's vision of
innocence and tried to sell the film as an upbeat action feature:

WHEREVER HE WALKED—ALL HELL BROKE LOOSE!

A BOMB BLASTS IN A CROWDED SAIGON SQUARE . . .
A TORCH IS PUT TO A WATCH-TOWER ON THE TAY NINH ROAD . . .
A BODY IS FOUND FLOATING IN THE RIVER . . .
—AND ALWAYS THE QUIET AMERICAN IS THERE!

Yes, he *is* there, but in no case is he the conscious agent of these
events, only their victim: the bomb blast was to discredit him,
the tower was burned in an effort to kill him, and the body
floating in the river was his. As with the war that we would
enter a few years later, the film was fobbed off on an unsuspect-
ing public with half-truths and gay promises of adventure.

I don't know whether *The Quiet American* ever plays on
television, but if it does, watch it: the effect, in broad terms of
national image, is like catching a glimpse of oneself in a crowd
scene on the evening news. The startled, embarrassed reaction,
however, is not "is that *me?*" but "Is *that* how I used to see
myself?"

The same reaction can be generated by sampling the contemporary reviews. From *Variety:* "Mankiewicz has delivered a
thoughtful script that aims primarily at contrasting political
points-of-view and, sometimes, showing their application in
human terms. . . . There are likely to be an awful lot of people
who'll come out of this film saying (about Indo-Chinese problems) 'Who gives a damn?' This may not be the 'right' attitude,
but—in terms of the mass audience—it's a forgivable one."
Where the *Saturday Review* had earlier complained that
Greene's novel was unfair ("even those of us who can imagine
how our well-off, liberal foreign policy has often seemed . . . *to
people who have spent themselves in history* will want to protest that there is more to us than Woodrow Wilson and the
Rover Boys"), it applauded the film as "more credible and truer
to the earnest, hard-working, apolitical types that [Mankiewicz]
found in Indo China" (a remarkable compliment, in that Mankiewicz had not been to Vietnam before he wrote the script).
"He has taken a large, expensive company out to the far East,"
Arthur Knight continued, "and brought back a picture hot with
the menace of Communist night-marauders. . . . If this is the

kind of picture that there isn't room for any more, the movies might just as well close up right now."

THE ADVENTURE GROWS MORIBUND

The winter of 1971. I've just seen *The Last Valley*, a costume epic set in an Alpine village during the Thirty Years' War or some other irrelevant fracas. An intellectual matches wits with a warrior, rich landowners contend with militarists for the right to exploit the peasants, girls are raped, humble cottages burned, and the pictorial and aural horrors of war evoked for all they are worth.

Afterwards, I meet a colleague in the lobby. A historian, he complains that the characters didn't act like types out of the early seventeenth century. I respond that they may be meant to stand for contemporary figures in Vietnam. My colleague quite justifiably snorts, wants to know what the parallel proves, how it works. I don't know, I tell him. It's just a hunch. Not until later do I remember that James Clavell, who wrote, produced, and directed *The Last Valley* had written, produced, and directed a film set in Vietnam during the Vietminh insurgency. That was *Five Gates to Hell* (1959), about a bunch of Red Cross nurses and doctors who are kidnapped by a Communist guerrilla chief. As in *China Gate*, there is a rather cavalier attitude toward the nature of the enemy. Where Lee Van Cleef was the master of a medieval castle, here the hulking Neville Brand (often cast as an Indian) plays the kind of brute who nails nuns to trees, turns his men loose to ravish helpless nurses, boasts in broken English "Soon I war lord of whole Vietnam," and falls inexplicably in love with the only American nurse in the group.

And the beautiful American is not just a pretty face stuck in as the female lead. No, the daughter of the American vice-consul at the Hanoi embassy, she is named Athena after the goddess of wisdom, fertility, and (my dictionary informs me), "prudent warfare." Wise Athena arbitrates the squabbles of the other nurses; fertile Athena announces she thinks she is going to have the guerrilla leader's child (the allegorical point of this escapes me); the prudent warrior leads the other nurses in their escape and has a unilateral shootout with Neville Brand (having just killed another nun, he is shot by Athena and pitches forward to die with the words: "I—I—can't kill—I love you"). Everyone loves Americans.

Rape, murder, sacrilege, kidnapping, and overweening ambition: these are the enemy's five gates to hell. More or less the same pattern is found in *Brushfire* (1962): guerrillas in an unnamed Southeast Asian country kidnap an American couple, demanding a ransom of weapons. But two American planters (John Ireland and Everett Sloane) decide that rebels must not be given their way, and set out to rescue the hostages. Though they are too late to prevent the brutal rebel leader from raping Easter, the American woman, the planters manage to kill him and rout the rebels. At film's end, John Ireland explains to Easter that the rescue effort (which cost her husband's life) was necessary to keep the brushfire rebellion from erupting into something bigger.

Produced and directed by Jack Warner, Jr., the scion of the studio that made more war movies than any other during World War II, *Brushfire* was a flimsy attempt to resurrect villains of twenty years past. "The story came out of rumors about actions in SE Asia which were taking place before we got in to the extent of placing troops there," the scenarist wrote me. "It came out of a very stupid bit of advice given to the producer by [Warner Brothers] that he try for an exploitation film—one that might have some shock values at the box office." The first shock is that the guerrilla leader is a former Nazi named Martin (Bormann?). Though the script was written by Irwin Blacker, a former CIA man who often writes on irregular warfare, the notion of Asian rebels trooping after an ex-Nazi seems highly unlikely and more than a little condescending.* Would such rebels need or want a white mercenary, much less a pure Aryan? Would a representative of the people who rewrote the books on conventional *mechanized* warfare make a good guerrilla?

And why is it that American civilians, and not locals, are called upon to crush the rebels and restore order? What does this all mean? That part of the psychological preparation for our actual involvement in Southeast Asia grew out of something as simple as casting practices dictated by studio wisdom which held that only those wars in which Americans lead the way are worthy of their print cost?

---

*Blacker has authored or edited books with such titles as *Behind the Lines: Twenty-Eight Stories of Irregular Warfare; Irregulars, Partisans, Guerillas; State of Siege; The Military Mind, Chain of Command,* etc. His novel, *Search and Destroy,* about American saboteurs in North Vietnam, was the source for an aborted film project discussed in the first chapter.

THE ADVENTURE COMES HOME ON THE EVENING NEWS

Harrison Carter MacWhite, the newly appointed American ambassador to the kingdom of Sarkhan, recounting his long-awaited reunion with his old war-time buddy, now a Sarkhanese nationalist: "Deong's a Communist. . . . Everytime he opened his mouth—right on the party line."

Mrs. MacWhite: "What about the present, the flowers—and—and—the note? Doesn't it mean anything?"

MacWhite: "Yeah—that means we have an excellent chance of losing Sarkhan, and then all the rest of Southeast Asia."

—The Ugly American

Curtis LeMay, advocating the bombing of North Vietnam: "I don't understand it. Here we are at the height of our power. The most powerful nation in the world. And yet we're afraid to use that power, we lack the will. In the last thirty years we've lost Estonia. Latvia. Lithuania. Poland. Czechoslovakia. Hungary. Bulgaria. China. . . ."

William Bundy: "Some people don't think we ever had them."

—Quoted by David Halberstam in *The Best and the Brightest*

Reporter, following rebellion in Sarkhan: "We gonna lose this country, sir?"

MacWhite: "Well, we never had this country."

—The Ugly American

It doesn't take long for Ambassador MacWhite to understand that Sarkhan, a mythical country bordering China and divided into a North and a South, is not ours to lose. Ah, but what a mess he makes before he catches on: he commits our Seventh Fleet, helps throw Sarkhan into outright civil war, and unwittingly sets the stage for the assassination of his old comrade-in-arms.

Like the Lederer and Burdick novel, *The Ugly American* is a tract warning us that our image is a trifle tarnished. Never, of course, does the film doubt that beneath the tarnish is the pure brass of American good intentions. There *is* criticism: Americans tend to be stubborn, impetuous, naive. It's like a syndicated horoscope: you read it and nod, Yes, that's general enough to apply to me. Then you read the funnies.

Before I begin to guide you through *The Ugly American,* I think you should be warned that the trip will be a long one befitting the significance of a film dedicated, in the words of a contemporary reviewer (Andrew Sarris), "to the platitudinous proposition that we had all better buckle down to win the Cold War."

Things have not been going well in Sarkhan. As the credits end, we see a peaceful ribbon of asphalt conveniently labled

FREEDOM ROAD
SARKHAN-U. S. A.
JOINT HIGHWAY PROJECT

But at the end of the road is a construction site plagued by politically explosive Communist sabotage. The outgoing American ambassador, a clammy flibbertigibbet, whines and squirms, as though burdened with previsions of what would harry LBJ back to the Pedernales.

Aide (played by Arthur Hill with the righteousness of Owen Marshall): "This may be your last chance to set the record straight—one clear, *sane* statement about why we're building Freedom Road."

Ambassador Sears: "It's not that simple—those reporters twist everything I say." It's not clear whether he's been giving *insane* answers all along, but the wishful thinking behind the aide's comment is clear: there must be some arrangement of words that will explain and justify America's role in Sarkhan.

Meanwhile, back in Washington, the media-bedeviled ambassador's replacement is being grilled in a Senate confirmation hearing. A metaphor is at hand. A warning to the working press. A prophecy. Something. In the novel, MacWhite had been a career diplomat; in the film he is a journalist-turned-publisher. Do you see what is about to happen? Reporters, like the one we met in *The Quiet American* and the one we'll meet in *The Green Berets,* spend all of their time harping about military and diplomatic blunders. So let's see how a member of the fourth estate functions when the spats are on the other foot.

Why is a journalist qualified to be an ambassador?, asks a Senator. "A good reporter has to win the confidence and the trust of people if he is ever to write anything perceptive about them," MacWhite explains, fiddling with his pipe. Besides, he has other qualifications: during World War II he had fought with the Sarkhanese underground against the Japanese and has kept in touch with his old comrade Deong, who emerged from the war as Sarkhan's national hero. Isn't Deong a Communist?, the Senator demands. MacWhite smiles in amusement, shakes his head. Not Deong. I know Deong.

Meanwhile, back in Sarkhan, Deong is on the soapbox. "We do not want the American military road. We do not want to be in the cold war." My old friend MacWhite will listen to us, he promises. Go to the airport. Carry signs. Be peaceful. Just stand quietly. Let him know how we feel, he instructs. And then the stirring nationalist slogan:"Sarkhan for the Sarkhanese!" Cheers. Cut to the welcome for Ambassador MacWhite: "America the Beautiful" on the soundtrack, a mob armed with placards on the runway ("Death to U. S. Imperialists," "War-mongers Get Out," "Yank Go Home"). A riot; MacWhite besieged in his limousine (shades of Nixon's Latin American crisis).

Cut to the entire diplomatic mission on the carpet, getting reamed out by their new boss: "The only thing that's clear at all is that there is no clarity." And: "Confusion, ignorance, and indifference will cease right now." He promptly stomps off for a reunion with Deong and gets stinking drunk for old times' sake. Deong, sensing the time is propitious and his friend well-oiled, puts in a plug for stopping the construction of that "American military adventure," Freedom Road. Easy-going MacWhite suddenly reacts like a knee-jerk USIA spokesman: "Freedom Road symbolizes development here," he lectures, "and once that happens, North Sarkhan can't take this country over because it's very difficult to subvert people who have enough to eat and an ability to defend themselves."

Deong grows nasty. He wants the United States to take its guns away from the puppet regime. The reunion sours, turns acid. The two old buddies, drunk on palm whiskey, shout slogans and counter-slogans at one another. MacWhite waves his finger under Deong's nose, Deong balls his fist, my right hand bears down on the pen, my left tenses to stop the reel should I need time to get it all down on paper. A hand touches my shoulder—I twitch and throw the machine into fast forward. Mac-White's slurred clichés turn into Donald Duck quacks.

I stop the machine, take off my earphones. It's the girl who's been watching the kinescope of a defunct television situation comedy at the viewing table next to me. A graduate student, probably roped into an unworkable thesis about the metaphysical significance of *Leave It to Beaver* or whatever it is she is spinning off that pile of 16 mm cannisters—but still able to giggle in the dark along with laughter canned before she was born. Perhaps she is revisiting her own lost youth, watching a program that once meant something different to her. None of this occurs to me at the moment. I just wonder why she dares break the anti-camaraderie of serious film scholarship.

She nods toward MacWhite, frozen in drunken bellicosity on the glass screen, his brief moustache a dirty blur on a face puffed and sweaty from drink.

"My God, is that *Brando?* Can I listen?"

I hand her the headset, and restore Brando to motion. He gets up, turns his back on Deong, pouts. A closeup of Deong. The fist shaking again, the mouth moving, but no sound coming out for me.

"Who's the other one? He's so . . . *intense.*"

"Eiji Okada."

"Um. What's he done?"

"He was the Japanese lover in *Hiroshima, Mon Amour.*"

"Um. Is this *Sayonara?*"

"No, it's *The Last Tango in Sarkhan.*"

The reel, having spun out its twelve-minute course, dies with the joke, clicks through the gates, flaps around on the take-up. I don't bother to rethread and backtrack over the minute or two I've lost to the girl's curiosity. I've seen it before, know that MacWhite's drunken reunion with Deong must end in recriminations and misunderstanding so everything can go to bloody hell in Sarkhan, so Deong can be pushed over the line of leading a nationalist rebellion behind which his Communist betrayers can come to power. Deong and MacWhite are only doing their dance.

The American goes home at the end of his first long day on the job, tells his wife that the United States is losing Sarkhan. Instead of trying to understand why Deong doesn't want Freedom Road, he sets out to prove to himself that the road is not an imperialist plot. At the end of the asphalt he finds the American road-builder, a cheerful, benevolent, but physically ugly (thus the book's title) American pragmatist played by Pat Hingle in his best down-home mode. And the builder's wife (Jocelyn Brando, Marlon's sister) is the kind of woman who tags along building thatch-roofed hospitals in her man's wake. Surely, Homer and Emma Atkins are not imperialists or military-adventurists.

Mrs. MacWhite: "What brought you way out here?"

Mrs. Atkins: "Oh, something Homer calls unfinished world business." She doesn't mean to conjure up a vision of used car lots and fast-food franchises stretching away to the vanishing point of Freedom Road, but the metaphor of "world business" smacks of uprooted midwestern chambers of commerce writ large.

HOLLYWOOD DIPLOMAT

Caution, Secrecy, Mark *The Ugly American*

The other day, with the camera turning, Mr. Brando, punctiliously in moustache, morning coat and striped pants, was having his first meeting with the Prime Minister of Sarkhan. But apart from the few lines of script that he recalled with difficulty during the shooting, Mr. Brando declined to discuss the movie.

"The studio mandarins," said George Englund, producer-director of the picture, "have decided on the policy not to discuss the contents of the movie." He continued, trying to look severe. "In the light of the present situation in Southeast Asia the picture has such volatility that it could easily—perhaps wilfully—be misunderstood.

Mr. Englund, a tall, agile man, swung himself into the seat behind the crane-mounted movie camera and was lifted about ten feet as he peered across the huge office built for the Sarkhan Prime Minister. Mr. Brando stirred a demitasse. . . .

In the short scene, Mr. Brando sips his coffee and brandy and prepares to suggest to the Prime Minister a plan dealing with the affairs of Sarkhan. . . .

As the bell rang to alert everyone for the shooting sequence. . . . an expert whispered excitedly:

"This will be the first time Brando will be so dressed up in a movie. The outfit he is wearing was bought from the same place that made President Kennedy's."

Mr. Brando studied his demitasse and strode once more across the polished floor toward the camera, ready to help his country in Southeast Asia.

—Murray Schumach, *New York Times,* 27 May 1962

Murray Schumach departs, Brando turns into MacWhite. Elegantly garbed, pointer in hand, he steps up to a wall map of Sarkhan to do a sales talk for the prime minister. His surefire plan: don't stop the road—change its direction. "Instead of the road moving east [slash] it should strike straight north [jab, jab], all the way to the Sarkhanese border. Now, that would produce two dynamic effects. One, it would open up this whole timber area [tap, tap] for development, which would benefit the economy, and it would drive a harpoon [swish!] right into the heart [thunk!] of the Communist concentration." The Sarkhanese prime minister, perhaps a student of *Moby Dick,* wants nothing of harpoons and rejects the scheme as too provocative and explosive.

MacWhite: "My government feels that this is an extremely worthwhile plan."

Prime Minister: "Will your government stand by its military commitment to Sarkhan in the event of trouble?"

MacWhite: "The United States stands by its military commitment everywhere in the world. But there is no reason to regard this as a military situation—it's purely a political maneuver."

Suddenly the scene turns into another kind of whale hunt, as the prime minister corners MacWhite and sinks his harpoon into the loose fish of American military aid: "Before you go on, have I America's absolute commitment to stand behind us in the event of trouble?" MacWhite, as the *Pequod* springs the first leak: "You have."

In their novel, Lederer and Burdick had put forth certain characters as experts on America's ideal battle plan against communism in Asia—a professional soldier from Texas, a Taiwanese official (Chiang Kai-shek is held up as a model of Asian leadership, of course), a huge Boston-Irish Jesuit, and Colonel Edwin B. (for Barnum) Hillandale—modeled on Edward Lansdale, the man who put sugar in Vietminh gas tanks. Hillandale's major contribution to American diplomacy is the employment of spurious astrological skills for tricking an impressionable and superstitious Asian leader into sending troops to the Chinese border, a ploy straight out of *A Connecticut Yankee in King Arthur's Court* that seems to have the full approval of the authors.

But the novel was published in 1958. By the time the location shooting in Thailand was finished in 1962, the first American had died in combat in Vietnam. Keeping a low profile, the filmmakers jettisoned the militant characters and took one American, the road-builder Atkins, to stand for innate American sensibility. Homer begs MacWhite to stop construction of Freedom Road temporarily.

MacWhite: "Well, I don't think we can quit, Homer, just because we have a couple of casualties. . . ."

Homer: "Well, we're not at war, sir."

MacWhite: "We are at war, Homer, and the more we back down, the more they'll attack." Homer swears the Sarkhanese will not die for the road. "Call this party off," he begs. "Give things time to quiet down a little." MacWhite: "That's the whole point, Homer—there isn't any time. None. There's only one way to go, and that's the way we're going."

While MacWhite has been stumbling deeper into the morass, Deong has been to a jungle summit conference with military and diplomatic representatives of Russia, China, and the People's Republic of North Sarkhan. The dedication of Freedom Road is interrupted by the outbreak of Deong's revolution, and the Sarkhanese prime minister warns MacWhite that his government will fall unless the Seventh Fleet puts troops ashore. Before MacWhite will call for help, he insists on reasoning with Deong. Good Idea, beams the prime minister, who offers to form a coalition government with Deong to forestall further bloodshed. Off goes MacWhite in his flag-bedecked limousine, siren wailing, to the other side of the war-torn capital where Deong is running the rebellion from his own front porch. The war in Vietnam had been smoldering or raging for more than a decade, and Hollywood still didn't know how such affairs were conducted or how Americans were to comport themselves within the battle zone.

MacWhite arrives just in time to warn Deong that the revolution has been betrayed and its leader marked for death. Enter Communist assassin to shoot Deong, who lives long enough for reconciliation with MacWhite.

Now I'm down to the last reel in the stack. It's been a long morning in a close room. Much is still unclear. Does the revolution succeed? Will MacWhite send for troops? We get not answers but a press conference, not solutions but a metaphor. MacWhite launches into a Big Speech: "We forget that the men who started our country had the same kind of passion that Deong had . . . and unless we recognize their fight for independence as part of our own, we drive them to seek understanding some other place." Is he trying to say, a reporter asks, that we are pushing Sarkhan toward communism? No, he is "blaming the indifference that some of us show toward promises.

If the cold war disappeared right now, the American people would still be in this fight against ignorance, hunger, disease—because it's right—it's right to be in it—and if I had one appeal to make to every American it would be that . . ."

[cut to MacWhite as seen on television in a "typical" American living room decorated in fake early American—as MacWhite's sincerity and fervor mounts, a man comes in gnawing on a piece of chicken, watches MacWhite, consults his *TV Guide* and reaches for the set . . .]

CLICK!

The set goes black. "America the Beautiful" rises on the soundtrack. The last frames slide through the gate. I'm embarrassed by the attack on complacency Brando has just delivered with such confidence, posturing like one of the Best and the Brightest from the staircase of the American Embassy, flanked by spiffy Marine sentries. We've had almost two hours of blunders, blindness, and buffoonery—now a superstar risen out of the Midwest tries to turn it all around with one sane speech building to one appeal to every American. And click!, the script throws the responsibility into the American living room, self-righteously blaming Mr. Typical Citizen for not wanting to get involved in another fight.

THE ADVENTURE GOES PROFESSIONAL

Here I am, more than halfway through my chapter on films set in Vietnam or thereabouts, and the United States has not yet been in formal combat. The cinematic struggle, to date, had been carried on by amateurs or diplomats. Now it was time to call in the Marines in two films made in the mid-sixties. Both were minor productions starring Marshall Thompson, a former theology student from Peoria whose war-film career began late in World War II with *The Purple Heart* (he was the kid whose parachute didn't open).

In 1963, Thompson went to Vietnam to direct and star in the first uniformed combat picture of the war: *A Yank in Viet-Nam.** Released in 1964 on a Lowe's circuit double-bill with Dean Martin's *Who's Been Sleeping in My Bed?*, the film starts out as a careful reflection of official policy in the early sixties. Americans are supposed to be simply observers and advisers; the Vietnamese are to do all the fighting. Thompson plays a Marine Corps major named Benson who is captured by the Vietcong when his helicopter is shot down. Rescued by friendly guerrillas† helping a beautiful Vietnamese girl find her kidnapped father, Major Benson adventures along with them fairly passively until the end, when he takes charge to save the

---

*The title follows the popular formula of *A Yank in Korea, Libya, London, Rome, Indo China, the RAF, on the Burma Road,* etc.
†The guerrillas are led by Enrique Magalona, the Filipino actor who played the North Korean prisoner in *The Hook* the year before; the other important male Vietnamese role is filled by Mario Barri, also Filipino.

day. The climax of the film mirrors what had actually been happening in Vietnam during the years when American military and political observers had grown impatient at the slow progress of the South Vietnamese government and were itching to get involved.

Though *A Yank in Viet-Nam* opens with the announcement that "the motion picture you are about to see was filmed entirely in South Vietnam, in the actual combat areas, during the present war against the Communist Viet-Cong," the story it tells could have been shot on a back-lot. It's literally a standard Western chase ("a marketable piece of merchandize," said the *Variety* reviewer). The film moves through the Vietnamese landscape too quickly for us to see the people who are the real sufferers, and reduces twenty years of war to a South Vietnamese guerrilla's complaint that "First came the Japanese, then came the French, and now the Communists." The Americans aren't on the list because their presence is, of course, welcome—an assumption Michael Wayne, the producer of *The Green Berets,* was to make in explaining the historical background of the conflict to Dan Wakefield: "These people . . . have been under the Chinese and under the French, but our troops are the first soldiers they really like."

In 1965, Marshall Thompson appeared in his second Vietnam film, *To the Shores of Hell.* Though made with elaborate Marine Corps assistance (footage of troops, helicopters, ships, landing craft, etc., at Camp Pendleton was converted on screen into an unopposed beach head at Da Nang), the film is basically a re-hash of the small-scale chase in Thompson's earlier effort. Where Major Benson helped rescue a South Vietnamese doctor from the Vietcong, Major Donahue sets out to rescue his brother, also a doctor, from the Cong. As in the earlier film, friendly South Vietnamese and a French priest are involved, and the rescue is successful, if the film is not.

The title was meant to evoke the Marine Corps hymn ("From the halls of Montezuma, to the shores of Tripoli"), the lobby posters stressed images of blasting artillery supporting tanks, helicopters, and men rushing into action under the bold promise that one would find "THE HELL-BUSTIN' SHOOT-THE-WORKS EPIC of the U. S. Marines," but it was all a Sell. Like the war, the movie flopped. It "enjoyed", the producer wrote me, "a number of domestic and foreign play dates. I do not know if it has as yet appeared on any local TV stations."

TWO FORGOTTEN ADVENTURES

Allied Artists, having released *A Yank in Viet-Nam* in 1964, tried its luck with *Operation CIA* in 1965. Kieu Chinh, who had played the Vietnamese doctor's daughter in the earlier film, now played a beautiful undercover agent, and the then-unknown Burt Reynolds starred as a CIA man sent to Vietnam after another American agent is blown up while trying to warn his superiors that something is dreadfully wrong in Saigon. Why a CIA man who has never been to Vietnam (or at least acts that way) is called in when the country is full of CIA men is not explained, but may be taken as a metaphor for a basic silliness in the conduct of the war and the film itself. Reynolds, who keeps getting beat up, kidnapped, and ambushed, eventually and implausibly prevails to discover that the Vietcong plan to dump nerve gas in the central air conditioning system at the American Embassy. Seventeen years had passed since *Saigon* and *Rogues' Regiment,* but little seems to have changed (except for the air conditioning, which Dick Powell didn't have). The Americans come in, solve problems, and depart.

In 1966, a film crew headed by the American Rolf Bayer turned up in Saigon to shoot *Run With the Devil,* a film involving buried gold, the CIA, Buddhist monks, and dozens of Vietcong guerrillas played by actual Communist defectors on loan from a government detention camp. Though the film was produced by a Manila-based outfit and never, to the best of my knowledge, shown in this country or anywhere else, some of the production details are worth noting, especially for the way they suggest growing sensitivity among American image-makers about how the war might look to outsiders (that is, American taxpayers and voters). For instance, the original version of the script, Neil Sheehan reported in the *New York Times* for 16 July 1966, had a Vietcong major assisting an American reporter and a Vietnamese woman psychiatrist in a search for a fortune in gold hidden by the late Ngo Dinh Diem.

To obtain cooperation from the United States military and civilian authorities [in Saigon], Mr. Bayer had to change this.

Officials of the United States Information Agency noted that audiences might deduce that the fortune had been obtained by diverting American aid funds, and this would create doubts about the use to which United States aid to Vietnam is put.

The information agency told Mr. Bayer to eliminate all references to the Diem regime if he wanted American cooperation, and suggested he have the Vietcong hide the treasure.

"But it didn't make much sense to have the Reds hiding it," Mr. Bayer said, "so I figured the French would do it."

The most novel thing about *Run With the Devil* is that it ended, or was supposed to end, with all the leading characters, "Communist, pro-government and American," getting killed.

DIGRESSION: SOMEONE ELSE'S ADVENTURE REVISITED

While unknown producers and directors were trying to exploit whatever interest the war might hold, the smart money was staying away. The Frankenheimers and Kubricks and Kramers had taken on the big issues—military and political conspiracies, nuclear catastrophe, the very End of the World itself—but Vietnam was too specific. The Aldrichs and Peckinpahs found enough action at home or just across the border in Mexico.

Then Mark Robson, who had directed two of the sternest calls to duty of the Korean era—*I Want You* and *The Bridges at Toko-Ri*—produced and directed *The Lost Command* (1966), a film that managed to sidestep the issues of Vietnam and yet exploit its topicality. Robson's strategy was simplicity itself: He dropped in briefly on a group of French officers at Dien Bien Phu, then followed them to Algeria, where, humiliated by the no-win policy of their civilian leaders, they exert a brutal vigor that wins their rough and ready peasant colonel (Anthony Quinn) his coveted promotion to general.* No criticism was intended, and little perceived at the time: "No matter what the issue," said Arthur Knight in the *Saturday Review,* "no matter how idealistic or morally reprehensible the cause for which they fight, the mere act of standing up to an enemy requires a kind of courage that one can only admire. When . . . Anthony Quinn provides his men with resourceful and inspiring leadership, he automatically becomes an estimable figure. He does not question the principles he is fighting for, and, the film implies, neither should we. He is just a simple peasant making good in an army whose officers, hitherto, had all been aristo-

---

*This was the second American film to treat the major French defeat in Vietnam. The first was Warner Brothers' *Jump Into Hell* (1955), based on an Irving Wallace script about the siege of Dien Bien Phu focusing on the motives and fates of four French soldiers who volunteer to parachute into the doomed garrison.

crats. So bully for him. If some of the men in his command commit atrocities in Algeria, it is merely their natural reaction to the slaughter of their comrades, not official policy."

The Lost Command looked away by looking back, but even in looking back it betrayed certain attitudes toward the conflict then growing in Vietnam. For one, it is in total sympathy with the French warriors and implies that had they been allowed to prosecute the war against the yellow-skins in Asia without hindrance, the brown-skins in Algeria would not have gotten the dangerous notion that a proud nation can be successfully challenged. Secondly, though the film hands us the loudspeaker rhetoric of the Vietminh ("our soldiers are smaller and less strong than yours, but they fight with more spirit because we have the truth, the only truth, on our side; you fight to keep humanity in the dark, we serve a just cause") and lets a disillusioned French officer provide a near-traitorous analysis of what kept the Vietminh going ("It wasn't fear at all—they wanted change, any kind of change. I don't blame them"), when we finally meet the enemy, they turn out to be central-casting Nips out of the old Warner Brothers hate-mill: threatening, posturing, full of inflated rhetoric—and helpless before the mystery of a jeep without keys.

PROLOGUE TO THE GREATEST ADVENTURE OF THEM ALL

July 1966—*The Lost Command* is beginning its first run. William Calley, flat broke in Albuquerque, joins the army. And John Wayne is in Vietnam, pressing the flesh in the boondocks, raising spirits in hospitals.

Soon Wayne would return to the States to begin *The Green Berets.* Starting at the top, he first cabled President Johnson in December 1966 to let him know the project was underway. Bill Moyers replied with an expression of the President's interest ("it sounded like an exciting venture"). Wayne then went to the Department of Defense with an eight-page list of the men and materiel he would need: troops of Oriental descent who could pass for Vietnamese, hundreds of Caucasian soldiers to play themselves, American armaments, captured enemy weapons, armored personnel carriers and cargo planes and helicopters and tanks and bulldozers and jeeps and trucks and ambulances and gee a whole big list of stuff that went on and on as though the people at Batjac had been sharpening their appetites on T. S. Eliot's "Triumphal March":

5,800,000	rifles and carbines,
102,000	machine guns,
28,000	trench mortars,
53,000	field and heavy guns,
I cannot tell how many projectiles, mines and fuses,	
13,000	aeroplanes,
24,000	aeroplane engines,
50,000	ammunition waggons,
now 55,000	army waggons,
11,000	field kitchens,
1,150	field bakeries.

In *The Green Berets,* one of the major characters is the "scrounger" played by Jim Hutton. Not only does he steal weapons and building materials from other units, but he himself has been scrounged—a lover of home comforts, he doesn't want to go back to Vietnam until blackmailed by Wayne and his men. The whole question of priorities should come up here, but doesn't. Hollywood had always treated the scrounger as a comic personification of Free Enterprise. Take what you need—the hell with anyone else's needs or mission; the hell with congressional appropriations, the hell with poverty at home. Hutton takes from other characters, Wayne takes from the military, the military takes from the taxpayer, and everyone has a gay time.

During the filming of *Tora! Tora! Tora!,* a House Military Operations Subcommittee hearing revealed, an Assistant Secretary of Defense for Public Affairs wrote the Secretary of Defense a memorandum showing "great concern about possible congressional criticism if a seaman were killed [seven had been burned, and several civilian pilots killed] or a carrier should take time off during the Vietnam war to simulate a Japanese carrier.... Assistance to *The Green Berets,* which the Navy (and Mr. Valenti) had brought up, was a different matter, as Public Affairs saw it. That film favored our role in Vietnam, and if a serviceman were injured or killed in the making, it would be easier to explain to the Hill."*

---

*This quote comes from the Subcommittee's report on *Military Assistance to Commercial Film Projects.* For a fuller account of DOD assistance to *The Green*

The Green Berets was just the kind of film the military wanted, and a grateful army eventually billed Wayne's production company a mere $18,623.64 for what Congressman Benjamin S. Rosenthal thought might have amounted to a million dollars worth of services: eighty-five hours of flying time by UH–1 helicopters, the use of countless M–16 rifles, mortars, grenade launchers, flamethrowers, and machine guns, tactical air support, locations at four different army posts, and 3,800 man-days of military personnel taken away from their regular duties.

"When are you going back to the States?" went the cast joke at Fort Benning, where most of the action was shot. But it was more surrealistic than funny: hundreds of young men filling in before the cameras to make a movie supporting a war they wouldn't have to go to if people like John Wayne had stopped pushing it.

THE GREATEST ADVENTURE OF THEM ALL

William Calley to John Sack: "I felt alive now, as I never had in America. I felt helpful, even if I couldn't build an SST, a spaceship, or something spectacular. I built wells, I showed the Vietnamese movies. I even showed them *The Green Berets.*"
—*Lieutenant Calley: His Own Story*

Here individuals of all nations are melted into a new race of men, whose labors and posterity will one day cause great changes in the world. Americans are the western pilgrims, who are carrying along with them that great mass of arts, sciences, vigor, and industry which began long since in the east; they will finish the great circle.
—*Letters from an American Farmer*

De Crèvecoeur's two-hundred-year-old prediction of our high national destiny is fulfilled—we pushed the frontier across the continent until we got to the Pacific, sat on the shore awhile making movies about the conquest, and then began looking across the water to Hawaii and beyond, to where the East is west of the West. For lack of a West to conquer, we have gone east, which may explain why *The Green Berets* ends with an old Western star walking off into the setting sun as it slowly

Berets, see Fulbright's *The Pentagon Propaganda Machine.*

sinks into the South China Sea to the east of Vietnam. That's not just bad geography but a sadly revealing metaphor for our hankering after lost frontiers.

Or did John Wayne simply want to make a Western? During the filming of *The Green Berets,* producer Michael Wayne told a *Variety* interviewer that "We're not making a political picture; we're making a picture about a bunch of right guys . . . Cowboys and Indians. . . . The Americans are the good guys and the Viet Cong are the bad guys. . . . Maybe we shouldn't have destroyed all those Indians, but when you are making a picture, the Indians are the bad guys."

The most popular American film genre because it portrays a vital and supposedly unambiguous period in our history, the Western has frequently provided a safe platform for commenting on current affairs. By extension, the ballad heard at the start and finish, Wayne's line to the effect that "out here, due process is a bullet," the Dodge City sign over the main gate to the Green Beret outpost, the cross-bow toting "native" scouts—and Wayne himself—all make the biggest and most important film about American involvement in Vietnam look as politically safe as a John Ford romantization of the old West.*

But then, *The Green Berets* looks like a lot of other movies. For one, it has scraps of old World War II films: a good old top kick named Muldoon and a dogface called Kowalski; an enemy general, in the tradition of the suave celluloid Nazi, flaunts fancy quarters, a French staff car, distinguished gray hair, a well-tailored uniform, and a decadent weakness for caviar, wine, and beautiful but helpless women. More specifically, as several film buffs have suggested to me, it is a reworking of *Back to Bataan,* in which John Wayne, twenty-odd years younger, also played a bird colonel who goes to the aid of a freedom-loving people strug-

---

*Employing a classic director of Westerns does not guarantee the safety of the platform, as the United States Information Agency learned when it asked the late John Ford to oversee production of *Vietnam! Vietnam!,* a documentary presenting a view of the war favorable to official American interests. The resulting film was shelved in 1971 and cannot be shown publicly in this country. Let Joseph McBride's description suffice: "Glib as it may sound, Ford's view of the war is reminiscent of a Western. The Vietcong are the bad guys, the peasants are the terrorized farmers, the Americans are the Earp Brothers come to clean up the territory so that decent folks can go to church and set up schools. Such an innocent vision of society is charming in the archaic context of the Western genre, but debilitating and ridiculous in a documentary of modern war." So with *The Green Berets.*

gling against foreign invaders. Similarities abound: the loyal "native" girl who spies on the enemy at the hazard of her reputation; the small allied force fighting in the hills against greater numbers, then attacking the invaders directly and escaping cross-country; the enemy itself, interchangeable automatons given to lemming-like attacks; and the loveable little native boy who receives American military insignia from Wayne's hands late in each film.

Back to Bataan celebrates America's earlier success working with guerrillas and partisans against a force superior in size and equipment who would complain: "We cannot find the enemy. We send a hundred men out, and they see nothing. We send ten men, and they don't come back." "Why have we failed to win the people over," asks a Japanese general, when "the guerrillas obviously have the complete aid and sympathy of the people?" By the time *The Green Berets* was made, Americans would be voicing the same kind of complaints. Suddenly we were on the wrong side.

Ah, but that our allies in Vietnam had been as heroic and selfless as the Filipino guerrilla (Anthony Quinn) who rejects the suggestion that his countrymen be evacuated nine days before a planned American invasion.

Quinn: "That'll give the Japs a pretty good idea where to expect the landings, won't it?"

Navy Officer: "There's nothing else we can do. We can't risk civilian lives."

Quinn: "There haven't been any 'civilians' here since the fall of Bataan. If it will save American lives and help make the landings safe, our people will not evacuate."

Officer: "I'm sure glad you guys are on our side."

John Wayne looks on paternalistically throughout this exchange, as he does in similar scenes in *The Green Berets*. But a quarter century later, the rhetoric is more basic. ARVN captain: "Kill all stinking Cong, then go home"; ARVN colonel: "We build many camps, clobber many Vee Cee. Affirmative?" Wayne: "Affirmative. I like the way you talk."

"I like the way you talk." This is Wayne's highest compliment to his Vietnamese counterpart, and may explain why *The Green Berets* is one of the wordiest combat films ever made. With the exception of the Vietnamese nationals, who stumble along in Pidgin English, everyone runs on at great length, and the intellectual freight of the film involves getting a dovish reporter (co-star David Janssen) to change the way he talks.*

Let's go to the start of the film. The ballad heard over the credits ends on the couplet "They mean just what they say—/ The brave men of the Green Beret," as we hear a voice speaking German. It is a Green Beret team leader identifying himself and his mission, displaying his proficiency in another language to show the international role of the Special Forces beyond Vietnam. Each of the men under him identifies himself in a foreign tongue, then translates, right down to the radio operator: "I speak Danish and have a working knowledge of Norwegian and English."

A working knowledge of English?! Where are we? At the

JOHN F. KENNEDY CENTER FOR SPECIAL WARFARE,

a sign proclaims,

FORT BRAGG, NORTH CAROLINA.

The occasion is a public demonstration of Green Beret talents —a reminder, really, that the army spends most of its time teaching, not fighting. The audience is a grandstand full of neatly dressed, polite civilians whose role is to applaud when Master Sergeant Muldoon (Aldo Ray) scores points against David Janssen and his fellow slow learners at the press table in front of the grandstand.

After Sergeant Muldoon introduces himself as an expert on Vietnam, a reporter asks him the kind of wife-beating question that no intelligent journalist would put to a lowly non-com: "Why is the United States waging this useless war?" Muldoon's answer exculpates the Green Berets from anything that might follow in the film: "Foreign policy decisions are not made by the military. A soldier goes where he is told to go, fights whom he is told to fight." Now David Janssen joins the sniping, aiming at Muldoon's black assistant: "Do you agree with that, Sergeant McGee? That the Green Beret is just a military robot with

---

*They even talk about the sounds of words. Luke Askew (who later returned as the bearded and bandannaed hitchhiker in *Easy Rider*) plays a gung-ho sergeant named Provo whose chief worry is that his name won't be "right" on a memorial should he die a hero's death: "Provo's Barracks, Provo's Commissary —ya see what I mean," he complains to Colonel Wayne, "it just don't sing." Predictably, he dies, and Wayne, declaring that "it sings," commissions a sign reading "Provo's Privy."

no personal feeling?" (Muldoon, in his most intimidating voice: "Can I have your name, sir?")

But McGee, played by the sensitive Raymond St. Jacques, must have his say, for with the exception of two black soldiers who are given step-'n-fetchit chores, McGee is the only black in the film (Wayne to *Playboy* interviewer: "I've directed two pictures and I gave the blacks their proper position. I had a black slave in *The Alamo,* and I had the correct number of blacks in *The Green Berets"*). McGee's "proper position" is to legitimize, in one soulful speech, our presence in Vietnam—and to stand for all the humane functions of the Green Berets (later we will see him ministering to an old Montagnard, spooning whiskey down his throat: "He's dying, poor old thing. Can't even keep his rice down anymore. . . . He's tired, bone tired"). McGee begins to answer Janssen's question very slowly and artfully in a quiet, reasonable voice. Yes, Green Berets have feelings—it's hard not to form them "out there." As soldiers, they can keep perspective on what the enemy does in combat, but (his voice and emotions begin to rise) the enemy's "extermination of the civilian leadership, the intentional murder and torture of innocent women and children . . ."

A woman reporter breaks in to stop the flood of feeling: "Yes, I guess horrible things happen in war, but that doesn't mean they need us or even want us." McGee neatly and patronizingly sidesteps the reporter's objection: "Let me put it in terms we can all understand. If this same thing happened in the United States, every mayor in every city would be murdered. Every teacher . . . every professor . . . every Senator, every member of the House of Representatives and their families. . . . But in spite of this, there's always some little fellow out there willing to stand up and take the place of those who've been decimated. They need us, Miss Sutton, and they want us."

Immediately, a woman (one of those little fellows willing to stand up?) rises behind the reporters, introduces herself with a deprecatory shrug as a housewife, and allows as how "It's strange that we never read of this in the newspapers." Muldoon takes charge again: "Well, that's newspapers for you, m'am— you could fill volumes with what you don't read in them" (big laugh from the gallery). Now Janssen rides to the aid of his profession: "That's sometimes very true, Sergeant. But how do you know we should be fighting for this present government? They've had no free elections. They have no constitution. Six months ago, a committee was appointed to form a constitution —still no constitution."

Clearly, battle lines have been drawn, and Sergeant Muldoon is no slouch. He launches into a response that once would have been accompanied by "America the Beautiful" or "The Battle Hymn of the Republic" on the soundtrack. There is no music, but Aldo Ray's normally rasping voice acquires a buttery wonder that does the trick: "The school I went to . . . taught us that the thirteen colonies, with proper and educated leadership, all with the same goal in mind, after the Revolutionary War, took from 1776 to 1787, eleven years of peaceful effort, before they came up with a paper that all thirteen colonies could sign. Our present Constitution."

When the enthusiastic applause dies down, Janssen, looking properly impressed at the rhetoric, allows a sarcastic compliment: "That's very good, Sergeant." But he underestimates his opponent, thinks Muldoon has exhausted his powers with one set piece speech. Janssen brings up the heavy artillery: "There are still a lot of people who believe this is simply a war between the Vietnamese people. It's their war—let *them* handle it." Muldoon has reserves, however, and literally throws them at the reporter. He takes captured enemy weapons from a display stand and begins to dump them under Janssen's nose, escalating his voice and intensity as the pile of Russian, Chinese, and Satellite armaments grows. "No sir," he concludes to wild applause, "it doesn't take a lead weight to fall on me or a hit from one of those weapons to recognize that what is involved here is Communist domination of the world!"

Janssen's humiliation is not complete. He goes up to John Wayne, who has been watching and smiling approvingly at Muldoon's handling of the reporters (he likes the way Muldoon talks).

Janssen: "Colonel, your brainwashed sergeant didn't sell me."

Wayne: "Didn't sell you what?"

Janssen: "Didn't sell me on the idea that we should be in Southeast Asia."

Wayne: "You ever been to Southeast Asia?"

Janssen: "No, I haven't."

Wayne: "Huh!" Fade out on Wayne walking away from Janssen, who, on the basis of that enigmatic "huh!" will decide to go to Vietnam and see for himself.

I've spent a lot of time on this opening scene because it makes clear that *The Green Berets* is not so much about winning the war against the Vietcong as it is about winning the hearts and minds of the American public. David Janssen is Wayne's co-star because his role is as important; Wayne merely kills the Cong, a simple enough feat given the way the enemy makes mass charges, but Janssen must kill his own doubts about America's destiny in Southeast Asia. Though Wayne has pro-claimed he intended *The Green Berets* to be purely entertain-ment, he may have meant that he intended to entertain himself by revealing that all those biased newspaper accounts of the war came from men who didn't know what they were talking about.

At the end of one of the spoke-like corridors that radiate out from the hub of the Pentagon is a large painting of Ernie Pyle, the model of the modern military reporter who travels along with the boys and leaves policy to the experts. By the last reel, the Janssen character will qualify for the Ernie Pyle Hall of Fame—we will see him (dressed in regulation fatigues instead of the modish white hunter outfit he wore earlier) shoulder a duffle bag and head back to the war that has come to mean something different to him. We never learn what it does mean, only that he has somehow had an Experience that allows this kind of post-battle exchange:

Wayne: "Whata ya gonna say in that newspaper of yours?"

Janssen: "If I say what I feel, I may be out of a job."

Wayne: "We'll always give you one."

Janssen: "I could do you more good with a typewriter." (The Pressbook explains at this point that "the former skeptic leaves to write about the heroic exploits of the American and South Vietnamese forces.")

The conversion of Janssen is managed almost entirely through a time-honored device that goes back to anti-Hun mov-ies of the Great War, the rape and murder of a child. Janssen accompanies the Green Berets to a friendly Montagnard vil-lage. But the Vietcong have been there, and have murdered the headman. How about the headman's granddaughter, asks Janssen, who had given the little girl a medallion. A village woman with an eye for detail reveals that the girl has been taken away by *five* guerrillas. Knowing what *that* means, Janssen gets one of his Excedrin headaches and runs off into the Georgia piney woods to find the body. Wayne comes up to console Janssen with a speech that's standard-issue when there's a tough propaganda job to be done. "It's pretty hard to talk to anyone about this country till they've come over here and seen it." He then launches into a little horror story of murder, mutilation, torture, disembowelment, bonecrushing, and the "abuse" of a chieftain's wife by no less than *forty* Vietcong.

Following the rape-murder of the girl, Janssen stops nit-picking about the justice of the war. The unspoken assumption is that Americans never rape or murder, and that simply showing a reporter what the enemy does will guarantee agreement that we should be involved in the war. With Janssen disposed of (except for several brief appearances that will demonstrate the conditioning still holds), and having justified any future violence in the name of the sanctity of childhood, *The Green Berets* moves directly into combat. The Vietcong attack Wayne's outpost like so many desparate Apaches. They die under a mortar barrage, they die in the minefields, they die doused with flaming gasoline, and on the barbed wire perimeter, and finally, having captured the outpost upon Wayne's withdrawal, they obligingly mill about like geese while Wayne calls in an airstrike (Pilot: "It'll only take a minute"), and die one last time. Wayne: "I believe we can move back in there tomorrow—God willin' and the river don't rise."

Interviewer: "Did you resent the critics who labeled [*The Green Berets*] a shameless propaganda film?"

Wayne: "I agreed with them. It was an American film about American boys who were heroes over there. In that sense, it was propaganda."

—Playboy

The film, like the war, goes on too long. The special effects and battle scenes are technically well done, like the war itself, elaborately and meticulously conducted, but not worth doing. "Never have a war and a movie complemented each other so appropriately," said one reviewer, meaning that the tedium, excessiveness, and extravagance of Vietnam found its artistic counterpart in Wayne's movie.

It is, bluntly, a stupid film, but not a vicious one, for its foolishness was blatant, its lack of reality patent to anyone with sufficient thumb-finger co-ordination to turn on the evening news. When I showed the film to students in 1972, even those who passed for radicals at the tail end of the war found the colonel played by John Wayne to be likeable because . . . well, because he was John Wayne. The Duke had been playing virtuous soldiers, sheriffs, and frontiersmen for decades, and here all the roles were balled into one. It wasn't his fault that the times had changed. So when he got his first Academy Award the following year for *True Grit,* the real true grit had already been shown in the hard-headed and unstylish courage he displayed in hitching himself, his fortune, and even his family (one of his sons produced, another played a can-do officer) to a cattle drive that went the wrong way.

Some will probably object that the outwardly innocent quality of the film made it doubly corrupt and insidious. Yet the explosive French radicals, who have a nose for such things, declined to attack. There was a good deal of critical pique (the *New York Times'* Renata Adler, commandeering a rhetorical overkill to match the film's, called it "a pivotal event" marking "the end of the traditional war pictures and a tremendous breakdown of the fantasy-making apparatus in this country"; others reviewed the war and not the film), and pickets sprung up across the land—New York and London, Paris and Rome, Munich and Tokyo and Stockholm. And in Minnesota, a lone protestor marched up and down bearing a sign proclaiming "I do not protest the war—just this picture."

Meanwhile, John Wayne let it be known that he had commissioned a seven foot tall monument to the Green Berets to be sculpted in Vermont and installed at Fort Bragg.

THE LAST ADVENTURE?

The Green Berets was the first major combat film set in Vietnam. As this book goes to press in the spring of 1974, it is still the only one, though others will surely appear as the war fades into the safer perspective of time. In 1970, a small independent firm, Fanfare Productions, went to the Philippines to make an exploitation pic about a motorcycle gang recruited to rescue a presidential adviser held prisoner by the Vietcong. The five bikers succeed, but all die violently and in gory slow motion in the process.

For the time being, the title of this film has the last word: *The Losers.*

FIVE

IN ENEMY COUNTRY— THE WAR COMES HOME

Marine captain, home after eighteen months in a POW camp, on being told that his fiancée has been wounded by a sniper while walking across a campus: "What's going on in this world? I thought I left all that insanity behind in Nam."
—*The Streets of San Francisco,* 31 January 1974

The film opens. A Vietnamese woman is crying, clutching a child to her. Americans move through her village, their Zippos out. The camera jerks, the scene changes. Carnage. Sorrow. And a persistent narrator grinds out a hackneyed radical denunciation of America's role in Southeast Asia.

Then we see that the footage is on a movieola in front of a group of students. To the side, yoga-like on an editing table, sits their instructor, Thad.

Mark, reacting to especially bloody scene: "Are you really gonna leave that in?"

Mike: "Look, I *want* people to be offended by this—it's a real war, not a TV program."

Robie: "Well, you want them to sit through it too."

Steve: "No, you've got to get into the psychology of it. They'll sit there and watch because they don't want to come off squeamish."

Penny: "And maybe one of them—just one—will come away horrified enough to get into the peace movement."

Mark: "All you're gonna do is make a lot of women sick to their stomachs."

Thad: "It's kind of brutal. [professorial pause] Don't you think you could have made your point some other way? I must say, I really didn't expect quite this much."

I squirm in the plush seat of the well-appointed little viewing room. "Christ, that's a pissy line"—I mock my own delivery: " 'I must say, I *really* didn't expect *quite* this much.' "

"It fits the character," the director says from behind his pipe. "It's *you.*"

I mumble an obscenity. The film cuts away from Thad to the movieola, where we see more scenes of the war in Vietnam, the protest at home.

Now, a lovemaking scene is intercut with the war and protest shots as the narrator intones, "Make peace, not empire; make love, not war."

Shot in Ithaca in the spring of 1970, shortly before the Kent State killings, *Thaddeus* is about a young college professor whose students have made a pornographic anti-war film. At issue was freedom of speech, but the war protest background was supposed to make it go, to give it savor and a topical peg.

As it turned out, such stories were in the air—before the year was out, I would see a mess of campus-upheaval films all plucked out of the same Zeitgeist that spawned *Thaddeus: The*

Activist and *Getting Straight, The Strawberry Statement* and *RPM* and *Zabriskie Point.* For one brief moment, Hollywood had thought there was money to be made by backing films about young people who were refusing to buy Vietnam. It was a message that filtered down even to the provinces.

Failing to find a market for his film, Peter Klinge, the director, made another in 1971 starring Ralph Meeker as a Vietnam veteran who goes berserk. Both are still unreleased, but serve to document the flood of films that brought the war home.

In the spring of 1970, not long after the Kent State killings and the revelation of our massacres in Vietnam, I spent an afternoon with Richard Condon, the author of *The Manchurian Candidate* and other bitterly effective investigations into the dark continent of the American psyche. Condon was at work that spring of our discontent on a film treatment entitled *Are They Singing My Song?* Punning on Songmy, the name of one of the hamlets purged by our troops, he was trying to put together a film dealing with a group of Weathermen who decide to wipe out a small town in New Jersey in retaliation for the Mylai atrocities.

Condon never found the backing needed; that farflung institution popularly known as Hollywood was, unlike SDS, remarkably loathe to bring the war home. The troubles of Condon, an old Walt Disney public relations man who should know how to put together a marketable package, set me to thinking: why have there been so few films about Vietnam's impact on American life?

The answer, I found, was that there were already several dozen films by mid-1970, but that with few exceptions they were low-budget efforts made on the periphery of the industry by newcomers and one-shots. By the time I closed my files in January 1974 to write this chapter, I had collected over seventy films dealing specifically with the war's influence at home.* As Thad would say, I really didn't expect quite that much. Yet I wonder how many more films died, like Condon's, in utero. Stirling Silliphant, the scenarist for such popular or critical successes as *In the Heat of the Night, Charly,* and *The Poseidon Adventure,* had also passed around an anti-war script entitled

---

*This number does not include films that merely allude to the war or its effect in passing, as does *Electra-Glide in Blue* when it offhandedly establishes its protagonist's identity as a Vietvet.

Groundswell. The title, Silliphant wrote me, "was a reference to the below-surface tide that was rising throughout the country among young people." Focusing on a college girl, the film was to involve radical retribution against the girl's father, the Chief of Staff of the United States Army. Set up for kidnapping by his daughter, the general is taken to an isolated little community on Long Island where he is put on trial for war crimes. The tribunal, composed of anti-war students and a Vietcong suicide squad put ashore from a Chinese submarine, invoke the principles established by the Allies at Nuremberg.

"The theme of the film," Silliphant wrote, "was that all political ideology—whether capitalist democracy or bureaucratic communism—is a pile of self-serving, power-and-profit motivated anti-human shit." "Anti-political and anarchistic," showing man as the "victim of his leaders—and ultimately of himself," the film was to be "Christ-like in its very simplicity—therefore something to be ignored."

With the country uneasy over what many saw as a threat from radical students in the late sixties, and given the way life often tends to imitate art, the major studios gathered the mantle of responsibility and sobriety more closely and passed up the Condon and Silliphant projects. So it was left to radical young filmmakers like Robert Kramer (not to be confused with Stanley) to bring the war home—Kramer's *The Edge* (1968) dealt with an attempt to kill the President in reparation for the slaughter in Vietnam, while *Ice* (1970) treated urban guerrillas in an imaginary future when the United States has gone to war in Mexico.

Just as Hollywood looked away from the war as it was being waged in Asia, it at first ignored the growing struggle in its own backyard, then began to exploit it in as many ways as possible. Perhaps the strangest example is *Chrome and Hot Leather* (1971).

Like many earlier AIP releases, this is a motorcycle epic, but with a twist. The good guys are four Green Beret instructors who pass themselves off as clean-cut bikers in order to avenge the death of their leader's fiancée (she was killed when her shiny Lincoln Continental was forced off the road by a hairy biker). The Green Berets take matters into their own hands because the law is slow. Illegally requisitioning explosion simulators, smoke grenades, rockets, tear gas, grenade launchers, radios, walkie-talkies, a command post tent, field rations, and a deuce-and-a-half to carry it all, they systematically but considerately ("watch your co-ordinates," warns their leader, "I don't want to kill anyone") violate the civil liberties of an entire motorcycle gang (headed by the same actor who led *The Losers* into Vietnam combat, William Smith) to punish one man. As the gang is being marched off to justice (and justice will probably demand their instant release), the soundtrack gives us a song: "Some day you'll want to go home again, home again, home again."

That we are to thank the methods proved in Vietnam for this sterling civic cleanup is established in the opening scene. Here we see an American unit that seems to be advancing on "natives" in black pajamas—they battle, and the GI's seem to be losing when Sergeant Mitchell, who will later lead the military bikers, stops the mayhem to explain what his students have been doing wrong under smoggy California skies. It is a simple matter to apply these lessons to the enemy at home, for home is also enemy country—as you will find in all of the other films in this chapter. And through this enemy country lurch the walking wounded, the men (and a few women) who are the casualties of the war, either because they went to it—or because they didn't.

On foot they came. Tens, then hundreds of thousands of young Americans invading an alien land, throwing the natives into panic. They wore a common uniform, shared common assumptions, and held guitars before them or slung over their shoulders like rifles. Perhaps *Woodstock* resembled Vietnam because the war had come to resemble *Woodstock*—a whole generation of long-haired youth blowing grass, listening to rock music, and flashing peace signs at the nearest cameraman. Whether in Vietnam or Woodstock, the participants were clearly at war.

PART ONE: THE WALKING WOUNDED
(PROTESTORS)

In the early years of the war, while dissent over Vietnam seemed anathema to commercial producers and directors in America, foreign filmmakers took the war to their bosoms. In 1967, when Silliphant was trying unsuccessfully to interest

Hollywood in *Groundswell*, England's Peter Brook made *Tell Me Lies*, a semi-documentary about three Londoners disturbed by the image of a mutilated Vietnamese child; Alain Resnais, Claude Lelouch, Jean-Luc Godard, and others collaborated on a documentary pastiche, *Far from Vietnam*, while Lelouch made *Live for Life*, with Yves Montand as a French journalist who goes to Vietnam to make a documentary.

As late as 1968, the year of *The Green Berets* and the year President Johnson was driven from office by dissension over the war, the only American films critical of our involvement were meant for basically radical or avant-garde audiences. Up to that time there had not been (nor would there ever be) any homefront film unequivocally supporting the war. In addition to Robert Kramer's above-mentioned *The Edge*, 1968 gave us Adolfas Mekas's *Windflowers*, in which a draft-dodger is hounded to his death by helicopter-borne police and FBI agents. But even in *Windflowers*, the Vietnam war was not specifically mentioned. Significantly, several critics assumed Mekas's film was definitely not about Vietnam because of the background conflict's length: "As the hero has been running for six years, his pacifist feelings predate the present war," wrote the *Variety* reviewer six years, two months, and one day after our first combat fatality in Vietnam. As I have said before, Vietnam snuck up on us. One reason it took so long for resistance films to appear, or even a major combat film, was that it was not clear that we were actually at war, because we hoped Vietnam would, like Dutch Elm disease and the Surgeon General's warning on our cigarette packs, just go away.

Beginning in 1968–1969, several broad varieties of homefront movies emerged. The veterans started making their mark on the screen, draft resistors and war protestors stood up to be counted, and Vietnam became visible as a shadow over life in America.

First, some of the early Zeitgeist flicks. Jim McBride's *David Holzman's Diary*, Andy Warhol's *Blue Movie*, and Haskell Wexler's *Medium Cool* all make explicit reference to the war as part of a general disaffection. In McBride's film, the soundtrack includes news broadcast references to America's growing role in the war, and "David Holzman"'s rationale for beginning his film is that he has just been classified 1–A by his draft board. There is enough generalized discussion of the war in *Blue Movie* for Warhol's program notes to proclaim it "a film about the Vietnamese war and what we can do about it" (the prescription, apparently, is to go to bed). Reversing the debriefing of the liberal journalist in *The Green Berets* a year earlier, *Medium Cool* is built around a detached TV newsman who slowly begins to realize that he and his medium cannot remain cool in a world gone crazy (the film is tied to the war through the newsman's affair with a woman whose husband is in Vietnam and through footage shot during the anti-war disturbances at the 1968 Chicago convention). Significantly, all three films were made by highly independent artists working on small budgets and for themselves.

"I'm not saying you never had it so good—but that's a fact, isn't it?" beams LBJ from a television screen in Brian De Palma's *Greetings* (1968), the film that initiated draft-dodging as a contemporary comic motif. A year later, two young men would pose as homosexuals to avoid induction in *The Gay Deceivers* and the draft would crop up as an occasion for mockery in *Alice's Restaurant* (Arlo Guthrie's zany physical and his eventual dispensation because of his "criminal" record for littering), and in 1971 *Drive, He Said* would have a running subplot about a student who pops pills and goes without sleep in preparation for his pre-induction physical.

By and large, however, the topic of draft-resistance or evasion found more serious treatment befitting the social havoc being wrought by the issue of the draft. In 1970, after the imprisonment of Joan Baez's husband for refusing induction, a documentary* *(Carry It On)* had followed the singer around the country as she gave concerts and talked against the war and the draft. Suddenly, the resistor was beginning to gain respectability, to provide a new hero for the times. That same year, *Cowards* traced youths who escape to Canada, stay to fight, or allow themselves to be dragged into the army ("a draft-resistance soap opera," the *New York Times* called it; "A Primer in the New Patriotism," it called itself). The next few years provided a little of something for everyone: *Prism* was about a lawyer who helps draft resistors, while *Parades* had AWOL soldiers in the mythical Fort Nix and *Outside In* had a draft-dodger come home for his father's funeral and get involved with another resistor and a Vietnam vet—and *No Drums, No Bugles* escaped into allegory via the story of a West Virginia

---

*Other resistance documentaries are *Terry Whitmore, For Example*, and *Deserters U. S. A.* (1969).

farmer who cannot or will not support the Union or the Confed-
eracy and goes into hiding for three years.* These were all
minor efforts by new directors with (excepting Martin Sheen in
the last film) unknown casts.

As the war wound down in late 1972 and early 1973, established figures began to get involved in the celluloid struggle:
Gregory Peck produced *The Trial of the Catonsville Nine* (Has-
kell Wexler was the director of photography, and Daniel Berrigan is credited for the screenplay), Jane Fonda and Donald
Sutherland made an anti-Vietnam USO show called *F. T. A.*
(*Free the Army* or *Fuck the Army,* take your pick), while Robert
Wise, one of the few major directors to touch the resistance
issue, produced and directed *Two People* with Peter Fonda as
a Vietnam deserter who, after sojourns in Russia and North
Africa, goes home to his punishment via the scenic route of
Casablanca and Paris (though the film may have suggested to
some audiences that deserters should give in, go back, and pay
up, the covert point being made is that the Vietnam exiles in
Canada, Sweden, Algeria, and elsewhere should not be kept in
limbo for they really love their country, etc., and want to get on
with their lives).

In all the years of the war in Vietnam, there seem to be only
three films about the draft and resistance set in the mainstream
of middle-class America, in small towns and suburbs and down
on the farm: *Hail, Hero!* (1969), *Homer* (1970), and *Summertree*
(1971). Before I discuss these key films, I think it important to
note that World War II and Korea inspired no films about resistors or slackers whose unstylish reluctance was tolerated
beyond the final reel. There was cynicism about the need for
individual participation in *Mister Lucky* and *Casablanca* and
other films in the early forties, but that cynicism was usually
a result of the protagonist's secret low opinion of himself, and
was washed away when the slacker found that he was genu-
inely needed. Similarly, such Korean War films as *I Want You*
and *The Bridges at Toko-Ri* set up reluctant warriors for conversion. The main role of homefront films during those two
earlier conflicts had been to motivate civilian soldiers, to prepare the public for war, and to funnel doubts and resistance

---

*Analogously, Robert Downey's comically surrealistic *No More Excuses* (1968)
had a Civil War soldier ramble in and out of the Vietnam-obsessed present.

toward belief and acceptance. For Vietnam, the process was reversed: the films explained why men stayed home, even turned home itself into a battleground.

Only one Vietnam homefront film tried to evoke the old motivational magic that had worked so well in *Sergeant York* to tell an affirmative story about a boy who opposes the war but goes. That was *Hail, Hero!*, the first and last effort to play both sides of the fence. An eminently safe film introducing Kirk Douglas's son Michael* and directed by David *(Lonely Are the Brave)* Miller, it was the only Vietnam-related film to play at Radio City Music Hall (where it was sandwiched between *True Grit* and *A Boy Named Charlie Brown*). Though none of the posters or newspaper slugs used the taboo word Vietnam and instead lured the general public with upbeat references to the generation gap as a "void from which a new force must emerge, a new hero," there was a special campaign to bring in young audiences. Touting it as the "first motion picture to deal with the sensitive issues of the Vietnam war and its relationship to the Generation Gap," the pressbook suggested distributors put posters for the film in record store displays of anti-war protest songs, run peace-poster contests, and otherwise market the film through the established anti-war movement.

And what did the doves find? Carl Dixon (Michael Douglas), the title's ironically hailed hero, has come home from Yale to the family ranch in Arizona bringing with him long hair, strange notions, and a Secret. The secret is that in spite of his recent history of active resistance to the war, he has inexplicably dropped out of college and enlisted in the army. He shares the secret with his grandfather's tombstone, a horse (or was it his dog?), and an old Mexican ranch hand:

Carl: "I've joined up."

Jésus: "Si, me join too, in Pancho Villa's time."

Carl: "But, Jésus, did you fight with them or against them?"

Jésus: "All-a the same, Carlos, all-a the same." Now that the audience knows, it can supposedly wallow in the lavish dramatic irony of Carl's later exchanges with people who don't know.

But why has Carl signed up? The answer is never made clear,

---

*Though Michael Douglas is only one of many Hollywood brats who acted in films critical of the war—others are Peter and Jane Fonda, Candice Bergen, Tisa Farrow, Kristoffer Tabori (Don Siegel's son), and Topo Swope (Dorothy McGuire's daughter)—he is the most ubiquitous, having also appeared in *Adam at Six A.M.* (1970) and *Summertree.*

but has something to do with the fact he accidentally crippled his hawkish older brother and with his desire to be loved by his stereotypically patriotic father, a man who seems happiest when remembering World War II (the father is played by Arthur Kennedy, who would suffer unto death through the same basic role in *Glory Boy* a few years later). Listen to them as Dad cuts away a pound or so of Carl's hair:

Dad: "Long hair on boys is one of the things wrong with this country . . .

Carl: "Everybody's so worried about how long hair is; nobody seems to care how long wars last."

Dad: (who usually gets the last good line in this kind of movie): "Sure they care—they know the war won't end if men can't see to shoot."

Carl: "Dad, what would you say to my joining up?"

Dad: "A kid like you? Don't make me laugh."

So why has he joined up? For the hawks, there are hints Carl is testing himself, not so much afraid of being killed as curious about whether or not he can kill. For the doves, there are hints he intends to bring his pacifism into the war. "What would happen," he asks a girl, "if every soldier on both sides would just try to love instead of hate?" Girl: "You can't even make your own brother love you—you expect to succeed with a stranger who can't even speak English?"

The confusion about motives, about which side Carl and the film are on, is a natural result of the script's attempt to give both sides a fair hearing and the film itself a fair chance at the box office. Finally, all the loose ends are brought together in the Dixon's baronial living room at an elaborate birthday party for Carl's brother. Picture a room hung with mementoes of war and the chase: flags, guns, swords, hunting trophies, and portraits of five generations of Dixon heroes from Guadalupe to Appomattox to San Juan to the Marne to Guadalcanal. "The stuffy and the stuffed," jokes Carl, knowing full well he will probably bring home a pair of black pajamas or a set of punji sticks to update the display.

From the film buff's point of view, the biggest trophy in the room is Teresa Wright, called out of a decade's retirement to play Carl's mother. Here, for those with long memories or the patience to puzzle out the finer points of casting, is a celluloid equivalent of apostolic succession, for Teresa Wright received an Oscar as Mrs. Miniver's daughter in 1942 and welcomed home Dana Andrews in *The Best Years of Our Lives* and Brando in *The Men*.

But on with the party. The chief guests are the local Congressman and Senator, there to provide the Establishment view.

Congressman: "I was too young [for World War II], but I was in Korea. What I'm saying is, we should do it the old way—go in there and wipe them out."

Dad: "You're damn right—we're the strongest nation in the world. The only thing they understand is force." More moderately, the Senator speaks of our good intentions being unable to stop aggression and the need to fight in order to save others. "Great power often brings responsibility."

After such gaucheries as taking a slug at the Congressman, presenting his brother with the dessicated corpse of an infant ("take another look before you envy me my chance to kill"), and asking the head of the old folks' home if he is having an affair with Mom, Carl ends up covering the side of a freshly painted barn with images of war and peace, including an American flag with hearts in place of stars.* Then he goes off to the army.

Where the party that climaxes *Hail, Hero!* is a bit heavy-handed in its symbolism (how many typical Americans live in a house full of martial mementoes going back to the war with Mexico and can summon senators to birthday parties?), *Homer* is believable for its affecting scene of a small-town farewell party for a boy about to go to Vietnam. The patriotic farewell, an event that brings the town together early in the film, is balanced by a patriotic eulogy upon his return in a flag-covered casket, a scene handled with dignity and without the cheap ironies that flaw most of the other films critical of the war.

The central character in this modest and well-received film is not the hapless warrior but a seventeen-year-old Wisconsin farmboy who protests the war in song and deed. The issues of the war are not important, only that it has killed Homer's friend. Note Vincent Canby's reaction to Homer's reply ("You don't understand, Pop—this is just something I have to do") when his father (a WWII veteran, naturally, who keeps his old uniform in the attic) wants to know why Homer has chained himself to the parking meter in front of the Veterans of Foreign Wars lodge: "This sounds very much like something that Gary Cooper's Sergeant York might have said before leaving the Tennessee hills to fight in World War I—which is the only

---

*The original version of the film had the parents come out to join Carl in making American graffiti, but this bold bridging of the generation gap was excised from the general release prints.

interesting thing about *Homer.*" What interests the *Times'* Canby is the film's dragooning of a classic pro-war device for "a comparatively anti-Vietnam war movie": "stereotypes of small-town American life and attitudes most often associated with simplistic propaganda in [support] of a strong United States commitment abroad."

Homer doesn't go to the war; neither does he go to jail. Nor is he punished for his resistance. The sheriff and the old-timers in the VFW post all respond casually, and though Homer leaves home at the end, we suspect he will return one day, a veteran of the internal war that turned out to be more important to America than the one across the seas. Vietnam has divided Homer from his family and town as it has divided the nation —but the film seems to present this division as something America can handle, not in the slickly affirmative manner of *Hail, Hero!* (which was released by the same organization, National General Pictures, a year earlier) but in a far subtler mode.

"Glib, cynical references to Vietnam—for the benefit of liberals only—have been cropping up in youth movies that lack the courage to confront the issues directly," wrote Stephen Farber in establishing the uniqueness of *Homer* as a film that "communicates the way in which this war, as it drags on and on, tears away at relationships and communities *within* America," as a film that "because of its simplicity and universality, *unifies* the audience, offers a shared experience—even if it is only a shared sadness for ruined lives." Alone among the films about resistors and protestors, *Homer* avoids the grotesque American stereotypes that divide audiences, stereotypes that *Hail, Hero!* ground out even as it rushed to deny their validity. But before you rejoice that Hollywood had looked out upon America and found it good, note that *Homer* was directed by a Canadian and that though it is set in a little Wisconsin town, the location shooting was done in Canada.

Finally, in 1971, after a decade of death, came the first, last, and (to be perfectly redundant) only major film devoted entirely to the issue of the draft and its effect. Directed by Anthony Newley, produced by Kirk Douglas, starring Michael Douglas (who had already enlisted, you'll remember, at the start of *Hail, Hero!*), and released by Columbia Pictures, *Summertree* followed the adventures of a college student who is dragged closer and closer to the maelstrom. At first, Jerry actually benefits from the war—he gets a job playing the guitar in a coffee house when the regular musician is caught in the draft, becomes the "big brother" of a little black boy whose older brother is in Vietnam, and the lover of a nurse (Brenda Vaccaro) whose husband is there. Then the little boy rejects him when his brother is killed, the nurse's husband comes home from the war, and Jerry loses his student deferment. He tries to make a break for Canada, but is stopped by his father (though Dad, who had been "hawking it up" earlier, no longer supports the war, he doesn't want Jerry to break the law).

At the end, months later, Jerry's parents are preparing for bed. Mom (Barbara Bel Geddes) comes into the bedroom and turns down the sound on the late news. Dad (Jack Warden) speaks: "You know something, Ruth? I bet I know what he's going to say when he comes home. . . . 'Goddamn, what a mistake I almost made, huh?' " Mom and Dad settle down contentedly in bed, kiss, and begin making love, oblivious of the Vietnam casualty report on the set in the background—and just as the television reporter's camera zooms in on Jerry (the continuity says he is wounded, but most viewers thought he was dead), a hand picks up the remote control and—remember the end of *The Ugly American?*—turns off the news.

INTERMISSION: LIMBO IS NO HAPPY ENDING

A generation ago, Mark Robson directed two of the Korean War's most important motivational films, the ultra-patriotic *I Want You* and *The Bridges at Toko-Ri*. In so doing, he had helped weaken civilian resistance to that war. In early 1973, at about the same time as the Vietnam cease-fire and the repatriation of prisoners, Robson's *Limbo*, an anti-Vietnam sermon in the form of a melodrama about the wives of pilots missing or imprisoned in North Vietnam, appeared just in time to be anticlimactic.

Look what time has done to the war film subgenre of the women who wait at home. An air force general opens a meeting of POW/MIA wives with "God bless you, and keep up the faith" —then hastily departs, leaving a vacuum into which rush alien, civilian notions. The film's chief spokesperson, a thoughtful mother of four named Mary Kaye Buell, a good church-going Catholic who has remained faithful to her husband, proclaims quite simply and without being effectively contradicted that her husband has wasted his most productive career and family years in a prisoner of war camp for "what I have come to believe is a totally unworthy cause." The sole counterargument, delivered in a sickly sweet Southern accent, comes from the rich, spoiled daughter of a retired colonel: "We are not going to surrender! We are going to have some kind of victory with some kind of honor, because all those men did not die in vain!" But Mary Kaye has the last word, last words being very important: "We can't justify it that way. . . . we made a mistake, why don't we admit we made a mistake and get out?" Admiral Tarrant is nowhere in sight.

Another wife is Sandy, the romantic lead. Married only weeks before her husband Roy shipped out, Sandy decides not to wait in limbo when she learns he is missing in action. She begins an affair with an ambitious, hardworking law student—no pampered long-hair, mind you, but a very straight young man earning his way through college by pumping gas at night—who worked for NASA until the government decided to spend "more on war and less on the exploration of the universe" (even a "liberal" university town audience hissed at the bald opportunism of that line—that *Limbo*'s makers felt they still needed a Protestant-ethic spokesman as late as 1973 in order to criticize the war did not inspire confidence in the film's commitment). The resolution comes (or, more properly, doesn't come) when Sandy's lost husband is found and repatriated. His airport homecoming is a media event, with a news director snapping out orders on camera placement. Roy's plane touches down, rolls to a stop. The door opens and Roy emerges, looking furtive, scared. His hair is too short, his uniform too big. He lurches down the steps. Sandy runs toward him as a television announcer stands to one side summarizing the whole movie for us, reminding the audience in the theater and the imaginary audience watching imaginary sets at home of all the sad cases of the men who won't come back. "It's nice to report," he proclaims dramatically an instant before the final music hits us and the image freezes on the reunion of Sandy with a man she does not really know or want, "it's nice to report *one* that has a happy ending."

Limbo is over, but what follows is not a happy ending. Not in real life or in the movies.

PART TWO: THE WALKING WOUNDED
(VETERANS)

Girl (Leigh Taylor-Young): "Did you ever kill anybody? I mean, you were in the army, you were in Vietnam, weren't you?"
Boy (Ryan O'Neal): "Yeah, for a while."
Girl: "Well, did you kill anybody?"
Boy: "I suppose so."
Girl: "Was it fun?"
Boy: "I never hung around long enough to find out. Listen, I wasn't trying to win any goddamn war, you understand? I just wanted to stay alive."
Girl: "Did you make it?"

—The Big Bounce

August 1970. Heading for Australia in the American summer of 1970, I change planes in Los Angeles. Our jet takes off before dawn, prolonging the night as it races away from the morning sun. So this is how going to Vietnam feels, I think. Most of the passengers on the plane are in khaki. Perhaps because of their uncertain destinies, perhaps because they had to wait for hours in a muggy terminal for an oft-delayed flight, they are quiet, somber. In Hawaii we part company, they to continue their journey into the combat zone, I to scholarly pursuits in Canberra and Melbourne. Later, departing the topsy-turvy Australian winter, I make connection with another planeload of soldiers. Now we race toward the dawn, but the gloom of the earlier flight persists. I resist asking the boy next to me if he's glad to be going home, half-afraid the question will betray naive condescension, half-afraid my seatmate may suspect a liberal interrogation lurks behind the solicitude.

The pilot announces our landfall, but no cheer goes up, not even a snicker or a hiss. Could it be they've never been away?

The little girl stands frozen in front of a tree. The pilot of the strafing plane does not see her until it is too late. Thus opens *Sundays and Cybele* (1962), the story of a French veteran of the war in Indo-China who has been left a shell because of his accidental killing of a child. Like the veterans in many of the American films I will now discuss, the protagonist of *Sundays and Cybele* dies in the last reel as a result of his experiences in the war.

Oddly enough, the first American film to present a veteran of

Vietnam was another Mark Robson product, *The Lost Command* (1966). George Segal played an Arab officer in the French army who goes home to Algeria, gets involved in the rebellion against French rule, and is killed by his old comrades. Before this chapter is over, we will find the same thing happening in the American homecomings.

I mention these two films about veterans of the French adventure in Vietnam because they provide a foretaste of the sad homecomings and unhappy endings that would greet America's screen veterans. Before I supply a context, let me inflict a handful of these homecomings on you.

Item (1967): The first celluloid veteran of Vietnam is the long-suffering Billy Jack in *The Born Losers.* "He had just returned from the war," the opening narration tells us. "One of those Green Beret rangers. A trained killer, people were to say later." Later is when Billy Jack takes the law into his own hands to protect the weak against vicious bullies and rapists in a motorcycle gang. Like the French veteran in *Sundays and Cybele,* he is shot by a policeman, but he survives to star in *Billy Jack* and the forthcoming *The Trial of Billy Jack.*

Item (1968): Opening with the theme song "No Communication," *Angels from Hell* has a war hero return to take control of his old bike gang. Using his combat experience to outmaneuver rivals, contemptuous of the "establishment" that sent him to war, defiant of all authority, he quickly goes power mad, ranting about how he will soon have an army of followers. "You're insane," says his girl; "I'm a genius," he retorts, but before the issue can be resolved, the hero has been blasted off his bike by a deputy. The film ends upon the ironic image of his body under a tag from Isaiah, "Come now, and let us reason together," while the theme song comments "no communication."

Item (1968): Johnny Taylor, a would-be actor, comes home from Vietnam armed with a filmscript given him by a grateful Hollywood writer just before he died. Trying to parlay the script into an acting role for himself, Johnny gets involved in various absurd adventures, including the rescue of a fair maiden from a Nazi-suited motorcycle gang. So much for a film with a title, *The Angry Breed,* that could have stood for a whole generation of disillusioned warriors.

Item (1969): In yet another Vietvet versus motorcycle gang epic, *Satan's Sadists,* Johnny Martin (according to the *Filmfacts* plot summary) "utilizes his combat training by smashing a mirror in the face of one of the thugs and drowning another in a toilet bowl." Later he flings a poisonous snake around the neck of another gang member and finally kills their leader with a knife through the throat.

Sum of items: four films, four chances to vary the story line. But in each case, the veteran is involved with motorcycle gangs; in each case, he is a catalyst for violence if not violent himself.

Green Beret Captain, speaking of Vietnam veteran who has just killed thirteen deputies: "He's as well balanced as you or I."

Police Chief: "I don't kill for a living."

Captain: "Of course not. You tolerate a system that lets others do it for you. And when they come back from the war, you can't stand the smell of death on them."

Chief: "At the start I didn't know he was in the war."

Captain: "But you saw he wasn't acting normally, and you didn't try very hard to find out why. . . . He gave up three years to enlist in a war that was supposed to help his country, and the only trade he came out with is how to kill. Where was he supposed to get a job that needed experience like that?"

—David Morrell's novel, *First Blood*

"When Johnny Comes Marching Home" is not only the title of a popular Civil War song; it is a symbol and a situation. It is a symbol with curiously ambivalent meanings. It signifies the return of heroes, of wars ended, of happy reunions after hard won but glorious victories, and of peace after battle. It is also a sign of dissension, of nervous uncertainty lest, in truth, we have not prepared a "land fit for heroes."

—Franklin Fearing, "Warriors Return: Normal or Neurotic?"
Hollywood Quarterly, 1945

Surveying the film treatment of veterans at the end of World War II, Fearing, a professor of psychology, concluded that "the meanings with which we clothe the bare facts of demobilization will reveal our basic conceptions of the war itself and the reasons for which it was fought." That thesis seems valid today, for the majority of films about veterans of Vietnam present them as violent drifters, brutalized and threatening figures reflecting (if not created by) unconscious attitudes toward the war and the men who fought it.

To put it another way: Vietnam has produced a large body of young men who practiced or witnessed at first hand the sanctioned use of violence—not surprisingly, film and television writers and producers have assumed the mass audience will accept the portrayal of veterans as constantly violent, given to handgrenade fraggings in hotel elevators and (even before the

New Orleans incident) sniping from rooftops. Though the films are rarely specific about the exact relationship between Vietnam and violent veterans, three general categories can be dimly perceived: the Vietnamese experience has turned healthy young men into sick killers; it has pushed latently violent men over the line or has transformed blatant maniacs into honored representatives of our culture; most commonly, it has embittered men (be they normal or neurotic) while teaching them skills that can be put to dangerous use.

And when the veteran is not busy maiming and killing others, he is a scapegoat or sacrificial figure, as in David Rabe's controversial play. *Sticks and Bones* opens with a blind veteran being turned over to his family by a sergeant who travels about the country delivering the sightless, the helpless, and the mindless in exchange for receipts. David, the veteran, proves so embarrassing and inconvenient to his all-American family (Ozzie and Harriet, his dad and mom, and Rick, his kid brother) that they talk him into killing himself in the living room.

These two extremes (violent or victim) are so prevalent that Robert Jay Lifton felt the need, apparently, for a disclaimer in the subtitle of his study of the psychological impact of the war: *Home from the War; Vietnam Veterans: Neither Victims nor Executioners.*

"Unlike the returning servicemen of earlier wars," wrote Murray Polner in the preface to *No Victory Parades: The Return of the Vietnam Veteran,* "they have not been celebrated in film or song; there are no more victory parades." There *have* been at least thirty films about Vietnam veterans, and more are sure to come, but the only thing they seem to celebrate is mayhem. In *Slaughterhouse-Five,* Billy Pilgrim's son goes off to war as shaggy rebel and comes back a neat and respectful Green Beret—but the audience knows that is only Vonnegut's joke.

For any viewer old enough to remember the sensitive films about homecomings following World War II, the shabbiness of the current crop is particularly startling. Our involvement in Vietnam was three or four times longer than that in the earlier war, yet Vietnam produced not a single film with a chance of aspiring to the heights of *The Best Years of Our Lives,* which won seven Academy Awards in 1946 for tracing three veterans —nor has even one of the dozens of Vietvet films come close to the kind of commercial and popular appeal represented by the

Oscar, that much maligned but indicative measure of what the film industry purports to respect. Significantly, the only film about a veteran to be awarded an Oscar during the decade or more of Vietnam, *The Subject Was Roses,* is about the homecoming of a soldier in the mid forties.*

World War II brought us together, largely silencing the kind of internal conflicts that tended to surface during Vietnam. As the popular arts of the forties supported our soldiers, the tensions of war and return were not as disruptive as they might have been. After World War II, films about veterans gave occasion for reflecting upon the healing values of our domestic and civic institutions. Thus, the major films about veterans in those years tended to present extreme handicaps—an amputee *(The Best Year of Our Lives)*, a paraplegic *(The Men)*, and blindness *(The Pride of the Marines)*. With the exception of *The P. O. W.* (1973), a film about a paralyzed veteran held prisoner to his wheelchair, Vietnam has not yet inspired films about physically disabled men, perhaps because the psychic wounds have been deep enough (and because the returned soldiers have needed all their strength for striking back at a society that is depicted as having betrayed them).

At the same time, there has been no serious examination of those psychic wounds, though some films make a half-hearted effort in that direction. In *The Stone Killer* (1973), for instance, a psychiatrist is trotted out to render judgment on a violent Vietvet. Lipper has no visible scars, he explains, but aggression is habit forming and Lipper has become an addict. Then the punch line: "Vietnam doesn't make heroes—it makes a generation of Lippers." There is no examination of this diagnosis, it is simply slipped in as a pseudo-scientific commentary on what follows.

The only attempt to deal seriously with the psychology of the returned Vietnam veteran is a television movie made in about 1971, *Welcome Home, Johnny Bristol.* Perhaps because it dealt with an escaped POW in a time when the plight of the captives was a topic on which Americans divided by the war could reach some agreement, *Johnny Bristol* more closely resembles the kind of affirmative "When Johnny Comes Marching Home"

---

*I'm not forgetting that Michael Corleone is a veteran, but that fact is incidental to the plot of *The Godfather.*

story that followed World War II than does any other film I will discuss here.

The film opens with Captain Johnny Bristol (Martin Landau) in a bamboo cage, the prisoner of the Vietcong. Only one thing sustains him: his memory of a happy childhood in a picturebook New England village. Prompted by another prisoner, a man without life-sustaining memories of home, Johnny repeats his stories, thus justifying nostalgic flashbacks to the town minister delivering a speech on peace and tolerance at the Fourth of July celebration in the town square.

Rescued by a helicopter raid, Johnny Bristol returns "home" by slow stages. First he must recover from wounds and malnutrition in an army hospital full of men who have not yet made it home—including a World War II veteran (Forrest Tucker) who has been there for a quarter of a century. When he is finally released in the company of a nurse, Bristol heads for his home town. As he nears his destination, he says to the nurse "Everything good that ever happened to me happened here, in Charles, Vermont." But Charles, Vermont (the combination of words will be repeated no less frequently than "Rosebud" in *Citizen Kane*) is not where he remembered it. Moreover, there is no record of any town with that name.

From that point, the film becomes Bristol's search for the truth about his own past. Eventually he learns that his memories of a Grandma Moses America are fantasies, that his true home is a run-down Philadelphia neighborhood at the intersection of Charles and Vermont Streets, and that the brutal murder of his parents when he was a child left him emotionally homeless. Charles, Vermont is the creation of a man whose real memories would have been of no comfort to him in foreign captivity. In other words, Vietnam has forced Johnny Bristol (and many other Americans) back into the idealization of an America that never existed except in the imagination.

In its treatment of the character played by Pat O'Brien, the film demolishes the patriotic type-casting that has marked that actor's screen roles. In search of his past, Johnny tracks down the old recruiting sergeant who had inducted him into the army seventeen years earlier. "You remember me, don't you?" In the more conventional film, we would expect the kindly old figure we know so well as priest or coach or father figure to solve everything with a bit of wise blarney. But Vietnam *has* soured our perceptions: "Do I remember you? Do I remember you? No, I don't," says Sergeant O'Brien, then sadly confesses that thousands of faceless and forgotten boys have flowed through his hands toward war and death.

As in most of the other returned veteran sagas or melo-dramas, the war in Vietnam is never an issue in *Welcome Home, Johnny Bristol.* We see morally neutral action scenes set there, we see the name on a map, we hear the word "Vietnam" once or twice on the soundtrack—but Vietnam's effect is pervasive. Johnny comes home to find the water and air poisoned, to find assassins walking the land—no wonder he begins to suspect that the army or the government is hiding the truth about what they have done with his home. Vietnam, then, is a kind of hallucinatory drug that makes him invent an ideal America; but it is also a truth serum which forces him to see through the false ideal.

Of course, even in a few films made after World War II, veterans came back to an America that was not quite the paradise the movies had promised. They came home to face racial or religious bigotry in direct contrast to the democratic ideals for which they had fought. Having cleaned up evil in the rest of the world, Hollywood found it easy to attack anti-semitism and the segregation of blacks when the victim was a veteran and tolerance could be sold as patriotic or anti-fascistic. Thus, the veteran-victims in *Gentleman's Agreement, The Home of the Brave,* and *Lost Boundaries.* By fade-out, however, some improvement had been made; the world was a better place.

Though there were fewer films about men who had been in the Korean War, their problems were proportionally greater— they came back to be courtmartialed in *The Rack* and *Time Limit;* they brought home war-induced morphine addiction in *A Hatful of Rain* or came back to little communities with big challenges to the racial status quo, as in *Japanese War Bride.* By and large, things worked out—they had their families, jobs to go back to, and a society at peace with itself.

The Vietnam film veteran, however, comes back to loneliness, unemployment, and a divided and violent society, themes most commonly represented by the motorcycle gangs that roared through the earlier films. Today's celluloid veteran finds that the folks at home, when he has a home, don't understand him, and that civic authorities and employers are indifferent, corrupt, or both. In short, today's films about veterans actually reflect the moral isolation of the combat soldier—an isolation created in part by Hollywood's reluctance to provide the kind of patriotic and emotional support for this war as for the earlier ones.

Though United States involvement had been growing since the early 1960s and the problems of veterans had been evident by the middle of the decade, not until 1969 did a major studio pick up on the theme. That was in *The Big Bounce,* released by Warner Brothers the year after that studio released *The Green Berets.* In his first feature film, Ryan O'Neal played a drifting survivor of Vietnam who gets involved in pointlessly sordid scrapes rather than going home to the conventional Mom and Apple Pie rewards of past wars, past films. He is first seen (in a newsreel clip of a "friendly" ball game at a migrant labor camp) belting a Chicano in the face with a baseball bat. Early on, he establishes his credentials: "I got my discharge down South two months ago. Fort Bliss. I guess I've been more or less on my way home ever since."

There is no motorcycle gang in this one, but that omission is more than compensated by the sexy psychopath played by O'Neal's real-life wife, Leigh Taylor-Young. She taunts the veteran to smash windows and break into houses, then involves him in a hit-and-run accident, a payroll robbery, blackmail, and murder. Though he rejects her at the end, he is still a migrant worker heading no-where from no-where, the recipient of the disgusted tribute of an up-raised middle finger from the girl who might have given his life a direction, albeit a criminal one.

Nineteen seventy saw the veteran-as-motorcyclist gimmick escalated into *The Losers,* in which two vets *return* to Indo-China as part of an ultra-violent five man team who ride their Hondas into the ultimate rumble—against the Vietcong. They all die in gory slow-motion in order to rescue a civilian presidential adviser who, in a grotesque parody of all high-handed official ingratitude, denounces them as trash.

The Losers was a low budget exploitation film seemingly meant for a particularly specialized audience of the disenchanted—not just veterans, but all those who have gotten the short end of the stick and take bitter solace in extreme representations of their plight. But 1970 also supplied an exploitation film for the more privileged disenchanted. *Getting Straight* tried to give them a hero in Harry, the graduate student played by Elliot Gould. Though the film ends with an armed confrontation in what is clearly enemy country, I hesitate to give more than passing reference to *Getting Straight,* for having been to Vietnam is just part of Harry's contemporary credentials. He's been to Selma, too.

"Your brother has the same personality profile as the Boston Strangler," a man tells his wife, speaking about an ex-Marine who has just returned from Vietnam. But the line, delivered by Dom De Luise, is played for laughs, the potential mass-murderer is only Glen Campbell, and the film Paramount's *Norwood* (1970), the first and last attempt to supply a comic homecoming reminiscent of those in films of the forties. Norwood gets innocently and humorously involved with a car theft ring headed by Pat Hingle, and after a transcontinental adventure in search of his Marine buddy Joe Namath, wins Kim Darby and a spot on the Louisiana Hayride (that's a radio program, for you folks not conversant with the dreams of the heartland).

After a brief flirtation with a happy ending in *Norwood,* the veteran films returned to small-scale violence and large-scale pessimism. A quick sampling will do. Burt Topper's *The Hard Ride* (1971), apparently the last of the bike gang pictures, opens with a white vet bringing his black buddy home for burial, and ends with the white vet being buried too. In *Vanishing Point* (1971) and *Journey through Rosebud* (1972) Vietnam veterans die in speeding cars. In MGM'S *Clay Pigeon* (1972), a soldier named Joe jumps on a grenade to save his buddies; the grenade doesn't go off, and Joe comes home with a medal, only to be used against his will by the police to trap a narcotics king pin—and to die in the bloodshed that has become almost obligatory in these films (Tom Stern, who produced, co-directed, and played the disenchanted hero had also died violently as the psychopathic veteran in *Angels from Hell* four years earlier). The title figure in *Jud* (1971) doesn't die in spite of the film's heavy sacrificial symbolism (the story is set at Christmas time, the hero's initials are J. C., and he is warned, "Jud, if you don't want to be crucified, don't stay around crosses")—tortured by the memory of having killed a child in Vietnam, Jud drifts aimlessly, putting his few remaining emotional reserves into savage fights and denunciations of the society he once defended.

In mid-1971 a major shift in the veteran stories began to become evident. The big studios and distributors were starting to take more interest in the genre, backing or buying films with positive endings. The most spectacularly successful example is the first: *Billy Jack.*

Flashback: to a crowded movie house near Times Square. I have come to learn something about *Billy Jack.* I had seen it with a small suburban audience during its first release in 1971. Now, in December 1973, it is playing at dozens of theaters in the

Manhattan area. The month before, *Variety* had reported that *Billy Jack* had grossed thirty million dollars in 1971 and might finish 1973 with a total of sixty million. I know that part of the film's success lies in the fact that Warner Brothers formed a subsidiary company headed by (among others) a former Assistant Secretary of Defense. I suspect another part of the success is the central character's appealing mixture of Christ-like attributes and readiness for physical combat. I did not, however, expect a full house at a midnight show—I did not expect an audience that included families with small children, middle-aged men in business suits, Puerto Rican teenagers filling whole rows.

Billy Jack ("a half-breed," the heroine tells us, "a war hero who hated war") is surrounded. One by one, a dozen men emerge from behind trees and form a circle around him. Brutal Boss Posner (good old Bert Freed, actually) steps up to mock Billy.

Posner: "You really think those Green Beret karate tricks gonna help you against all these boys?"

Middle-aged black man next to me: "Well, it don't look to me like I really have much choice, now does it?"

Billy Jack: "Well, it doesn't look to me like I really have any choice now, does it?"

Posner (laughing smugly): "That's right, you don't."

Man next to me: "Then you know what I'm gonna do, just for the hell of it?"

Billy Jack: "You know what I think I'm going to do then, just for the hell of it?"

Posner: "Tell me."

Man next to me: "Tell 'um, Bill-eee Jaack!"

Billy Jack (all by himself now, for my neighbor wants to hear this one): "I'm going to take this right foot and I'm going to whop you on that side of your face—and you want to know something? There's not a damn thing you're going to be able to do about it."

Posner: "Really?"

Billy Jack and the man next to me, in unison: "Really."

WHOP!

Billy Jack preaches non-violence, but takes its excitement from the hero's ability to teach others not to get violent with him. At the end, Billy Jack is de-programmed, defused, disarmed—agrees to trust the system, to stand trial for the violence he had been driven to use against an enemy that (like the dirty Nips and Krauts of old) rapes schoolmarms, murders cripples, and oppresses children. Billy Jack is the only popular celluloid hero to come out of Vietnam, is the era's equivalent of the succession of roles played by Flynn and Gable and Wayne. But look: his heroism is seen only on the homefront, another sign of the extent to which America has become the enemy country in which it is easier to work out heroic fantasies without political controversy.

The veteran who puts his martial talents to socially acceptable use, or nearly so, also proved a fertile subject for the black box-office in the early seventies. In *The Bus is Coming* (1971), a black officer named Billy Mitchell comes home to find that his brother, a civil rights leader, has been murdered. Avoiding taking sides with either the black militants or those who counsel patience and trust in the law, Billy begins his own investigation into his brother's murder. Though Billy is shot before he can implicate two corrupt policemen, the honest white police chief has reached the same conclusion and restores order. Like Billy Jack, Billy Mitchell has become an agent of social order who "pays" in blood for working on his own. Films with bigger budgets and casts soon appeared. Jim Brown returns as the titular hero of AIP's *Slaughter* (1972) to find his parents murdered. A former Green Beret captain, Slaughter goes to work for a federal agency (FBI? CIA?) that encourages him to use his military expertise to destroy the enemies of his parents and country.* In 1973, Slaughter returned in *Slaughter's Big Rip-Off* and another Green Beret captain, Gordon Hudson (Paul Winfield) comes home from Vietnam to find his wife has OD'ed on heroin. He beats up a pusher, gets beaten up himself, then declares *Gordon's War*. With three other former Green Berets (shades of *Chrome and Hot Leather*), he battles with fists, explosives, shotguns, cars, and spray deodorants (useful for setting the bad guys on fire). After cleaning up the black pushers and money men, Gordon and his men go after the white Mister Big in his tower office on Park Avenue. Directed by Ossie Davis for Twentieth Century–Fox and starring an Academy Award nominee, *Gordon's War* is indicative of the extent to which the

---

*Less "acceptable" action by militant black veterans (led by Jim Brown) is also seen in *Black Gunn* (1972).

violent veteran had become a respectable and profitable gambit.

January 23, 1974. Earlier this month, taking time off from writing the preceding chapter, I turned on *Columbo*—within three minutes, a hired killer tells his employer not to worry about a murder contract: "I fragged a couple of hundred in 'Nam." A few nights later, I drive twenty miles to see *Charlie Varrick,* and another killer says roughly the same thing. Last night, tired of struggling to compress the sheer bulk of veteran sagas into meaningful shape, I turn on *Hawaii Five-O* in time to catch a returned hero blow up himself, his father, and a narcotics lab.

Vietnam veteran: "I felt sorry. I don't know why I felt sorry. John Wayne never felt sorry."
—quoted by Lifton in *Home from the War*

Before 1971, the gratuitously violent veteran had been found only in exploitation pictures produced cheaply and quickly. The major studios and distributors had been more restrained, as in *The Big Bounce* and *Norwood.* But as the war became sufficiently unpopular to be attacked indirectly and as the violent veteran stereotype had been worked and reworked without provoking the mass audience or special interest groups, established figures in the industry began to move where only AIP had tred before. Now negative stories would begin to reach larger and more varied audiences.

The first major negative film has its roots back in that watershed year, 1968. Stanford Whitmore was working at Universal down the hall from Philip Waxman and Abraham Polonsky. "We'd have lunch and talk and of course denounce the war," Whitmore wrote me, "agreeing that this time slogans and lies couldn't hide the truth as before." Waxman owned the screen rights to John Sanford's *The Old Man's Place,* a 1935 novel about three veterans of World War I. "Sanford's novel . . . had all the brutality-from-disillusion of WWI, but we got to wondering about the brutality-from-*realization* by those forced into Vietnam." The studio gave the go-ahead, and Whitmore adapted the novel. Universal then turned the script down, and Waxman eventually sold the project to Cinerama, which released the film in the summer of 1971, at the same time as *Billy Jack,* another project that had bounced from studio to studio like a triple play (AIP to Fox to Warner Brothers). First released as *Glory Boy,* it was reissued a year later as *My Old Man's Place.*

Remember *War Hunt* back in Chapter Two? That film played on the difference between what is acceptable in war and in peace, in the foreign combat zone and at home. "IT HAPPENED ON A RAGING BATTLEFIELD BUT HE COULD HAVE BEEN A MURDERER STALKING A CITY'S STREETS" and "NOT ALL MEN CAN BE GIVEN A GUN," proclaimed the posters. "It doesn't take a vocational guidance counselor to make plain that a homicidal maniac can use his special aptitudes to great advantage on the battlefield," wrote the *Newsweek* reviewer in 1962. "He takes real joy in his work, finds opportunity for socially useful self-expression, and, the world being what it is, seldom has much trouble obtaining employment." The only flaw in *War Hunt* was that it took the easy course of having the insane Endore killed in the war zone. A more revealing story would have been the account of his return to the States and his impact upon a society with few legitimate outlets for the psychopath. But in 1962, the ends had to be tied up neatly. War had to stay where it belonged.

So when Stanford Whitmore, who wrote *War Hunt,* sat down to adapt that World War I novel, what he was really doing was bringing Endore home as a be-ribboned psychopath named Sergeant Martin Flood. Sergeant Flood could equally well be *The Steel Helmet's* Sergeant Zack, grown older and wiser— where Zack went to the aid of a Korean woman who turned out to be a man, Flood has returned home to hostile San Francisco to be lured into an alley by a mugger disguised as a woman— the ploy doesn't work, and the "woman" gets soundly stomped.

At first, the homecoming is pointless. Brutal Sergeant Flood (Mitchell Ryan) and comic Private Pilgrim (William Devane) accompany sensitive Private Trubee Pell (Michael Moriarty) to his father's isolated farm where they raise conventional hell— drinking, fighting, dynamiting fish, running nude races, and swapping fake memories. Things come to a head when a girl arrives on the scene. A pacifist student from Canada (herself in enemy country, you see, a volunteer at an anti-war headquarters identified as Pentagon West), the girl is played by Topo Swope, the daughter of Dorothy McGuire. But where the mother had welcomed a disfigured Robert Young home from World War II in *The Enchanted Cottage* (1945) and sent World War II veteran Dana Andrews back to war in *I Want You,* the daughter is beaten and raped by Sergeant Flood before he is finally gunned down.

Despite Andrew Sarris's judgment that *My Old Man's Place* was "one of the most explicit statements on the Vietnam war I have seen on the screen," what this film says about Vietnam's effect is not clear: whereas the "bad" guy is a certifiable psychopath and no evidence is given to make us think this particular war has made him the way he is, Trubee Pell, the gentle "good" guy, is haunted by the memory of killing a Vietnamese woman and emptying his weapon into her corpse. A safer reaction is that of the reviewer for *Cue:* "This strange, unusual film points out how the routine of killing in a far-off land might influence domestic efforts at love and normalcy."

The real point of the film is to be found in a major change from the source. In the novel, old man Pell had been totally opposed to his son going off to the Great War, but in the film he has been transformed into a gung-ho World War II veteran played by Arthur Kennedy, who gets top billing. In the film, Trubee brings the professional soldier home to mock his old man. "He'll like you," he tells Flood enigmatically, knowing the old man will soon understand that beneath the erect façade and impressive decorations lies brutish cruelty. Trubee wants to punish his father for sending him off to war with glorious yarns:

Flood: "He talked you into signing up?"
Trubee: "He lied me into it."
Flood: "And you expected a John Wayne movie?"
Trubee: "I never expected to kill a woman."
Flood: "She shoot first?"
Trubee: "Doesn't make any difference."

Here, as in *Hail, Hero!* a few years earlier, Arthur Kennedy is used to represent the continuity of citizen-soldier attitudes from the last great war. From the confirmed anti-militarist of the novel, he has become pathetic living proof that the title of the most honored World War II film, *The Best Years of Our Lives,* was no exaggeration. The scene in which he devours the cock and bull story of how Flood and Pilgrim saved his son's life in a rice paddy is a terribly sad and revealing moment in the history of the American war film. He searches for points of contact between his war and theirs, feeds them lines, and talks himself into believing that their experiences are perfectly analogous to his own. Even when the first unsettling bloodshed erupts, he tries to maintain the illusion in a scene with an old crony, the local sheriff. While the sheriff blasts away at clay pigeons, keeping his marksmanship in shape for appropriate civilian use, the old man makes allowances for the recent violence out at his place by reminding the sheriff of their own problems in adjusting to peace following *their* war. After assorted beatings, an attempted rape, a shooting, and a completed rape, the film ends with old man Pell and Sergeant Flood blasting each other to death, thus rather easily resolving the issues raised by the notion that Vietnam is the love child of America's affair with World War II.

The old soldier gambit of *My Old Man's Place* surfaces in Elia Kazan's *The Visitors* (1972) as well. Harry Wayne, a middle-aged writer of pulp Westerns whose fondest memories seem to be of killing Japanese in the Pacific, is immediately attracted to two young veterans who come to visit his despised son-in-law, a former buddy who turned them (and two others) in for raping and murdering a Vietnamese girl. Though some reviewers lumped *The Visitors* and *My Old Man's Place* together on the basis of the World War II veteran figure and their rape and revenge conclusion, Kazan's film deserves special consideration.

For one, to date it is the only film specifically about Vietnam's impact by a really top rank director. Secondly, because Kazan is established and had his choice of projects, he did not need to risk his reputation with a topic almost immediately doomed to critical and financial disaster, yet he did. Thirdly, and most important, Kazan's film is almost casual in its delineation of the war's effect: though the visitors were sent to Leavenworth for the rape-murder, they are now free, released on a legal technicality. They are not even particularly frightening figures —indeed, James Woods, the actor who plays Bill, the "good" veteran, projects a sinister quality resembling that of the cadaverous killer in *In the Heat of the Night,** while the two visitors are more personable, especially Sergeant Nickerson, a clean-cut all-American boy who insists he's no criminal ("Damn it. . . . I was an honor student in high school").

---

*January 30, 1974. "Uh, oh," says my wife, who's watching *Kojak* on the other side of the long room I work in. "Come see this. It's the kid who was in that movie about the veterans." She pulls out the monitor so I can hear. James Woods, now another veteran home from Vietnam, has just crept up on a pawnbroker and stabbed him. "Right through the heart and lungs," says the medical examiner, admiring the artistry of the job.

If anything, the buddy who turned them in is the outcast, the guy who doesn't fit. When his father-in-law learns that Bill did not join in the gang-rape, he allows as how he always did think Bill was half queer. Bill blames himself for not trying to stop the rape rather than causing his buddies to be punished afterwards: "The Vietcong do exactly the same thing. Everybody does. Every day. Why blame those guys? They were my friends, my buddies."

The visitors profess no ill will, watch football on television with Harry, shoot a neighbor's dog as a favor to him, beat up his son-in-law (who starts the fight), rape his daughter, and go their way. It is all very casual and realistic, unlike the majority of the returned veteran stories that build to violent and generally fatal climaxes. No one gets seriously hurt in *The Visitors*, for it is not a film that takes refuge in the kind of extreme catharsis or violent resolution audiences have been trained to expect. Where the rape of the girl in *My Old Man's Place* is immediately punished by death, the double rape here elicits only the last line, spoken by Bill to his wife: "Are you all right?"

In the propagandistic movies before and during the two world wars, rape was a convenient device for making the "enemy" hateful figures who could be disposed of with dispatch. John Wayne tried to work this trick with the rape of the little girl in *The Green Berets*. Now rape becomes something one does *to* the enemy.

More than any other filmmaker who has approached Vietnam, Kazan brought the war *home,** and made it a family affair. His son wrote the script and produced, Kazan financed it with his own money, and shot it at his own country home in Connecticut. The very fact that *The Visitors* is set in remotely suburban Connecticut brings it home in another sense, for almost all of the veteran films are set in the Southwest, with about twenty in the never-never land of California. Which brings us to our next film.

Four Green Berets enter a sleeping hamlet at dawn. All is quiet, peaceful. Suddenly, the muzzle of a weapon sticks out a window. The Green Berets start shooting. Within minutes, the male villagers, all armed, are shooting back. After pacifying

---

*Kazan calls *The Visitors* a "home movie" and the working title was *Home Free* (which had to be abandoned because of alleged conflicts with *Born Free* and *Living Free,* the lion movies).

the hamlet (that is, killing everyone in sight), the Green Berets gather around their leader for a map reconnaissance: "We've got a problem," he says, pointing to a spot on the map. "Heavy enemy concentration here." So far, we seem to be watching a standard-issue war movie. The odd thing is they are looking at a roadmap of New Mexico, for the town they've just trashed is smack dab on U. S. Route 82, due south of Springer, Ernest Medina's birthplace, and southeast of Albuquerque, where a hot-shot Army recruiter talked William Calley into joining up. Waiting for the end, the Green Berets listen with amusement to a radio news announcer speaking of the town they've massacred as "Mylai, U. S. A."

So, several years after Richard Condon gave up seeking a backer for *Are They Singing My Song?*, Songmy had come to America. But it wasn't brought by protestors or radicals or Vietcong. The war was brought home in Twentieth Century–Fox's *Welcome Home, Soldier Boys* (1972) by four guys as dog-friendly and neatly diversified as any you'll meet in a conventional war movie: Danny (Joe Don Baker), the sergeant, big, competent, and hell with the girls; Shooter (Paul Koslo), his silent, hawklike sidekick; Fatback (Elliot Street), the chubby comic relief; and of course the Kid (Alan Vint), the youngest, smallest, most idealistic—the kind of role Richard Jaeckel played for twenty years. It's the kid who carries the dream, who sustained them through the terrors of Vietnam with his stories of his old man's three hundred acres in California. Like a reverse *Easy Rider* or a modern *Grapes of Wrath*, the film follows them from an army separation center in Arkansas toward the promised land. Instead of Captain America's bike or the Joad's truck, their transport is a second-hand Caddy, a funereal black limousine named "As Is" and loaded to the fins with souvenirs: grenades, rifles, rocket launchers, machine guns, and ammunition.

They never make it to California. Misunderstood, rejected, cheated, persecuted, and bored silly, they have a little psychological accident and wipe out the population of Hope, New Mexico (the real name of a real town, grateful to the filmmakers for buying up and burning down abandoned property).

Hopeless, they put on their uniforms to face the National Guard troops who come in to destroy them, but not before they have a chance to shoot down an army helicopter, something our boys haven't gotten to do in Nam. In other words, they've become honorary Vietcong. At the end, the National Guardsmen are seen moving through the desolate town, securing it as had the four Green Berets. Now *they* are the veterans.

Where earlier films had pinned the violence on bad apples or had justified it through the veterans' willingness to fight for a just cause against drug pushers, bigots, or slavering rapists on motorcycles, *Welcome Home, Soldier Boys* does neither. Instead, the Green Berets are presented sympathetically. Oh, they do throw a naked woman out of the speeding car without pausing to see whether she survives, but she *had* tried to exploit them. Everyone tries to exploit them: the used car salesman who sells them the run-down limousine for five thousand dollars,* the cross-roads mechanic who charges them fourteen hundred dollars for repairs when the engine explodes, the motel manager who gleefully totes up a seven hundred dollar bill for a night's fun. That they are foolish with their money is beside the point—they are back in God's country and expect to be treated fairly and with gratitude for what they have done. Instead, they find people consider them freaks or worse. "When we were in the service," says a middle-aged hick in a Texas road stop, "nobody came back till the war was *over*. . . . Now, they put in a couple of easy months and they come back and nothing's done. . . . No wonder that damn war's gone on for ten years. Ought to get the *old* army back there. . . . Shit, you watch television—all they do is kill the damn civilians." Welcome home, soldier boys.

Brother-in-law: "I've always wondered. I mean, was it hard? All that killing?"
Danny: "Yeah. In the beginning. [Pauses.] But I got better at it."

Girl: "You become what you do."
Danny: "I'll tell you what I've done. The only thing I've ever done."
Girl: "What?"
Danny: "I've killed one hundred and thirteen people . . . maybe more. That's the official count."
Girl: "Then you're a killer. A—killer."
Danny: "That's kinda what I've been thinking."
—*Welcome Home, Soldier Boys*

Before Vietnam, America did not feel threatened by her veterans. It was assumed that when boys were sent away to war

---

*Veterans also get stung with bad cars in *The Visitors* and *My Old Man's Place.*

they would kill and when they came home they would stop. Following World War II, there was no film tradition of veterans being brutal, of them needing a special debriefing. Shortly after the Korean War, Samuel Fuller made a film about a paramilitary operation employing the violent talents of former soldiers —but *House of Bamboo* (1955) was set in Japan. After Vietnam, filmmakers felt no need to keep afar the men who could not turn off the inner war. There was a place for them right at home, as in *The Stone Killer* (1973) in which a Mafia capo commissions a small army of Vietvets to massacre the opposition—such men, someone points out for the slower members of the audience, have the required talents and ability to follow orders, but lack criminal records. That *The Stone Killer* is. based on an English detective novel that doesn't even mention war, Vietnam, veterans, or syndicate rubouts, is only further proof of the growing popularity of the Vietvet as a gimmick for passing off violence as social commentary.

But the difference between films that use the veteran as a gimmick and those that actually explore rather than exploit the effects of the Vietnamese experience is hard to define. *Welcome Home, Soldier Boys, The Visitors,* perhaps even *My Old Man's Place* are in the second category. As we drift into the mid-seventies, it would seem that the returned veteran genre has begun to attain its maturity, having outgrown the simple release of action with or against motorcycle gangs or the dreary aimlessness of the emotionally stalled heroes of *Jud* or *The Big Bounce*. The Vietvet is beginning to assume epic stature. Two films about to enter production seem indicative of the genre's future.

The first, *Rolling Thunder,** is to open with an upbeat quote from Richard Nixon: "Our returning prisoners-of-war are examples of the high moral fiber . . . which will help make this a nation . . . free from crime." What follows is not quite the ironic reversal that one expects, for the ex-POW hero does indeed help remove a goodly number of criminals, though he does take a few innocent bystanders with him.

After an emotional airport celebration (the crowd bursts spontaneously into "God Bless America" as the first POW sticks his head out of the plane), we go home to Corpus Christi with good old Charlie Rane, an air force colonel returned after seven

---

*The title comes from the code name for air operations over North Vietnam. *Rolling Thunder* will be made by AIP, which has graduated from cheap exploitation films to more expensive ones (*Dillinger, Slaughter,* etc.).

years in Hanoi. Rane's is not the sordid, lonely, homecoming of the typical veteran film. Instead, he comes back to a brand new red Cadillac convertible (a present from the local businessmen who are exploiting him in their own way), a new color TV, a mod wardrobe, and a check for $124,000 in back pay.

TV reporter: "What are you going to do with all this money?"

Rane: "Well, I ain't gonna put it in no bank."

Things aren't particularly good at home, however. Rane doesn't understand his son, now a long-haired teenager. He is impotent, his wife plans to divorce him as soon as he has adjusted, and he feels as though "they sent back an empty body and I wasn't in it. Just another coffin."

After twenty-seven pages of balancing Charlie Rane's outwardly successful but inwardly painful homecoming, the script begins to get interesting when four Spanish-speaking thugs show up at Rane's isolated house looking for the money Rane said he wasn't going to put in no bank. They pistol-whip him, singe his face with a butane lighter, grind off a hand in the garbage disposal. But Rane is in his element, being tortured. Failing, they threaten to shoot his wife, not knowing they are only driving him deeper into resistance. After they kill the wife, Rane's son tells them where the money is hidden. Not wanting witnesses, the intruders shoot Rane and the boy.

Rane survives, of course. In the hospital, he tells the local, state, federal, and military investigators that he remembers nothing, blames being shot in the head. But when the camera catches him sharpening the stainless steel hooks that replace the mutilated hand, we know that all is well. Rane leaves the hospital far happier and more confident than before the slaughter of his family. For now the rules are clear—he is back at war against a tangible enemy, one that can suffer, bleed, and die.

In joyous anticipation of gory revenge, he goes off in search of the killers. We are back on the beam now, about to have a gay adventure. At his side in the flashy red Eldorado is a pneumatic blonde named Linda, who exists in the plot chiefly to prove that Rane's impotence has disappeared. After tracking his prey to a house in El Paso where John Wayne once lived, he gives away his medals and picks up Johnny Vohden, another former POW who had managed to get all the way home to find it wasn't worth the trip. Johnny is glad to abandon his dull family to their chatter of garage sales and the relative merits of Japanese television sets.

Putting aside dull cares and Linda, Charlie and Johnny don

their pretty blue uniforms and haul ass down to Mexico where the killers and their cohorts are celebrating the big rip-off in a whorehouse. And what fun our heroes have! Rane slits a man's throat with his hook. Johnny gratuitously pistol-whips a Mexican prostitute. Rane opens the wrong door, discovers an innocent American businessman in bed with a girl, blasts them both anyway. Eventually, they kick in the right doors, shoot the right people, until no one is left alive but Johnny, who is seen blazing away at a corpse until his .45 is empty, then continuing to pull the trigger until the image freezes. "Johnny is caught mid-trigger pull," the script closes, "his mouth frozen open in a never-ending scream. Keyed up, ready to go. A force in motion, unable to stop. Pure energy."

Rolling Thunder, its author wrote me, is to work on a "fantastic, dream-like level, like a nightmare unfolding." With an enthusiasm approaching poetry, Paul Schrader describes his hero as an all-American figure of revenge: "racist, fascist, lean and obsessive." The film is "full of the paraphernalia of death," Schrader tells me. "If one makes a film about Nazis, he shoots scenes of boots, flags, and swastikas; if he makes a film about American death, he shoots red Caddys, blue AF uniforms and chrome-plated .45 automatics. A pure fantasy of American death. And a well-deserved death at that."

Whether or not the completed film will, as Schrader hopes, find "its audience among servicemen . . . wallowing in the American creed of death" and perhaps help them "to see themselves in a little perspective," or whether it "will be just another gore show and an extension of the problem itself," *Rolling Thunder* clearly does nothing to support the optimistic prediction I ventured in an earlier discussion of film veterans: "I suspect the return of our POW's may unleash a small flood of non-violent films, both good and bad, intelligent and melodramatic. . . . There has been no clear military victory in Vietnam and great division remains concerning the morality of the war—but the return of the prisoners is an occasion for something approaching national agreement and relief."

No such hopeful and healing films have appeared, nor are any in production as far as I know.* And yet, one project scheduled for filming as this book goes to press seems capable of presenting with understanding and dignity both a violent vet-

---

*Only at the last moment did I learn that Twentieth Century–Fox was about to release *Vrooder's Hooch,* a comedy about a veteran's adjustment to peace.

eran and the self-absorbed society to which he returns. If the adaptation Martin Ritt is preparing for Warner Brothers follows David Morrell's novel, *First Blood* will be not only the first major film to work out fully the way in which the war and the never-give-an-inch attitudes that caused it have rebounded on America, but the first to present that national catastrophe in terms that approach tragedy. For *First Blood* has the seeds of purest American graffiti, a stylized conflict—a war, really—between two of the screen's most popular heroic types: the romantic individualist who will not be pushed and the honest, straightforward lawman determined not to back down before threats to social order.

In Morrell's novel, Rambo, a shaggy, tattered drifter, is a super-vet: an ex-Green Beret, a former POW, and a Congressional Medal of Honor Winner. But police chief Wilfred Teasle doesn't know this when he sees Rambo hitch-hiking, picks him up, drives him through the center of town, and deposits him at the town line. Not particularly wanting to visit Madison, Kentucky, but tired of being pushed around, Rambo walks back into town. Escorted to the town line once more, he returns. The third time it happens, he is arrested for vagrancy.

Rambo's experiences as a Green Beret and POW become organic to the plot when he is brought down to the basement of the jail to be washed, shorn, and locked away for thirty-five days. The dampness, the cramped space, bring back his captivity: "The hole. . . . water seeping through the dirt, the walls crumbling." Rambo goes berserk, kills a deputy, races from the police station in the nude, knocks a gawking rider off his motorcycle, and escapes into the wilderness.

Not until Rambo has shot down a police helicopter, picked off the tracking dogs, and killed most of the posse, does Teasle learn he is chasing a Green Beret hero. Before the first stage of the chase is over, Rambo has killed a dozen pursuers; the only survivor is Teasle, who won the Distinguished Service Cross as a Marine sergeant in Korea and remembers the lessons of night patrol.

Now the Kentucky National Guard (conveniently scheduled for war games that weekend) is called in to cordon off the area. And a Green Beret officer, the man who trained the men who trained Rambo, arrives to advise the hundreds of police, guardsmen, and local sportsmen on how to contain "the best student we ever turned out." But the killing goes on, the body count mounts, and Rambo breaks through the cordon, returns to Teasle's defenseless town, burns down Main Street, dynamites the courthouse and police station, mortally wounds Teasle, and is himself killed by the Green Beret officer.

January 31, 1974. Having just followed Teasle and Rambo to their destinies, but too tired to write a conclusion to this chapter, and not even sure that a conclusion is possible at this still early date, I settle down for a few hours of television before attempting a midnight finale. Luck is with me. A campus sniper moves across the San Francisco rooftop, his M–16 at the ready. He fires, hits a girl—a flesh wound. He escapes across campus, takes up another position, kills a professor. At first the victims seem randomly selected, then Michael Douglas learns the wounded girl was having an affair with the professor and that her fiancé, a Marine Corps captain, is still recovering from eighteen months of internment in North Vietnam. Suspicion builds. There is a classic motive for violence, and the capacity: "You ever hear of a Marine who made captain who couldn't handle a rifle?" asks Karl Malden.

But this story has a happy ending, of sorts. The veteran really wasn't the killer. He was simply stuck in to mislead viewers trained to expect the worst from the boys they sent away to war. That is a happy ending, isn't it?

SIX

WHAT GAY DREAMS OF HOLOCAUST— HOLLYWOOD AND THE BOMBER

Gary Cooper: "One of these days half the world will be in ruins from the air. I want this country in the other half."
—*The Court Martial of Billy Mitchell*

I

[Billy Pilgrim] turned on the television. He came slightly unstuck in time, saw the late movie backwards, then forwards again. It was a movie about American bombers in the Second World War and the gallant men who flew them. Seen backwards by Billy, the story went like this:

American planes, full of holes and wounded men and corpses took off backwards from an airfield in England. Over France, a few German fighter planes flew at them backwards, sucked bullets and shell fragments from some of the planes and crewmen. They did the same for wrecked American bombers on the ground, and those planes flew up backwards to join the formation [to be continued].

August 18, 1973. On this bright New England summer afternoon just a few days after the halt of the bombing in Cambodia, we take our children for an outing at our local Strategic Air Command base. The occasion is the annual open house— Rotarians on the runways, congressmen in the grandstand, children in the cockpits, whole families among the Phantom jets.

We wander through acres of bombers, interceptors, tankers, transports, helicopters, and fighters, never once seeing a bomb. Daddies hold up babies in the yawning bomb-bays to see where the eggs go, but there are no eggs, not even the ones that say "Here come de judge" or "When you care enough to send the very best."

Everywhere in evidence is the SACred motto that many viewers of *Doctor Strangelove* assume to be an ironic conceit original with Stanley Kubrick: "Peace Is Our Profession." Cool sea breezes, stereotypically appropriate to the gay mood, blow past the Portsmouth Naval Ship Yard, the band plays rousing airs, the Goodyear blimp drifts overhead, the air force precision flying team does its insane thing, and a good time is had by all.

On our way back to the car we pass the monument at the main gate. "What is that, Daddy?" asks Joshua, who is now four. "A flying hard-on," I start to say, but bite my tongue and examine the monument with him. The bronze statue on top does look like a flying erection, a winged incubus aimed at the very heavens. On closer inspection, it turns out to be a very stylized atomic mushroom borne aloft on equally stylized falcon's wings.

Below this un-airworthy apparition is an explanatory tablet:

178

DEFENSOR VINDEX

The 509th Bombardment Wing—a unit with an unparalleled history and tradition. As the 509th Composite Group, its mission—to deliver the world's first atomic weapons. In 1945 the Hiroshima and Nagasaki drops by the unit unquestionably hastened the end of World War II. It furthermore set the stage for a credible SAC deterrent posture, making it clear to all mankind that differences among nations must be settled by means other than all-out nuclear war.

With B–29, B–50, B–47, KB–29 and KC–97 aircraft the unit has meritoriously contributed to the Strategic Air Command's "Mailed Fist" concept of Peace Through Strength. It is the sincere hope of its personnel that it will never again be necessary for mankind to launch nuclear weapons in anger.

"What is it, Daddy?" he asks again. "A flying hard-on," I answer.

The bombing, they say, is over. For the first time in more than a decade we are not dropping high explosives on anyone. But the bombs keep falling on the Late Late Show because Tyrone Power and Pat O'Brien, John Garfield and Dana Andrews, Van Johnson and Clark Gable, and a whole host of others are up there giving the Fascists hell. Or Rock Hudson and Jimmy Stewart are hanging in there waiting for the Commies to make the first move. Or Sterling Hayden and Slim Pickens have stopped waiting.

Winter, 1972. Sleepless after the eleven o'clock news chronicling the continuing saga of our bombers over Hanoi, I flip channels on my bedside Japanese portable and find myself witnessing an odd ceremony in which downed American airmen are being tried by an Asian court for bombing civilians. This is no radical hallucination, but the most patriotic of movies: *The Purple Heart,* a 1944 propaganda fantasy speculating on the fate of American bomber crews captured after Doolittle's Tokyo raid.*

The Purple Heart actually admits, by what it tries to hide, more than its makers intended. It quickly drops the question of whether or not American airmen are guilty of murder if they

---

*Sixteen bombers struck Japan on April 18, 1942; eight men were captured, tried, and sentenced to death, but the sentences were commuted to life imprisonment for five. The other three were executed in October 1942, and a fourth died of malnutrition. The remaining four survived.

drop bombs on cities and inadvertently kill civilians (the "atrocity" evidence produced by the Japanese prosecutor is so patently false that foreign correspondents in the courtroom cry foul). "When you bombed schools and hospitals," says a Japanese general, "you were only acting under orders. It is your commanding officers who are guilty, it is they who should be on trial." To the surprise of the defendants, he moves that the charges be dismissed.

The speech is only a trick, of course, for not even the Japanese believe the Americans guilty of any wrongdoing—they simply want to know where the bombers came from so they can strike back.

When our boys see the plot behind the general's speech and decline the gambit, their tempter commits suicide in frustration. Dana Andrews, the senior American, delivers this final speech before he and the others are led off to be executed:

It's true we Americans don't know very much about you Japanese, and never did—and now I realize you know even less about us. You can kill us—all of us, or part of us. But, if you think that's going to put the fear of God into the United States of America and stop them from sending other fliers to bomb you, you're wrong—dead wrong. They'll blacken your skies and burn your cities to the ground and make you get down on your knees and beg for mercy. This is your war—you wanted it— you asked for it. And now you're going to get it—and it won't be finished until your dirty little empire is wiped off the face of the earth.

Out of these two random exposures to rhetoric—to the Orwellian double-talk of a "Mailed Fist" concept of Peace Through Strength encountered under the candid sun of the first summer of a new peace, and to Dana Andrews's self-righteous proclamation of doom witnessed in the final bleak midnight winter of the late war—come two reminders of something we often choose to forget: not just our accountability as a nation for what we do or allow to be done in our name, but the tremendous gap between our perception of ourselves now and the perception reflected in that movie of thirty years ago. Rare in 1944 was the kind of thoughtfulness found in James Agee's review of *The Purple Heart:* "I feel extremely queasy watching fiction—especially persuasive fiction—which pretends to clarify facts that are not clear, and may never become so. Conditioned by such amphibious and ambiguous semi-information, we are still more likely than otherwise to do things to defeated enemies which, both morally and materially, will finally damage us more deeply even than them."

America has been growing old at the movies. Nowhere is this more evident than in the changes observable in a single generation of films about aerial bombardment. My starting point is fairly obvious, for the films of tactical or strategic bombing, like the actual techniques themselves, are a product of World War II.

But first, a confession is in order. I grew up with the films I will discuss, saw many of them at a tender age, accepted their messages wholeheartedly, and even today one half of me is attracted to their gay and violent simplicities while the other half still cannot fathom how their terrible implications passed largely unnoticed.

Finally, I am writing these words shortly after a war in which we dropped more tons of explosives on the enemy than during World War II, a staggering record set without benefit of a single celluloid celebration of the fact unless we include Mark Robson's *Limbo* (1973), which opens with a split-screen black-and-white sequence showing fighter bombers on the left, North Vietnamese gunners on the right. Then individual frames of a bomber and a missile merge into one image across the whole screen. The bomber explodes, the credits begin, and the film turns into a homefront melodrama. The cold war inspired films about the Strategic Air Command, but the last films touching on SAC or depicting modern bombers were released *before* the massive bombing of Vietnam began in the mid-1960s. Just as Hollywood has looked away from the war in Vietnam, so has it ignored a major tool of that war.

II

The formation flew backwards over a German city that was in flames. The bombers opened their bomb bay doors, exerted a miraculous magnetism which shrunk the fires, gathered them into cylindrical steel containers, and lifted the containers into the bellies of the planes. The containers were stored neatly in racks. The Germans below had miraculous devices of their own, which were long steel tubes. They used them to suck more fragments from the crewmen and planes. But there were still a few wounded Americans, though, and some of the bombers were in bad repair. Over France, though, German fighters came up again, made everything and everybody as good as new [to be continued].

As Americans prepared for war in 1941, three interlocking interests resulted in the bomber becoming a popular subject for films. The Army Air Corps, anxious to put itself before the public after years of obscurity and tight budgets, made men and equipment available; producers and directors responded enthusiastically to the possibilities of fast-moving air power stories; and the public, fascinated by this new toy, took pride in the national attempt to catch up with and by-pass the rest of the world in the production and use of bombers.

It all started with the most achingly titled of success stories, *I Wanted Wings,* in early 1941. Well before Pearl Harbor, the American Dedalus was preparing to fly toward the rising sun as Ray Milland and William Holden learned to pilot Flying Fortresses. But peacetime aviation, even in the name of national preparedness and even with an exciting training crash thrown in, was not enough. As American filmmakers couldn't wait to start bombing the Axis, Tyrone Power was promptly dispatched in Darryl F. Zanuck's *A Yank in the RAF.* Originally, the film was to end with the American pilot's death in a raid over Germany, but Zanuck, one of the most active Hollywood interventionists, gladly gave in to the British Air Ministry's request that the Yank be allowed to live. Showing Americans getting killed in defense of Britain would make poor propaganda, except for the isolationist cause, so Tyrone Power returned from the near-fatal raid to the arms of Betty Grable.

The following year came *Joe Smith, American* and *Wings for the Eagle,* both about men who work in bomber factories. In the first, young Robert Young is kidnapped by Nazi agents who want blueprints for a new bombsight; in the other, a father builds bombers while his son flies them (what, Dedalus again?). In spite of its rousing title, *Flying Fortress,* also made in 1942, was a conventional reformed playboy story made for Warner Brothers in England.

Not until 1943 did Hollywood hit its stride with a clutch of films reflecting direct American involvement in the war. RKO's *Bombardier,* the first film to explain how bombs are actually dropped, dramatized the transition from low-level to high-altitude bombing and the training of men on the Norden bombsight. *Bombardier* rewarded its audience for sitting patiently through the educational part by ending with a fiery raid on a Japanese aircraft factory, a raid jazzed up by the selfless act of a downed flier (Randolph Scott) who survives torture, escapes, and sets a huge fire as a beacon for a wave of bombers. The man who incinerates himself to light the way for others had been a critic of high-altitude precision bombing—his sacrifice, then, implies the death of skepticism and burning faith in the efficacy of the new technique.

A bigger, more important film was Warner Brothers' *Air Force,* about the crew of the Mary Ann, a B–17 flying across the Pacific at the time of the attack on Pearl Harbor. Made by Howard Hawks at the request of the new Army Air Force, the film focused on the personalities and problems of the crew, especially on John Garfield as the gunner who dropped his cynicism and became a team player. Not until the conversion of Garfield is the Mary Ann and her crew ready for the big climax, an imaginary battle in which a Japanese fleet is sunk (I call this action imaginary for I recall no such stunning victory over Japanese sea power in the first week of the war).

In the summer of 1943 came the film that sent me into the ranks of boys building the little models that air craft spotters were to use in identifying enemy planes over our cities. Walt Disney's *Victory Through Air Power* opened with a narrator announcing "Our country in the past has struggled through many storms of anguish, difficulty, and doubt. But we have always been saved by men of vision and courage, who opened our minds and showed us the way out of confusion." One such man, the narrator continues, was General William Mitchell. Then comes a live action newsreel clip in which the patron saint of the Strategic Air Command proclaims air power "the dominant feature of military operations." Immediately, Disney's narrator chimes in to dedicate the film to "the memory of Billy Mitchell, pioneer and prophet of air power."

What follows is a grotesquely oversimplified working-out of Major Alexander de Seversky's theories of *strategic* bombing (the technique of striking at the enemy's cities and populace) as opposed to *tactical* bombing (direct attacks on enemy troops in support of ground action). Disney interrupts the animation at several crucial points to allow de Seversky to speak directly to audiences that until recently had lapped up *Bambi* and *Dumbo:* "America should not hesitate to place its destiny in the hands of [our gallant airmen]. For with the strategy of air power they will make the enemy fight on our terms, against the weapons of our choosing, at our time—but on his soil."

Today, when Congress has just gotten around to taking a chunk of our destiny out of the hands of Billy Mitchell's protégés, *Victory Through Air Power* seems a snake in our Eden. Back then, however, it all sounded so clever, so easy, so *safe*. And before one had a chance to think, Disney wrapped up the Major's message in a powerful little vignette of patriotic animation that I can still remember: the American Eagle, representing air power, attacks and kills the enemy octopus sprawled across the globe, its tentacles like the rays of the rising sun on the Japanese flag. Victorious, the eagle settles protectively upon the globe and in a flash of lightning turns into the imperial bird on the staff of the American flag.

It is, or was, a moving piece of legerdemain, and one wonders why *Victory Through Air Power* was not included in the recent Disney retrospective at Lincoln Center. One suspects that it would have been shown were the Master still alive, for, as Richard Schickel points out in *The Disney Version*, Walt produced the film with his own money and out of that peculiar attraction toward strategic bombing held by "people of rightist political leanings," the kind of people who presumably voted for Curtis LeMay, the former chief of SAC, when he was George Wallace's running mate in the 1968 presidential race. "It is perhaps not amiss," muses Schickel, "to note that any philosophy that views the human aggregate as a mob incapable of choosing its own destiny and therefore in need of totalitarian leadership can easily be stretched to accommodate a certain indifference to massive, unselective destruction of that inconvenient mob."

Schickel's reaction to *VTAP* is almost uniquely a product of the sixties. Contemporary reviewers tended to find the film inspirational, and James Agee seems to have stood alone when he fretfully wondered whether Major de Seversky and Citizen Disney knew what they were talking about. Though he did not feel technically competent to question the film's validity, he felt he had been "sold something under pretty high pressure . . . and I am staggered by the ease with which such self-confidence, on matters of such importance, can be blared all over a nation, without cross questioning."

What particularly bothered Agee about *VTAP* was something that films dealing with strategic bombing studiously avoid: the fate of the people on the ground. De Seversky spoke of using air power to strike at the "heart of the beast," and Disney brought the abstraction of "the enemy" to life as, literally, a beast. Only in films about our allies did we see the human meaning of aerial bombardment from the point of view of the bombed civilians (*Mrs. Miniver, A Journey for Margaret,* etc.).

Following the lead of Disney/de Seversky, the studios got right to work striking the Japanese beast in the heart.* Early in 1944 came *The Purple Heart,* which opened with the crash landing of a bomber after the Doolittle raid and ended with the crew being sentenced to death by a Japanese court. Directed by Lewis Milestone, who created the great anti-war film *All Quiet on the Western Front,* and produced by Colonel Darryl F. Zanuck, who would later collaborate with his erstwhile enemies to make *Tora! Tora! Tora!, The Purple Heart* is probably the most bloody-minded and overtly self-righteous American propaganda film to come out of the war.

As I have indicated earlier, the Japanese torture the American fliers not simply to force them to admit to alleged atrocities but to learn whether they have flown from carriers or land bases. Had the captors waited a bit, they would have found the answer in *Thirty Seconds Over Tokyo,* also released in 1944, a detailed and purportedly factual recounting of the training of Doolittle's Raiders, their takeoff from the deck of the carrier *Hornet,* the bombing of Japan in B–25s (called Mitchells in honor of Billy), and the recovery of crews after crash-landings in China. Employing real names and events, the film is based on the personal account of Captain Ted Lawson, who lost a leg as a result of the raid—Captain Lawson's sacrifice and his hospital re-union with his wife added just the right romantic touch to the story and put the emphasis on the human suffering of the attackers rather than on the attacked.

The script writer, that old pacifist Dalton (*Johnny Got His Gun*) Trumbo, had to get around the problem of motivating a nice guy like Ted Lawson to go out and drop high explosives on a city. Here, in a speech delivered by Van Johnson, is Ted's solution: "I don't pretend to like the idea of killing a bunch of people—but it's a case of drop a bomb on them or pretty soon they'll be dropping one on Ellen." Note the sleight of hand: the enemy has become a vague "they" with civilians and soldiers lumped together. To demonstrate that Lawson and his colleagues have properly considered the moral issues involved, Trumbo has Doolittle (Spencer Tracy)

---

*Perhaps in reaction to the humiliation inflicted at Pearl Harbor, all of the major fiction films about strategic bombing produced *during* the war deal with the air war in the Pacific—not until *after* the war did we get films about bombing Europe (*Command Decision, Twelve O'Clock High,* etc.).

call for an examination of conscience: "Let me repeat what I have previously said: *You are to bomb the military targets assigned to you and nothing else.* Of course, in an operation of this nature, you can't avoid killing civilians, because war plants are manned by civilians. If any of you have moral feelings about this necessary killing of civilians . . . drop out. . . . No one will blame you for your feelings." Here, probably for the first time in film history, the central moral issue of modern war is faced more or less head-on: civilians are going to get killed, but *you* don't have to kill them—you can just get up and walk out of the briefing and no one will even think to call you chicken or berate you for wasting our time and money in training you.

Much of the moral justification for the bombing of Hiroshima and Nagasaki a year later are to be found in these two films: it's the enemy's war, he hit us first, he asked for it and he's gonna get it; if we don't do it to him, he'll do it to us. The only argument not used is the one advanced after the atomic bomb was used against Japan; that the bombing of civilian populations breaks the will of the people to keep fighting and thus saves lives, theirs and ours.

Ironically, the very next fiction film about bombing after *The Purple Heart* and *Thirty Seconds Over Tokyo* was *The Beginning or the End* (1947), a dramatized account of the development of the atomic bomb and its deployment. Only a small part of the film dealing with the flight of the *Enola Gay* touches directly on bombing, but the whole impetus of the film is toward delivery of the weapon.

The advent of the atomic bomb marked the end of the fairly simple, positive stories of dropping high explosives on cities. Instead, films would deal with command decisions or, in the case of *Catch-22* and *The War Lover,* would treat bombing negatively or at least ambiguously. The stakes were suddenly higher, and the kind of massive effort needed for getting "conventional" bombs to their targets seemed unrewarding when compared to the spectacular results obtainable from the new weapon.

The first in the series of films about nuclear war that would culminate in *Fail Safe* and *Doctor Strangelove, The Beginning or the End* seems as naive as the legend on the B–29 accompanying the *Enola Gay: "Necessary Evil"* (Witness this exchange over Hiroshima: "They'll never know what hit them." "We've been dropping warning leaflets on them for ten days now. That's ten days more warning than they gave us at Pearl Harbor."). James Agee found it "a horrifying sample of what American movies will be like if the state interferes with them much": "you learn less about atomic fission from this film than I would assume is taught by now in the more progressive nursery schools; you learn even less than that about the problems of atomic control; and you learn least of all about morals." In short, Agee thought, *The Beginning or the End* might have been better titled *Tom Swift and His Giant Ego.*

Not until six years later, in 1953, did Hollywood attempt another film about the nuclear bombing of Japan—that was *Above and Beyond,* the story of Colonel Tibbetts and the *Enola Gay,* the film that inaugurated a decade of factual fantasies about the Strategic Air Command.

But before Hollywood went on with films about the future, it had to get World War II out of its system. *The Best Years of Our Lives* attempts to say good-by to the bomber: the film opens in the nose of a retired bomber bringing our heroes home, and Dana Andrews, as the boy who rose from soda jerk to air force captain and fell back to earth again, is later seen wandering through a scrapyard full of junked war planes that we presumably wouldn't need again. But we couldn't junk them all, for within a few years Twentieth Century–Fox had purchased hundreds of surplus fighters and bombers so Colonel Zanuck (Retired) could make *Twelve O'Clock High* (1950), the second in a pair of important films focusing on the administration of bomber commands.

The first, in 1949, was *Command Decision* in which a young general played by Clark Gable battles his superiors and a host of enemies to continue a costly daylight bombing campaign against jet plane factories in Germany. When his bombers hit the wrong town and sustain great losses, General Dennis is ordered to cut down on raids and losses until Congress has voted a new budget for the Army Air Force. This order comes from Walter Pidgeon's politically wise older general (aptly named Kane), a contemporary of Billy Mitchell who has been through the air arm's lean years. But General Dennis, acting on the assumption that military prudence and logic demand he stop production of jet fighters before they have a chance to shoot down other bombers, makes a command decision to go after the target.

The real battle in this film, though, is not against enemy fighters; the war with Germany is only the transitory occasion for big-time military gambling. The conflict is between the army and the navy, between ground and air forces, between the military and the Congress, the military and the press. In the novel on which the film is based, cunning old General Kane momentarily envies his nominal enemies, the Germans, who have everything needed for a good war: "a docile, industrious people, a press that knew its place, no congress, no allies, and a leader who loved war and warriors."

As the air force shifts from outdated B–17s, General Dennis, who has said damn legality, damn orders, damn the losses, damn public opinion, damn Congress, is relieved of his post and ordered back to Washington in disgrace. But before the audience has a chance to get restless at this cowardly bureaucratic mistreatment of Clark Gable, new orders come: he is to proceed directly to virtue's reward, a B–29 command in Asia.

Daylight precision bombing of Germany is also at issue in *Twelve O'Clock High.* Again, the central character is a general officer rather than a pilot or bombardier. But where Gable's General Dennis must fight his superiors and other outsiders, this general must lick his own men. Young General Savage (Gregory Peck) takes over a dispirited, problem-ridden command, whips it into shape, and cracks under the pressure. Taken together with *Command Decision,* in which General Dennis is relieved of his command for exceeding his authority, these two films provide a link between the simple stories of bombing in World War II and the dramas of generals under stress in *Fail Safe* and, more spectacularly, *Doctor Strangelove,* in which General Jack D. Ripper both cracks up *and* exceeds his authority.

Unlike *Doctor Strangelove,* however, *Command Decision* and *Twelve O'Clock High* both treat their generals with great sympathy and understanding. Moreover, *Twelve O'Clock High* was written by two former air force colonels, Sy Bartlett and Beirne Lay, who have cornered a large share of the market on bomber films. Lay wrote *I Wanted Wings,* the first of the genre, as well as several later sagas *(Above and Beyond, Strategic Air Command).* Bartlett, who entered the war as an aide to General Carl Spaatz and is reputed to have been the first American to drop a bomb on Berlin, later served as deputy commander of a SAC base and eventually produced the last and most important of the officially sanctioned films about SAC: *A Gathering of Eagles* (1963).

Twelve O'Clock High, one of the first films to treat World War

II with nostalgia, and still a television favorite today,* is seen from the point of view of a middle-aged American veteran played by Dean Jagger. The film opens long after the war, with Jagger shopping in London where he happens to find a cracked Toby mug bearing the face of an early pilot. His memory jogged, he takes a sentimental journey into the countryside, biking through peaceful lanes until he arrives at a deserted airfield, its runways broken and weed-choked. As he stands there alone, remembering, the sound track gives us bits of old songs ("Bless Them All," etc.), and then hits us with revving engines. We see the grass around the lonely man wave, the camera looks up at the sky to reveal a flight of B–17s coming in, and suddenly we've been transported back to 1942.

I have summarized this opening passage in some detail because it represents the best Hollywood has to offer in the nostalgia line (Dean Jagger won an Oscar for his portrayal of the middle-aged officer) and because it foreshadowed a large part of the new strategy that filmmakers would employ in stories about bombing after the war ended. During the war, the psychological conditions of the time helped supply a natural appeal for overtly propagandistic or patriotic films. After the war, Lay and Bartlett manipulated the emotions of the audience to put it in sympathy with General Savage, whose agressive drive, whose passion for maximum effort, whose very name could be used to create a monomaniac monster or a figure of satire. But in 1950, as we recovered from World War II and girded for the cold war, Hollywood could still portray the Savages heroically.

III

When the bombers got back to their base, the steel cylinders were taken from the racks and shipped back to the United States of America, where factories were operating night and day, dismantling the cylinders, separating the dangerous contents into minerals. Touchingly, it was mainly women who did this work. The minerals were then shipped to specialists in remote areas. It was their business to put them into the ground, to hide them cleverly, so they would never hurt anybody ever again [to be continued].

---

*In 1964, shortly before the bombing of North Vietnam began, ABC turned the basic story line of *Twelve O'Clock High* into a television series. Borrowing heavily from *Command Decision,* the series trotted out senior generals and dumb politicians as heavies—one episode for instance, involved a senator who opposed daylight bombing.

Even as I write this, B–52s thunder over my head. They are coming from (or going back to) the SAC base I mentioned back at the start of the chapter. Furthermore, that base is the last home of the 509th Bomb Wing, the group that dropped the eggs on Hiroshima and Nagasaki under the leadership of Paul Tibbetts, whose name heads the list of 509th commanders on the monument at the gate. Which brings us to Tibbetts's own story and the start of the Strategic Air Command cycle of films: *Above and Beyond* (1952).

I call this film the start of the cycle because it not only deals with SAC's forerunner, the Strategic Air Forces, headed by Curtis LeMay, but also presents LeMay in the person of Jim Backus, who would soon become universally loved as the voice of Mister Magoo. Though *Above and Beyond* seems a reprise of *Thirty Seconds Over Tokyo*—the secret training, the leader who cannot explain the reason for the training—it is actually the first in a series of domestic melodramas about men who lead double lives, men caught between the stresses imposed by their duties and by their wives. In the films made during World War II, wives were usually abstractions back home; if they actually appeared on screen, they were sweet, supportive, and in the case of Van Johnson's bride in *Thirty Seconds,* blissfully pregnant. With *Above and Beyond,* however, begins the tradition of the confused, angry, and long-suffering whiner and nag. Thus Tibbetts (Robert Taylor) can't tell his wife (Eleanor Parker) what he is up to, and much of the dramatic force of the story has to do with whether or not Mrs. Tibbetts will eventually get it all together and realize that Men Have Their Work To Do.*

Not that the issue is ever very much in doubt, for Mrs. Tibbetts narrates the story of her husband's mission as she awaits his return to Washington after the Hiroshima raid. Eleanor Parker reflects how often she has waited for him—now she wonders whether they still have a marriage. Does Paul still want his home, does he still want her? Where did it all begin? Suddenly her off-camera voice takes on a dramatic newsreel tone as she guesses it all began two years ago over Africa on a

---

Above and Beyond, for all its moral vapidity, inspires two burning questions. First, is the real reason Tibbetts named his bomber after his mother rather than his wife because mom *understood?* Second, could it be that there is a deeper connection between the decline of the American military in recent years and the concurrent rise of female consciousness than we have previously admitted?

raid. . . . At the end, his plane arrives and they are gloriously re-united, for the killing of a city has restored domestic order, has justified Paul's near-desertion of his family and explained why he was always snapping at her over the smallest things, as when she looked at their sleeping children and said she was sad at the idea of children elsewhere being killed by bombs: "Lucy, don't ever say that to me again. Look, let's clear up one little piece of morality right now—it's not bombs alone that are horrible, it's war, not just weapons. . . . to lose this war to the gang we're fighting would be the most immoral thing we could do to those kids in there. And don't you forget it."

If you question the continuing significance of *Above and Beyond*'s domestic dilemma, then check the first of the films about bombers in peacetime, *Strategic Air Command*. Jimmy Stewart plays a professional baseball star called back to active duty at the peak of his career; June Allyson is the dutiful wife who first seethes over the sudden disruption of her comfortable existence, but then gives in when she sees how important it all is to Jimmy. She even has a baby at the right moment to prove her dedication.

Norman Mailer puts *Strategic Air Command* at the head of his list of prime artifacts of Shit, the new art movement replacing Camp ("movies about the Strategic Air Command with Jimmy Stewart, Hubert Humphrey speeches, old Lawrence Welk records, news photographs of Mayor Wagner, Senate testimony by Robert McNamara, interviews with J. Edgar Hoover"). The test for Shit, says Mailer, is this: "is this object, happening, work, event, or production more resonant [today] than it was yesterday?" Well, *SAC* is nothing if not resonant, both full of literal sounds and figurative reverberations.

Start with the casting of Jimmy Stewart (himself a full colonel commanding B–25s in World War II) as a big league ballplayer (third base), a real team player joining all the other boys on the Big Team. It's a jock metaphor, but one most viewers respond to: baseball represents the American duality of competition and team spirit and is essentially harmless. We will all sleep better with Jimmy Stewart up there, the film whispers to us.

Beyond the sports metaphor is the theme of teamwork versus individual action, a theme that runs through the earlier films about bombers but becomes obsessive in the SAC fantasies and finally reaches its comic apotheosis in *Doctor Strangelove* (where whole echelons of mindlessly functioning teams radiate down from General Turgidson to General Ripper to Major

Kong) and *Catch-22* (in which Yossarian ultimately discards the team colors and stops playing ball).

At first resentful at being dragged back into the service, Stewart quickly changes his mind as he gets his hands on the new equipment. Building the story around a retread provides a neat excuse for familiarizing the tax-paying audience with the peacetime role of SAC, how bombers and tactics have changed, and so forth. (Coach: "What's SAC?" General: "The air force's global bombing command." Coach: "You're the guys who drop the atom bomb?" General: "We hope we won't have to.") And Stewart is just right in this grand apologia pro nostra SAC, trotting out his best boyish amazement and enthusiasm, very aw shucks, gee whiz, mumble-mumble-I-mean-I-didn't-KNOW-they-were-so, you-know, BIG. Eventually, after a glorious flaming crash in Greenland and some support from his all-American wife, Stewart is ready to sign up for permanent duty and only a slight physical problem results in his being sent back to the *other* big league.

In spite of some unintentional humor (the chief of SAC, modeled clearly after C. E. LeMay, is E. C. *Hawkes*), *Strategic Air Command* is a serious, even ponderous work. Flippant types might call it a recruiting poster, but the film's own flacks were naturally more respectful, as in this press release: "Although technically we are now at peace, there hangs over everyone the fear of a surprise attack from without, and here is a picture to build up our confidence in our protective devices and allay some of our uneasy feelings." One of the devices used to instill confidence and awe is described by the *Time* reviewer in terms that might later have been used to describe the first vision of the great space ship in Stanley Kubrick's *2001:* "In the end, *SAC* passes from the understandably lyrical to the outright reverent. When the camera glides in for its first look at a B–47, the sound track bursts into organ peals of religious music, a strangely sacred serenade to one of the world's most powerful instruments of destruction."

One wonders if the unholy exhaltation rendered the space ship in *2001* might not be traced back to *SAC* through Kubrick's *Doctor Strangelove,* a film that mocks the traditions of the SAC film (the inflight refueling that opens *Strangelove* was first seen here) while making inevitable celluloid obeisance to the technology that so outshines the dull fools who administer it. Kubrick rediscovers the visual beauty of aerial weaponry in *Strangelove* and *2001,* giving back to us in slightly different terms what Bosley Crowther found in *SAC:* "the great . . . jet bombers and the nexus of bases and fields are truly the most photogenic and exciting things to be seen"; "the airplanes, the roaring engines, the cluttered cockpits, the clouds and the sky" are "the things that make your eyes bug and your heart leap with wonder and pride."

Again and again, contemporary reviewers commented on the visual spectacle of this film: the machines, the vapor trails, the aerial photography, the dramatic action scenes created by Anthony Mann. Having recently run the film for myself, I found *Strategic Air Command* still an impressive experience in spite of such lapses as sending Stewart off on his first flight to the tune of "A Stranger in Paradise"—and in spite of the fact that I was hunched over a scratchy copyright print on a Steenbeck viewing table rather than seeing it in its original form on the Vista Vision screen. This process had been introduced the year before for *White Christmas,* a Bing Crosby vehicle unequal to the giant screen's potential. Vista Vision's grandiose technique needed an appropriate story, so Hollywood turned to the one source (in those days before the space race) of great noise, speed, power, and danger.

Or was it that SAC turned to Hollywood? Just as in the early days of the budget wars when the Army Air Corps courted Hollywood, turning producers, directors, writers, and actors into officers and gentlemen, SAC in the middle of the Eisenhower years wanted films that demonstrated in simple but acceptable terms where hundreds of millions of dollars were going. The films never questioned the wisdom or morality of maintaining SAC, but set up tidy little problems to be neatly solved before the last reel: will Jimmy Stewart learn to do his duty willingly, will Rock Hudson get a good efficiency report?

Or was it that they needed one another—that SAC fed off the established propaganda machinery of Hollywood, and Hollywood off the new images SAC could supply and the raw power of the military itself? In those days, television was making ever bigger advances into the film audience. Desperate remedies were needed, and there was money to be made in exploiting the fascination and the strange pride that Americans could feel in the notion that their countrymen were carrying the seeds for global destruction around the stratosphere.

A cozy symbiosis developed. The air force provided men, facilities, advice, and equipment; Hollywood furnished glamor and romance. *Variety* announced that General LeMay "has given the film his endorsement to the extent that his outfit will join in exhibitor promotion—providing military bands or equipment displays for the bally." The invitational world premiere, held under the auspices of the Air Force Association, brought out senators, generals, and the very cream of Hollywood, from Danny Kaye and Grace Kelly to Spyros Skouras and Adolf Zukor. An air force general gave Jimmy Stewart a citation for distinguished public service, and everyone settled down to watch the greatest public service announcement of the cold war.

Later that year (1955), Hollywood reached back in time to educate the American public on the roots of our strategic air power in *The Court Martial of Billy Mitchell.* There was plain-talking, trustworthy Gary Cooper proclaiming SAC's chief article of faith: "One of these days half the world will be in ruins from the air. I want this country in the other half." A noble aspiration in those days when Americans were busily planting fall-out shelters where victory gardens once grew, when few came forward to ask seriously why it had to be assumed that aerial destruction was a foregone conclusion.

So the time was ripe for every American child to hear the story of Billy Mitchell: reduced in rank and put out to pasture because he persisted in the view that air power would one day sink navies and stalemate ground forces, because he broke rules imposed on him in an experiment—in 1921 he set out to sink a captured German battleship by bombing it from five thousand feet with thousand-pound bombs. When that wouldn't work, he sent his planes in at low level carrying two-thousand-pounders and sank the ship.

When Kubrick's General Ripper oversteps his authority and sends planes to attack Russia, we are horrified. When General Lavelle sends his bombers on unauthorized missions, we grow weary. But when Gary Cooper's General Mitchell breaks through the rules and red tape, the audience rejoices and it is only the hidebound traditionalists and the pettifogging prosecutors who are allowed to insinuate that Mitchell has acted lawlessly and unreasonably. *The Court Martial of Billy Mitchell* reaches back into safe history, into safer hindsight, to present a hero who could strike away the chains that have shackled the true American Prometheus.*

---

*Other films reach into fantasy. Thus, the Messianic American scientist/admiral played by Walter Pidgeon in *Voyage to the Bottom of the Sea.* He plans to destroy the Van Allen Radiation Belt (which has mysteriously burst into flame) by socking it with a Polaris missile. The nit-picking United Nations rejects the

In 1957, building on the enthusiasm generated by *Strategic Air Command,* and following its own success with *Billy Mitchell,* Warner Brothers released a paean to the work horse of the nuclear age: *Bombers B-52.* About a sergeant (Karl Malden) who is tempted to leave the air force for a higher-paying civilian job, the film is little more than a recruiting poster cataloguing the advantages of being an enlisted man—the sergeant lives in a nice little house, takes nice vacations, and has a nice daughter (Natalie Wood) who is loved by a nice colonel (Efrem Zimbalist, Jr.). The end product was a film so bad, so dull, so pointless, that it took another six years before Hollywood would again approach the bomber.

Then, in 1963–1964, appeared a clutch of films reflecting a troubled nation's growing confusion about air power. In the years that Vietnam first became a major issue in American life, the years that saw the war escalated, came a major film made under the auspices of SAC *(A Gathering of Eagles),* two films that suggested SAC might get out of hand by machine or human malfunction *(Doctor Strangelove* and *Fail Safe),* and the first film to criticize a World War II bomber pilot for bloody-mindedness *(The War Lover).*

A Gathering of Eagles was produced by Sy Bartlett, SAC's man in Hollywood, from his own story. Bartlett, you will remember, was reportedly the first American to bomb Berlin and was later deputy commander of a SAC base. Bartlett claims that when he set out to produce a Big Film about SAC, he had plenty of great technical details (missile drills, twenty-five-ton B-52s taking off at fifteen-second intervals, command posts full of blinking lights and clacking machines), but he did not have a story line until Curtis LeMay suggested he go along on an Operational Readiness Inspection. "That was it," Bartlett explained to the *New York Times.* "Suddenly everything fell into place. Short of war, the O. R. I. provided just what our drama needed."

The result was a melodrama about a young colonel (Rock Hudson) who—shades of Bartlett's *Twelve O'Clock High*—takes over a SAC base that has failed a surprise alert, surprise alerts being serious business as we learn in *Doctor Strangelove* and *Fail Safe. A Gathering of Eagles* ends by taking us to the brink that we would stumble across in those two later films—Hudson

---

plan, but the admiral *knows* he is right, so he sets out in a nuclear submarine. When the United Nations sends submarines to prevent the missile launch, our hero leads the pursuers into such great depths that they explode.

has so honed his crews that they can pass the dreaded Operational Readiness Inspection to prove their ability to go to war with dispatch.

The film tries for a touch of humanity by having Hudson (who has been insisting that his men work by the book) break a few rules, including sending a malfunctioning bomber into the air, so his command can pass that magical O. R. I. Only a giant step away, of course, is the decision of *Strangelove*'s General Ripper to break a few more rules and send his bombers all the way.

If I keep coming back to *Doctor Strangelove* and *Fail Safe* it is because *Eagles* looks forward to them in that it focuses on issues and symbols that will acquire new and sinister meanings the following year. Take the Red Phone, for instance. In *A Gathering of Eagles*, the young colonel's omnipresent link with the higher authority that can send his command to war is simply an inconvenience, a dramatic symbol of the conflict racking his marriage to Mary Peach: "The Red Phone," scream posters and newspaper ads, "His Mistress . . . Her Rival . . . Hurling him to the edge of space . . . freezing her love on the edge of time." A year later we would find telephones metamorphosed into larger symbols of the difficulty of and need for communication (remember Peter Sellers trying to place a collect call to the White House or Henry Fonda listening to the high-pitched whine of the American Embassy phone that melts when Moscow is obliterated?).

The seeds of *Strangelove* and *Fail Safe* were in the air, as the reaction of reviewers shows: the *Time* reviewer had a moment of doubt as he recounted the inefficient goings-on that Rock Hudson must stop ("Is SAC really all that sick?"), but he rushed headlong into optimism: "The film provides impressive evidence to the contrary." The *Newsweek* reviewer, however, seems to have intuited that the tensions of *Eagles* (tensions resulting from mechanical and human failure, including vanity, laziness, alcoholism, jealousy, and resentment) did indeed signal a great sickness: "Without the distinction of Hudson's preternatural charm, it is appallingly clear that only a maniac can run a SAC wing properly."

Which brings us to a SAC wing run by a maniac. When Jack D. Ripper decides to nuke the Commie Menace that has been poisoning his vital essences, he is acting out the great nightmare implicit in *A Gathering of Eagles:* that a single madman might send the world to war. *Fail Safe* tried to demonstrate that the System contains checks making it impossible for a madman to start a war (the corollary, that only a sane man can do so, is a conundrum worthy of *Catch-22*)—and then promptly created a situation in which a malfunctioning machine leads to the obliteration of two great cities.

Madman or malfunction, no matter which—and no matter that *Strangelove* opened and *Fail Safe* closed with Department of Defense disclaimers that what happens in the films could not actually happen—the gay dreams of holocaust that Agee saw in Walt Disney's *Victory Through Air Power* had become a terrible national nightmare in these two films produced immediately after the Cuban Missile Crisis. The bomber films of World War II had been happy stories because they were about Us doing It to Them; the early SAC films had been joyous celebrations of our safety behind a stratospheric Maginot line manned by Jimmy Stewart. But by 1964 the national subconscious was beginning to murmur: "If *we* have these weapons because the Russians have them because *we* have them, where will it all end?"

Kubrick attempted to answer the question with Armageddon: the accidental "delivery" of one American bomb setting off a Russian Doomsday Device. *Fail Safe,* released the same year by the same studio (Columbia), may have been meant to undercut the dark vision of *Doctor Strangelove*—everything turns out reasonably well when the destruction of Moscow is atoned for by the sacrifice of Manhattan. Where Kubrick's President Muffley (Peter Sellers) is a weak fool who allows the world to fall apart around his egg head, *Fail Safe* gives us Henry Fonda as a no-longer-so-young Mr. Lincoln for a nuclear age. *Strangelove's* generals are comic monsters; *Fail Safe's* are tough-minded but compassionate (the general in SAC Headquarters who grows sad contemplating the death of his Russian opposite-number's family, the general who bombs New York personally to spare his subordinates the pain).

Both films face the unthinkable—not simply that global nuclear war could erupt, but that America might trigger it. *Fail Safe,* a far more "serious" film than *Doctor Strangelove,* is ultimately weaker and shabbier because it turns disaster into an excuse for national pride. The disaster itself is blamed on a machine instead of on the men who put so much trust and pride in their toys; the hero of the piece becomes the brave American president who does what must be done, and the tragedy is that the Empire State Building becomes ground zero. The Burdick and Wheeler novel refers to the president's sacrifice of New York as "the most sweeping and incredible decision that any man had ever made," and ends on a patriotic and upbeat note as the president orders a Medal of Honor citation be prepared for the general who bombed New York: "Have the citation read simply: for the highest act of courage and the most supreme conception of duty to his country and to mankind."

In spite of my fondness for some of the images, characterizations, and incidents in *Fail Safe* (the final freeze-frames as New Yorkers enjoy their last instant of existence; the portrayal by Walter Matthau of Groteschele, President Fonda's Kissinger; even the SAC general's soppy farewell to his Russian counterpart), I will assert that this is a morally and intellectually dangerous film because it simplifies and romanticizes the issues of national responsibility: the president takes America's share all on his Kennedyesque shoulders, then lectures the Russian premier to the effect that they, president and premier, must use their remaining powers to prevent the same set of circumstances from occurring in the future—and it is all done neatly, cleanly, and quickly on the telephone.

At the very heart of *Fail Safe* is the maudlin cliché that provided the human drama in a whole decade of other "serious" films about strategic warfare—the melodramatic love/duty dilemma. *Fail Safe* opens with a SAC general being awakened from a nightmare in his Manhattan apartment by his loving wife; before his long day is over, he has bombed the city, thus killing his wife (and, to make things even more dramatic, the president's). The general immediately commits suicide, of course, but not even his personal sacrifice can stay this cynical viewer from pointing out that nukeing a long-suffering wife only escalates the cliché.

Doctor Strangelove, conversely, is something new. It takes the same stereotypes and breaks the mold. The love/duty cliché is laughed to its grave in General Buck Turgidson's affair with his secretary. "You can't call me *here,"* he squeaks when she calls him in the War Room under the president's glare. Of course he loves her, George C. Scott protests; of course he respects her mind. But though the bikini-clad secretary is lubriciously awaiting his return, Buck Turgidson has no dilemma: he would clearly prefer to make war, not love. Or is it that War is Love? Strange Love? Look at that directory of erotic perversions, the names of the central characters: Buck Turgidson, Jack D. Ripper, Ambassador de Sadesky, Major "King" Kong (a strange lover if there ever was one), and the three characters played by Peter Sellers: Group Captain Mandrake ("Get with child a mandrake's root," commanded John Donne), President Merkin Muffley (a merkin is a pubic wig), and Strangelove himself.

Kubrick has hit upon something here that was below the surface in many of the other films, where the wives of crews and commanders had been presented as unreasonably jealous. *Strangelove* suggests there may have been some cause for that jealousy. The film opens with planes as sexual objects* (a bomber coupling with a tanker); Jack D. Ripper's fear of International Communism is deeply involved with his sexual fears, and his resulting decision to attack Russia and purify his vital essences unleashes joy in Major Kong, who experiences a flash of concupiscence as he opens his survival kit ("one hundred dollars in rubles; nine packs of chewing gum; one issue of prophylactics; three lipsticks, three pair of nylon stockings—gee, a fella could have a pretty good weekend in Vegas with all that stuff") and later rides the world's biggest erection down to that old whore, the earth (the target, you will remember, is the Swiftian *Laputa*), thereby unleashing the cataclysm that inspires Doctor Strangelove's vision of subterranean copulation. Suddenly Doctor Strangelove's virility returns, he lurches forth miraculously from his wheelchair, and we see an orgasmic montage of nuclear blooms as we hear a girl with a bedroom voice promise "We'll meet again" on the soundtrack.

When Kubrick let the Doomsday Device rip at the end of *Strangelove,* he killed all those coitus interruptus peacetime SAC films by giving audiences what they had secretly coveted all along: gay images of holocaust. Films about bombers must thrive on action, violent action—and after one has seen Jimmy Stewart crash in flames or Rock Hudson make a tense landing after a fuel line breaks during inflight refueling, one lusts for something more. So Kubrick went back to the World War II films that were like Fourth of July celebrations in the town square (a lot of talk, then the fireworks) and copied their explosive endings. Films like *Air Force* and *Bombardier* had built toward a practical application of those elaborate techniques the young crews had so laboriously perfected. In the cold war

---

*Compare the end of *The War Lover* as Steve McQueen tries to talk his crippled bomber into gaining altitude: "Alright, baby, we're alone now. We're gonna make it. Get me up. Get me up. Come on. Get me up."

years, however, films had shown crews learning ever more ar-
cane techniques for controlling ever greater power. A tension
had been building toward crisis, and Kubrick was clever
enough or bold enough to release it on celluloid.

IV

The American fliers turned in their uniforms, became high school
kids. And Hitler turned into a baby, Billy Pilgrim supposed. That
wasn't in the movie. Billy was extrapolating. Everybody turned into a
baby, and all humanity, without exception, conspired biologically to
produce two perfect people named Adam and Eve, he supposed.
—Kurt Vonnegut, *Slaughterhouse-Five*

It has been almost a decade since *Strangelove* and *Fail Safe*
were released. In those years we have heard Curtis LeMay, who
rose from Chief of SAC to Chief of Staff of the whole air force,
advocate bombing the North Vietnamese back to the Stone Age.
We have witnessed growing uncertainty, both in and outside of
the air force, over the wisdom of mass bombing. Our papers
were full of scandals—secret unauthorized raids, accidental
bombings of friendly civilians and troops, blatant dissatisfac-
tion in the ranks of the air force itself.

Surely there was great material for a film about the Vietnam
air war, but no one came forward. In 1966, shortly after his
retirement from the air force, it was announced that Curtis
LeMay was working with Sy Bartlett on a project dealing with
Vietnam. The story never reached the screen, and Bartlett soon
turned his attention to *Che!* (if you can't lick them, make movies about them). Bartlett's description of the proposed film,
quoted back in Chapter One, is worth repeating here: "it dealt
with an approach to end the war in Vietnam by kidnapping the
Chinese General who called all the shots for Ho Chi Minh. It
propounded the theory that this would end further bombing
and bring an abrupt end to the bloodshed."

For several weeks I pondered the connection between Le-
May's background and this particular story line, on which,
Bartlett assured me, "General LeMay and I had the fullest cooperation." Slowly, very slowly, I saw the meaning: many who
believe in strategic bombing believe in magical, bloodless victories. When Disney's *Victory Through Air Power* was in pro-

duction, there was some fear in military quarters that de Seversky's views, if well presented, would weaken our determination to attack Europe directly. Now LeMay, who had masterminded the great fire raids on Japan (sixteen square miles of Tokyo set ablaze in one night and other marvels) and had overseen the bombing of Hiroshima and Nagasaki, strategies that supposedly led to the capitulation of Japan before it was necessary to send in ground troops, was casting about for another gimmick that would stop the war.

Meanwhile, back in Vietnam, the air war was expanding without affecting the will of the North Vietnamese and Vietcong to pursue the conflict. Billy Mitchell, his eye on the Holy Grail, had promised that air power would be the "dominant feature of military operations" and make the enemy "helpless to resist," but the enemy was not playing by Billy's rules. Without anyone really noticing, the pendulum had swung and air power had grown from a vital young giant to a tired old ogre, and David Halberstam was to offhandedly complain (in *The Best and the Brightest*) that "the Air Force believed in air power and bombing, *old-fashioned,* unrelieved bombing."

Suddenly, the strategy of the future was the impotent cliché of yesterday and we entered a period when Hollywood looked away, looked back. Instead of directly criticizing current air force activities in Vietnam, filmmakers looked back to World War II. First, there was *Catch–22,* about a bombing war that never seemed to end. But instead of leaving audiences with a horror of air power's ability for casual destruction, Mike Nichols's film enchanted them with nostalgic images—scruffy flight jackets, jauntily cocked caps, and creaky old B–25s struggling into the air. The same thing happened in 1962 to *The War Lover* when it resurrected a pack of B–17s—it's hard enough to make an anti-war film, and impossible if the chief tool of war is something as appealing as an antique bomber.

Then there was *Slaughterhouse-Five,* which attempted to treat the horrors of strategic bombing from ground level but somehow forgot to point out that the primary sufferers in the infamous Dresden raid were *Germans;* by focusing on an American character, the film fell right into step behind *The Purple Heart* and *Thirty Seconds Over Tokyo,* in which Yanks are shown to suffer tremendously following raids upon the enemy. By ending with the celebration at the birth of Billy Pilgrim's son, *Slaughterhouse-Five* managed to look away from both America's past and present, and by ending with Billy on the distant planet Tralfamadore (rather than in the rubble of

Dresden, as does Vonnegut's novel), the film achieves a double remoteness.

If Hollywood is to re-examine the meaning of bombing in World War II, if it will insist on depicting this bombing's effect on American characters, then it might do well to employ the approach of John William Corrington's 1970 novel, *The Bombardier*. Corrington takes the myth of American strength through diversity and turns it to show the opposite face, to show the seeds of national psychosis. He does this through the linked stories of five minority-group Americans—a Jew, a Black, a Pole, a Greek, a Catholic from the South, and a musician—who come together to bomb Dresden in spite of the fact, as one character muses, "We had no more in common with one another than we did with the Germans." Then Corrington skips ahead a quarter of a century to show the same individuals coming together for diverse political or social reasons at the 1968 Democratic National Convention in Chicago (one is a delegate, another a lobbyist, a reporter, a cop, and a rioter) to demonstrate that the teamwork and energy it took to bomb Europe and Japan was simply a re-channelling of our own internal hatreds. Thus, the black ex-bombardier throws a Molotov cocktail on the Polish American ex-bombardier, who is now a cop contemplating beating up the Jewish ex-bombardier. And so it goes.

But why should Hollywood make an allegorical film to undo the stereotypes it so carefully and firmly established in the 1940s? Besides, the tension, the danger, the potential for spectacular personal obliteration, the need for teamwork and competence and courage and all the values that marked twenty years of bombing films, found an outlet in our struggles to outstrip the Russians in the space race, a struggle that found its chronicle on television, not in the film.

The massive American effort to get men on the moon first was co-terminous with Vietnam; both the fire on the moon and the fire in the paddies were the legacy of Kennedy administered by Johnson and Nixon. Whether we call the Space Race a moral equivalent of war, or view it as a medium of aggression parallel to the war in Vietnam and the stockpiling of missiles at home, is immaterial. What is crucial is that not since Pearl Harbor had there been such an emotionally powerful national challenge as that supplied by the launching of Sputnik in 1957.

It was a challenge that could reinforce strange alliances. In *I Aim at the Stars,* the 1960 film biography of Werner von Braun, the crisis comes when an American officer, whose children were killed in V–2 raids (Germany's last stab at strategic bombing), insists that von Braun, a leading scientist at White Sands, should be tried as a war criminal. Before the film can suitably resolve the moral issues involved, the Russians launch Sputnik and the prototype for Doctor Strangelove becomes a hero by sending the first American satellite into orbit. The very fact the filmmakers thought it safe to employ this particular gimmick to end the film is a clue to America's secret moral bookkeeping and as sure a sign as any that nothing personal is involved in strategic warfare. "Good-by, von Braun," says the scientist's converted enemy at the fadeout, "and good luck with the universe."

December 6, 1972. I am sitting in front of the family television to watch the last Apollo mission set out for the Moon. Launch time passes, my wife drifts off to bed, and I am alone. Slowly the spectacle begins to take the shape of a movie by Stanley Kubrick—a malfunctioning computer prevents the launch and has to be de-programed and over-ridden by its human masters. Then midnight passes and suddenly I realize it is December 7, the thirty-first anniversary of Pearl Harbor. Now the movie changes for me—it's no longer about Keir Dullea lobotomizing HAL, it's Slim Pickens jiggling that bomb loose over Laputa. It's a movie to give America the visual thrills and release and rapture she has not been vouchsafed since the Bomb went underground and died at Amchitka.

As the night sky lights up from the rocket's blast, I am reminded of another night over twenty years before in New Mexico when I had sat up most of the night to watch an atomic fireball light the horizon. The soldier who had "won" the last big war had just become our President, we had just made an acceptable truce in Korea, the Russians were far behind in the armaments race, all was right in the world.

Whole families were gathered that night in the foothills and desert to witness something strange and beautiful. We didn't need an air force band or a precision flying team. We had all we wanted—the expectation of raw release, the momentary flashing proof that the secrets of the universe were ours, the long afterglow, and (if we were lucky) a clear view of the mushroom cloud rising above the horizon to be lit by the first rays of the morning sun.

Ah, what a dream we had.

Durham, New Hampshire
July 1973—March 1974

APPENDIX 1

In 1967 Vinh Noan, the Vietnamese filmmaker identified in Chapter One, tried to interest American producers in this treatment for a film depicting the idealism of the "typical" South Vietnamese peasant and his commitment to the unceasing struggle against communism. Making only small changes for the sake of clarity, I present Vinh Noan's aborted project as a souvenir of the war.

A NIGHT OF TERROR

by Vinh Noan

INTERIOR OF A HELICOPTER—AT SUNDOWN

A few helicopters are flying over a mountainous area in a remote district of South Vietnam. They are on a reconnaissance flight and are on their way back to their base.

Like any other afternoon in South Vietnam, the sky is covered with heavy, dark clouds. At times the pilots can see each other; sometimes they can't because they are separated by thick, opaque clouds.

Inside the last helicopter, we can see two American officers: one is Second Lieutenant John, the pilot. The other, Captain Herbert, is reading a map with two Vietnamese officers. There is also a journalist newly arrived from America, blond Carol Bower, seeking for the truth of the war.

Suddenly, Lieutenant John turns to warn Captain Herbert that he has seen something in the forest they have just flown over. They decide to skim the ground for better observation. If they notice something important, they will inform the rest of the squadron.

As they descend, they see a great number of communist soldiers gathering in the forest below them. Even though the communists disperse rapidly when they hear the whirr of motors, many smoking fires and broken branches are left on the ground.

Herbert picks up the microphone and, as he tries to call the squadron, is wounded by a blast of machine-gun fire from the ground.

In the helicopter, broken bits of electronic equipment fly

around. One of the Vietnamese officers is killed on the spot. The transmitter is inoperative and the other Vietnamese officer is trying to stop Herbert's bleeding with a field dressing, while John is looking for a spot to make an emergency landing because the helicopter has also been hit by ground fire, and cannot fly farther.

CREDITS

INTERIOR OF A HAMLET—AT SUNDOWN

From a sentry box erected on the roof of a hamlet pagoda, a youth is scanning the surrounding landscape. Suddenly he notices the signals made by a young shepherd standing on the back of his buffalo.

While he is trying to decipher the shepherd's signals, a helicopter appears from a thick cloud and performs an emergency landing on a spot near the hamlet with a deafening *whirr*. The villagers are gathering by a bamboo wall to observe the helicopter. They guess that the craft is in trouble as the landing is not smooth and its fuselage is riddled with bullet holes.

Because of machine-gun fire and the landing of the helicopter, the chief of the hamlet immediately knows that the enemy is nearby. He orders the women and children evacuated to shelters and the youths on the alert.

With a nurse and four young men, the chief rushes to the helicopter to help the crew.

As they bring Herbert out of the craft, the noise of tocsins and drums warns that the enemy is marching to the hamlet.

With the wounded captain, the group can only withdraw slowly to the hamlet as the Viet Cong start shooting. The hamlet chief is mortally wounded by gunfire as he approaches the gate. He is finally rescued by Minh, the courageous young military leader of the village.

The hamlet is now entirely besieged by the VC who launch a violent attack with mortar shells to intimidate the inhabitants. Inside the hamlet, houses are destroyed under the rain of shells.

Darkness is falling.

In an underground shelter, the dying chief is sobbing out his will, pleading with Minh to fight to the last man.

His eyes filled with tears, Minh bites his lips and looks at the dark reality surrounding him.

Lieutenant John, who is used to fighting with airplanes, with modern equipment and arms, is suddenly caught on a battlefield with a group of underdeveloped people whose arms consist of an assortment of knives, spikes, spears, a few bird guns—and only a few submachine guns. Analyzing the situation logically and practically, John sees no hope of the hamlet resisting the attack. He hastily asks Minh to show him the communications center so he can send out messages for help from other friendly posts. His heart sinks when he sees the transceiver: the battery is dead and a shell fragment has broken another part of the equipment. His hope to communicate with the outside evaporates.

Ignoring John's anxiety and completely detached from the gravity of the situation, Carol, the typical journalist, starts to type the exciting story for her publisher back home.

Meanwhile, Herbert clenches his teeth, sweating all over as the nurse cleans his wound with alcohol.

After the initial attack, the communists pause to issue a warning through a megaphone: if the hamlet's inhabitants agree to hand the Americans over to them, they will leave at once; otherwise the hamlet will be destroyed.

After Minh translates the terms into English, Herbert and John discuss the alternatives. They do not want to see the children and women die because of their presence. So they decide to surrender. But there's Carol to be considered. Only then does the non-violent girl realize that her immunity to violence has never existed. However, she flatly refuses to give herself up to the VC in order to save a group of people she doesn't know!

While the hamlet is deliberating, the VC resume their harangue: "They are foreigners and consist of only three persons —you, people of the hamlet, must realize that it's senseless to sacrifice the lives of five hundred people for them."

Since the hamlet chief has been killed, Minh replaces him in accordance with the regulations. He uses a megaphone to ask the VC to cease fire for an hour so that they can make their decision.

Knowing that airplanes and regular forces cannot come at night to assist the hamlet, the VC accept the proposition. They also need time to dig trenches in preparation for their attack.

The whole hamlet boils with conflict. Shall they hand over the Americans or fight to save them? Minh, true to his promise to the old chief, decides to fight. But his younger brother, Long, is the head of the group which chooses to hand over the Americans to the enemy.

The two American officers then raise their voices, asking the inhabitants to stop the discussion because they have the right to decide their own fate and they don't want to ask for unnecessary protection since other people's lives are menaced. They offer to surrender themselves.

Minh strongly protests that idea; he thinks that anyone who enters the hamlet must follow its regulations, as all passengers aboard a ship must obey the captain's order. In a word, the Americans must respect the law of the village.

Before the villagers vote, Minh speaks: "The enemy outside will sacrifice everything, crush everything, in order to reach their aims. For them, men are mere figures—they will exchange five hundred Vietnamese for three Americans! But in this struggle our ideal is different from the VC: we respect the 'human being.' For us, men are not mere figures. . . ."

Long interrupts his brother, angrily pulling a suckling infant from its mother's breast and holding it up as he speaks: "I want to know who has the right to sacrifice this baby's life for those foreigners? The men outside give us a chance to make a choice because they don't want to kill all of us unnecessarily. Why should we sacrifice our lives meaninglessly?"

Minh smiles, picks up the baby and speaks calmly: "As my brother said, this is an example for us: who has the right to sacrifice this baby for these foreigners? But look at the problem from another angle: if we hand over the Americans, the lives of five hundred inhabitants will be saved; on the other hand, if we don't obey they will kill five hundred Vietnamese, including this baby, to get these Americans at any price. This is the difference in the two beliefs—we don't sow terror and misfortune around us in our attempt to reach goals as they do."

John expresses his opinion: "In these critical minutes, you are being completely idealistic. From my practical point of view, you better try to solve this urgent problem. If you want to fight, what means are at your disposal? Can we resist an enemy many times stronger than we? You must understand that without reinforcements, we have no hope of surviving."

Long plays on the American's point of view: "The Americans themselves admit that we are in a hopeless situation. Everybody will die if reinforcements do not come to relieve us. So, I ask you to vote NO."

Minh concludes: "First, to answer our American friends— we're discussing idealism because we want to make clear the purpose of our struggle. For example, I wonder if the guerrillas outside have the right to choose whether or not they will kill hundreds of their compatriots in order to get a few foreigners. But in here, in a few moments, we are prefectly free to choose whether we will turn these friends over to the enemy or take the risk to defend them. In fact, we have this choice and I think this kind of liberty is what we are fighting for up to now. Also, these fellow soldiers, the Americans, are here to help us keep that precious right of freedom. The burning flame of liberty in our heart will lead us to the final victory."

The villagers begin to cast their votes. The outcome is YES, which means they want to fight!

Minh gives orders and explains the tactics they must employ: "First, we must understand the enemy's tactics: they always apply the 'one slow and four fast' tactic. This means that before attacking, they first apply the 'one slow.' The attack preparation must be long and minute. Then they apply the 'four fast': fast advance, fast attack, fast battlefield recovery, and fast retreat. Right now, they outnumber us so they underestimate us and won't make a careful preparation. We also have the advantage that they don't know our surface and underground plan of defense. In brief, they don't know the layout of our trenches, obstacles, mine fields, and hideouts."

"So we have two parts in this battle. First, let's use all our strength to smash the enemy's massive attack—if we fail we'll apply another tactic. Then we apply the guerrilla tactic. Even if the enemy can enter the hamlet, it doesn't help them at all because we have the advantage of fighting at night. The enemy can't get anything because we will continue to fight from one trench to another, from house to house, and if we can resist until sunrise, the communists will retreat because they are not strong enough to occupy the hamlet during day light—they're afraid of the counterattack made by airplanes and regular army soldiers."

"Women who don't belong to the active resistance must carry out the plan of hiding food and drugs. If the enemy enters the hamlet, children and invalids must strictly apply the non-cooperation policy."

Minh now asks John to repair the transceiver in order to communicate with the outside world. A few smart young boys assisting John go down into a safe shelter to do the assigned job. Because of his wound, Herbert is carried into the shelter, but he refuses to stay idle and offers to repair the transceiver so John can help a group of young men lay mines and traps in a more effective way.

Emotionally affected by the brave decision of the people inside the hamlet, Carol offers to join the relief group.

The other able-bodied men and women are divided into groups to fight at different defense points.

When they call Long, he has disappeared! In fact, he is an enemy agent. When the hamlet voted to fight, Long defected to the enemy by a secret underground passage, bringing a layout of the defenses with him.

Nga, the nurse, is most shocked at the news, having never known that her lover was a traitor. She had always declined Minh's love because she was fascinated by Long's mysterious attitude, by his fanaticism which appalls her now: his willingness to sacrifice everything to obtain the so-called liberation and happiness of humanity.

Now the situation becomes worse. Because the enemy's knowledge of the underground defense lines makes extended resistance impossible, Minh begins to order the only underground passage leading to the outside destroyed.

But before he can finish his order, the Viet Cong launch their violent attack. To open passages through the obstacle-filled mines, they first dig shallow trenches to the hamlet's bamboo barricade and set it on fire with gasoline. The flames rise very high, and the strong wind quickly transforms the fences surrounding the hamlet into a sea of fire.

Then the VC tie the young shepherds and their buffaloes together and push them through the mine fields surrounding the hamlet. Buffaloes are blown to pieces as they walk on the mines, thus clearing a path for the Viet Cong.

The enemy attack is violent, but the hamlet's resistance is very heroic.

Grenades burst everywhere; the communists take cover behind the buffaloes killed by mines as they proceed toward the hamlet, but they suffer heavy losses from the barrage fire of the hamlet's soldiers.

John, Minh, and many others prove to be excellent marksmen. Among them is a North Vietnamese refugee, his whole fortune consisting of a water pipe (inherited from his father!) on which are carved seven dragons. After taking his last puff of smoke, he becomes a brilliant marksman: none of his bullets miss the target!

After the first attempt has failed, the enemy, having suffered heavy losses, tries another tactic: they use mortars to shell the points of resistance and fluster the defenders while their men dig tunnels under the mine field to enter the hamlet.

Inside the hamlet, the losses are also very high. Many dead

lie on the mounds of earth. Carol and Nga set up an underground dressing station.

In the next shelter, Herbert is doing his best to repair the transceiver. He remembers that there is a good battery in the helicopter. But how can it be brought to the hamlet? The craft must be well guarded by the VC or perhaps even destroyed by now!

The children who are working with him volunteer to get the battery. The children's spirit of sacrifice causes Herbert's eyes to fill with tears and he realizes what a grave responsibility he bears for these people's lives. The children leave, their only weapons one grenade and unflinching courage.

Meanwhile, amid explosions and the whizz of mortar shells, Minh counts his men and reorganizes the resistance line to face a second attack. Suddenly he hears a noise under his feet: the enemy are digging tunnels to enter the hamlet. From what points did they start their digging? How much have they dug? How can he face such a tactic? These questions are not easy to answer. From afar, in his peculiar dialect, the man from Central Vietnam warns Minh: "They are digging underneath."

The atmosphere of the hamlet is tense, anxious, and hopeless . . .

Mortar shells explode everywhere, raising dust and sand . . .

The pipe smoker has a suggestion: "The enemy are digging tunnels to get in—why don't we dig to get out?" His suggestion is rejected because if everybody is digging, no one will be ready to fight when the enemy launches a second attack. Even if the people of the hamlet were able to get out, the ground outside is flat and offers no possibility of cover. To leave the hamlet now would be suicidal.

Everybody is nervous and is anxiously awaiting the enemy's next move.

John and a few boys are crawling from one place to another to lay grenades and traps . . .

In an individual trench, a young man holds a rifle in one hand and a black dog in another, applying his ear to the ground to follow the digging noises of the enemy. He waits anxiously, and in order to dissipate his fear, he tries to smoke. He lights a match, but his hand is shaking so that he cannot light his cigarette. The dog seems to understand the situation and licks his master's hand as if he wants to share his anxiety! The young man moves his body and a grenade drops. The dog picks it up with his mouth and brings it to his master—he wants to say he's fighting on his master's side.

Meanwhile, older people prepare hot tea and bring it to the combatants in the trenches. Among them, we can see Minh's mother looking at her oldest son with pity: he is dirty, untidy, as he busily organizes the resistance. And then she thinks of her second son . . .

John, who is deeply touched by the attitude of the people, drinks his tea with great pleasure: from a highly mechanized and scientific world, he suddenly finds himself in a rudimentary hole in the ground fighting alongside a people he had never dreamed of encountering—yet now he will perhaps die with them. Pulling a picture of a silvery-haired girl from his wallet, he lights a cigarette in order to glance at his sweetheart back in New York. Perhaps it's the last time he will look at her picture! The image of the beautiful girl disappears with the light of the match. The explosion of a mortar shell by his trench brings him back to the murky reality.

The children leave the hamlet by means of a drain pipe which is just large enough for them to squeeze through. According to the plan, as they approach the helicopter they will throw a grenade as a signal for the soldiers in the hamlet to open heavy fire and shout loudly to simulate a counterattack and distract the enemy. During the commotion, the children will climb into the helicopter to remove the battery and bring it back to the hamlet.

The children successfully complete their mission, but by the time the battery reaches Herbert, the enemy have forced entries at many points.

Hand-to-hand combat is taking place in every corner of the hamlet. Even though the VC have entered the hamlet, they can't subdue it because the defending snipers keep up a steady fire from well-concealed positions. The VC are forced into the trenches to fight.

In the hamlet, confusion reaches its peak. No one can tell friend from enemy, nor the friendly trench from the enemy's. There are alternate moments of noisy disorder and complete silence as the adversaries search the darkness for glimpses of each other.

In one shelter, the mother of the nursing baby is killed by an enemy bullet when the baby cries out loudly, revealing the mother's hiding place. The baby continues to cry, so his five-year-old sister crawls to him and tries to comfort him, but the baby will not stop crying. Frightened, the young girl pulls up her shirt and tries to nurse her brother, but the baby cries more loudly! Panic-stricken but resourceful, she picks up a peeled coconut, makes a hole in it with her little finger and gives it to her little brother to suck: he stops crying at once!

As the fighting goes on, Herbert begins to smile because the transceiver finally lights up. The children crawl out to fix the antenna.

Inside a zigzag fortified trench, one side is held by our men, the other side by the enemy. In the night nobody knows when and who he must shoot. The man from Central Vietnam argues politics loudly with the VC standing at the other end of the trench. In a flare of anger, he sticks his head out of the trench and is killed on the spot!

Not far away, the pipe smoker shoots an enemy sniper down. On hearing the communist's cry of pain, the pipe smoker is touched and wants to crawl to help his victim, but is afraid of being shot. Finally, he holds out his pipe to the wounded sniper and invites him to smoke. Even though he cannot see his unusual guest, he can hear the purring of his pipe and smiles with satisfaction.

Thanks to this charitable act, the guest smoker uses his last bit of strength to shoot down a VC who tries to kill his unknown host.

John and another man carry Minh, who has been wounded in the chest, into the nurse's shelter. Suddenly, Long and two other communists appear. Nga cries out excitedly and tries to cover Minh with her body, but Long shoots them in cold blood. Carol quickly throws a bottle of alcohol at Long, and John opens fire with a submachine gun and kills Long and the other communists.

Minh caresses Nga's hair which has fallen over his face. As he touches her wound, he clenches his jaws in anger at his helplessness.

In the next trench, a man with the black dog sees a group of communists progressing toward him. He takes the grenade handed to him a few minutes ago by his dog, throws it at the enemy. The dog, thinking that his master is playing with him, rushes toward the grenade to bring it back. Appalled, the young man forgets the danger, dashes out to catch the dog. A burst of gun fire cuts him down on the spot and a big explosion kills the dog and the communists.

As the resistance continues, the VC set fire to the houses and the hamlet becomes a sea of fire . . .

Crouching in the flickering light, Herbert sends his first message. As he speaks, the communists arrive at his position. Even though he is badly wounded, he still tries to send his message before he falls by the transceiver which continues to ask for further information . . .

The rising sun finally appears over the sea of fire and the cries are gradually drowned out by the noise of approaching airplanes.

The communists retreat in a great hurry to the forest, leaving behind them a hamlet full of corpses and wounded after a night of terror.

When the armored tanks and the paratroopers arrive to pursue the enemy, Minh's mother has just finished burying Long. In her prayer, the old woman says: "If there's no difference about the concept of happiness, maybe I should have had a happy family with my two sons."

A jeep comes to pick up John. He shakes Minh's hand warmly and, before leaving, shouts to Carol to come along. She, unmindful of his call, is seated on a broken chair, already at work on her completely new dispatch about a group of people of different nationalities who fought for a noble ideal: liberating the country and MAN . . . during a night of terror.

APPENDIX 2

The following list was supplied to me by the Pentagon. Though it covers only the two decades ending in 1968 and does not include every film receiving minor assistance, it does give some idea of the variety of films which received Department of Defense support. An equally revealing document would be a list of the films and projects refused assistance by the military. The dissertations by Shain and Suid (see Bibliography) supply additional information on DoD assistance to commercial filmmakers.

APPROXIMATE LIST OF COMMERCIAL MOTION PICTURES ON WHICH THE DEPARTMENT OF DEFENSE RENDERED ASSISTANCE 1949–1968

TITLE	RELEASED BY	YEAR RELEASED
Above and Beyond	M-G-M	1953
Air Cadet	Universal	1951
All Hands on Deck	20th Century-Fox	1960
All the Young Men	Columbia	1960
Ambush Bay	United Artists	1966
American Guerrilla in the Philippines	20th Century-Fox	1950
Anchors Away	M-G-M	1953
Annapolis Story	Allied Artists	1955
Anzio	Columbia	1967
Armored Command	Allied Artists	1961
At War with the Army	Paramount	1951
Away All Boats	Universal	1956
Bamboo Saucer	Fairbanks	1967
Battle at Bloody Beach	20th Century-Fox	1961
Battle Beneath the Earth	M-G-M	1968
Battle Circus	M-G-M	1953
Battle Cry	Warner Bros.	1955
Battleground	M-G-M	1950
Battle Hymn	Universal	1957
Battle of the Coral Sea	Columbia	1959
Battle of North Atlantic	Universal	1967
Battle Stations	Columbia	1956
Battle Taxi	United Artists	1955
Battle Without Front Line	DiLaurentiis	1967

215

TITLE	RELEASED BY	YEAR RELEASED
Battle Zone	Allied Artists	1952
Beachhead	United Artists	1954
Beach Red	United Artists	1967
Beardless Warriors	Universal	1964
Beast of Budapest	Allied Artists	1958
Bedford Incident	Columbia	1965
Between Heaven and Hell	20th Century-Fox	1956
Big Lift, The	20th Century-Fox	1950
Blood Alley	Warner Bros.	1955
Bold and the Brave	RKO	1956
Bombers B-52	Warner Bros.	1957
Breakthrough	Warner Bros.	1950
Bridges at Toko-ri	Paramount	1955
Bye Bye Birdie	Columbia	1963
Caine Mutiny	Columbia	1954
Call Me Mister	20th Century-Fox	1950
Capt. Newman, M.D.	Universal	1963
Cease Fire	Paramount	1954
Chain Lightning	Warner Bros.	1950
Citizen Soldier	Republic	
Combat Squadron	Columbia	1953
Command Decision	M-G-M	1949
Court Martial of Billy Mitchell	Warner Bros.	1955
Cry for Happy	Columbia	1961
Darby's Rangers	Warner Bros.	1958
Day the Earth Stood Still	20th Century-Fox	1951
D-Day Sixth of June	20th Century-Fox	1956
Deadly Mantis, The	Universal	1957
Decision Before Dawn	20th Century-Fox	1952
Deepfreeze	Disney	1958
Deep Six, The	Warner Bros.	1958
Devil at Four O'Clock	Columbia	1961
Devil's Brigade	United Artists	1968
Disorderly Orderly	Paramount	1964
Dondi	Allied Artists	1957
Donovan's Reef	Paramount	1963
Don't Give up the Ship	Paramount	1959
Don't Go Near the Water	M-G-M	1956
Easy Come Easy Go	Paramount	1967
Enemy Below	20th Century-Fox	1957
Eternal Sea	Republic	1955
Extraordinary Seaman	M-G-M	1968

TITLE	RELEASED BY	YEAR RELEASED
Face of War	Eli Landeau	1968
Father Goose	Universal	1965
55 Days at Peking	Allied Artists	1963
Fighter Attack	Allied Artists	1953
Fighter Squadron	Warner Bros.	1948
First to Fight	Warner Bros.	1966
Fixed Bayonets	20th Century-Fox	1951
Flat Top	Allied Artists	1952
Flight from Ashiya	United Artists	1962
Flight Nurse	Republic	1954
Flying Leathernecks	RKO	1951
Francis Goes to West Point	Universal	1951
Francis in the Navy	Universal	1955
Francis Joins the WACS	Universal	1955
Fraulein	20th Century-Fox	1958
Frogmen	20th Century-Fox	1951
From Here to Eternity	Columbia	1953
Gallant Hours	United Artists	1960
Gathering of Eagles	Universal	1963
Giant	Warner Bros.	1956
GI Blues	Paramount	1960
Girl He Left Behind	Warner Bros.	1956
Girls of Pleasure Island	Paramount	1953
Glenn Miller Story	Universal	1954
Glory Brigade	20th Century-Fox	1953
Go for Broke	M-G-M	1951
Goldfinger	United Artists	1964
Great Escape	United Artists	1963
Great Impostor	Universal	1961
Green Berets	Warner Bros.-7 Arts	1968
Halls of Montezuma	20th Century-Fox	1951
Happiest Millionaire	Disney	1966
Heaven Knows, Mr. Allison	20th Century-Fox	1957
Hellcats of Navy	Columbia	1957
Hellfighters	Universal	1968
Hello Dolly	20th Century-Fox	1967
Hell is for Heroes	Paramount	1962
Hell to Eternity	Allied Artists	1960
Here Come the Jets	20th Century-Fox	1959
Here Come the Marines	Monogram	1952
House of Bamboo	20th Century-Fox	1953
Hunters	20th Century-Fox	1958

TITLE	RELEASED BY	YEAR RELEASED
I Aim at the Stars	Columbia	1960
Ice Station Zebra	M-G-M	1968
Incredible Mr. Limpet	Warner Bros.	1964
In Enemy Country	Universal	1965
In Harm's Way	Paramount	1965
In Love and War	20th Century-Fox	1958
It Came from Beneath the Sea	Columbia	1955
I Was a Male War Bride	20th Century-Fox	1949
I Was an American Spy	Allied Artists	1951
Jet Pilot	Universal	1957
Joe Butterfly	Universal	1957
John Paul Jones	Warner Bros.	1959
Judgment at Nuremberg	United Artists	1961
Jumping Jacks	Paramount	1952
Jump into Hell	Warner Bros.	1955
Kings Go Forth	United Artists	1958
Last Blitzkrieg	Columbia	1959
Last Time I Saw Archie	United Artists	1961
Lieutenant Robin Crusoe	Disney	1966
Lieutenant Wore Skirts	20th Century-Fox	1956
Longest Day	20th Century-Fox	1962
Long Gray Line	Columbia	1955
Manchurian Candidate	United Artists	1962
Marines Let's Go	20th Century-Fox	1961
McConnell Story	Warner Bros.-7 Arts	1955
Men of the Fighting Lady	M-G-M	1954
Merrill's Marauders	Warner Bros.	1962
Mio Alley	Allied Artists	1953
Mister Roberts	Warner Bros.	1955
Monster That Challenged the Earth	United Artists	1957
Mountain Road	Columbia	1960
Moon Pilot	Disney	1962
Mystery Submarine	Universal	1950
Naked and the Dead	Warner Bros.	1958
Never Wave at a WAC	RKO	1953
Nobody's Perfect	Universal	1967
No Man Is an Island	Universal	1962
None but the Brave	Warner Bros.	1965
Not with My Wife, You Don't	Warner Bros.	1966
Nutty Professor	Paramount	1962
Off Limits	Paramount	1953

TITLE	RELEASED BY	YEAR RELEASED
Okinawa	Columbia	1952
One Minute to Zero	RKO	1952
Onionhead	Warner Bros.	1958
On the Double	Paramount	1961
On the Threshold of Space	20th Century-Fox	1956
Operation Haylift	Lippert	1950
Operation Mad Ball	Columbia	1957
Operation Petticoat	Universal	1959
Pacific Highway	Disney	1958
Parrish	Warner Bros.	1961
Pawnbroker	Allied Artists	1965
Perfect Furlough	Universal	1959
Pigeon That Took Rome	Paramount	1962
Private's Affair	20th Century- Fox	1959
Private Navy of Sgt. O'Farrell	United Artists	1968
Proud and Profane	Paramount	1955
PT-109	Warner Bros.	1963
Rack, The	M-G-M	1956
Red Ball Express	Universal	1952
Retreat Hell	Warner Bros.	1953
Run Silent, Run Deep	United Artists	1958
Russians Are Coming, The	United Artists	1965
Sabre Jet	United Artists	1953
Sad Sack	Paramount	1957
Sailor Beware	Paramount	1951
Sands of Iwo Jima	Republic	1950
Screaming Eagles	Allied Artists	1956
Sharkfighters	United Artists	1956
Shoes of the Fisherman	M-G-M	1968
Skirts Ahoy	M-G-M	1953
Soldiers in the Rain	Allied Artists	1963
Somebody Up There Likes Me	M-G-M	1957
Sound Off	Columbia	1953
South Pacific	20th Century-Fox	1958
Spirit of St. Louis	Warner Bros.	1957
Stalag 17	Paramount	1953
Stars and Stripes Forever	20th Century-Fox	1950
Steel Bayonet	Allied Artists	1958
Strategic Air Command	Paramount	1955
Submarine Command	Paramount	1951

TITLE	RELEASED BY	YEAR RELEASED
Surrender Hell	Allied Artists	1959
Take the High Ground	M-G-M	1953
Tanks Are Coming	Warner Bros.	1951
Tarawa Beachhead	Columbia	1958
Target Earth	Allied Artists	1954
Target Zero	Warner Bros.	1955
Task Force	Warner Bros.	1949
Teahouse of the August Moon	M-G-M	1956
Thirty-Six Hours	M-G-M	1965
Thousand Plane Raid	United Artists	1968
Three Brave Men	20th Century-Fox	1957
Time for Heroes	Universal	1966
Time Limit	United Artists	1957
Tobruk	Universal	1965
To Hell and Back	Universal	1955
To the Shores of Hell	Riviera	1965
Tokyo Joe	Columbia	1949
Torpedo Alley	Allied Artists	1953
Torpedo Run	M-G-M	1958
Twelve O'Clock High	20th Century-Fox	1950
Twenty-Fifth Hour	M-G-M	1967
Ugly American	Universal	1963
Up Periscope	Warner Bros.	1959
Wackiest Ship in the Army	Columbia	1960
Wake Me When It's Over	20th Century-Fox	1960
War Lover	Columbia	1962
West Point Story	Warner Bros.	1950
What Am I Bid	Liberty International	1967
Wild Blue Yonder	Republic	1951
Willie and Joe Back at the Front	Universal	1952
Windjammer	DeRochmont	1959
Wings of the Eagle	M-G-M	1957
X-15	United Artists	1961
Yellow Rolls Royce	M-G-M	1965
Young Lions	20th Century-Fox	1958
You're in the Navy Now	20th Century-Fox	1959
Yours, Mine and Ours	United Artists	1967

APPENDIX 3

EXTRACTS FROM DEPARTMENT OF DEFENSE
INSTRUCTION 5410.15 (NOVEMBER 3, 1966):
"DELINEATION OF DoD AUDIO-VISUAL PUBLIC
AFFAIRS RESPONSIBILITIES AND POLICIES"

I. Purpose

This Instruction delineates Department of Defense responsibilities and policies on releasing DoD generated audio-visual material to the public and furnishing assistance to non-Government agencies involved in the production of audio-visual materials insofar as they help sustain public understanding of the DoD. . . .

IV. Responsibilities

The Assistant Secretary of Defense (Public Affairs) is the sole authority for the approval and implementation of all DoD assistance to non-Government agencies in the production of audio-visual materials. . . .

V. Principles Governing Assistance to Non-Government Audio-Visual Media

A. The production, program, project, or assistance will benefit the DoD or otherwise be in the national interest based on consideration of the following factors:
1. Authenticity of the portrayal of military operations, or historical incidents, persons or places depicting a true interpretation of military life.
2. Compliance with accepted standards of dignity and propriety in the industry.
B. There can be no deviation from established DoD safety standards.
C. Operational readiness of the Armed Forces shall not be impaired.
D. Official activities of military personnel in assisting the production must be within the scope of normal military activities, with exceptions being made only in unusual circumstances.

E. Diversion of equipment, personnel and material resources from normal military locations or military operations may be authorized only when circumstances preclude the filming without it, and such diversions shall be held to a minimum and without interference with military operations, and will be on the basis that the production company will reimburse the Government for expenses incurred in the diversion.

F. DoD material and personnel services will not be employed in such a manner as to compete with commercial and private enterprises.

SELECTED BIBLIOGRAPHY

Agee, James. *Agee on Film, Volume I.* New York: Grosset and Dunlap, 1969.
Seemingly alone among major film reviewers during World War II, Agee
maintained an intellectual and emotional distance from the patriotic gore of
Hollywood's attacks on the Axis.

Alloway, Lawrence. *Violent America: The Movies 1946–1964.* New York: The
Museum of Modern Art, 1971.

Arlen, Michael J. *Living Room War.* New York: Viking Press, 1969.
Though this book deals with television, many of its insights can be applied
to film.

Barsam, Richard Meran. *Nonfiction Film: A Critical History.* New York: Dutton, 1973.
See Chapter Seven, "World War II on Film."

Barthel, Joan. "John Wayne, Superhawk." *New York Times Magazine,* 24
December 1967.
On the making of *The Green Berets.*

Behlmer, Rudy. "World War I Aviation Films." *Films in Review,* 18 (August-September 1967), 413–33.

Belmans, Jacques. "Cinema and Men at War." *Film Society Review,* 7 (February 1972), 22–37.
By a French critic; international in scope.

Bergman, Andrew. *We're in the Money: Depression America and Its Films.*
New York: New York University Press, 1971.
An account of how Hollywood responded to another major American crisis.

Corliss, Richard, William Johnson, and Max Kozloff. "Shooting at Wars, Three
Views." *Film Quarterly,* 21 (Winter 1967–68), 27–36.

Daniel, Joseph. *Guerre et Cinema.* Paris: A. Colin, 1972. Limited to the French
war film.

Deming, Barbara. *Running Away from Myself: A Dream Portrait of America
Drawn from the Films of the Forties.* New York: Grossman, 1969.
As its subtitle suggests, a study of the decade which produced more war films
than any other. See particularly the chapter on war heroes, " 'I'm Not Fighting for Anything Any More—Except Myself,' " and the one on the heroes'
return, " 'I've Got to Bring Him Home Where He Belongs.' "

Dempsey, M. "War as Movie Theater." *Film Quarterly,* 25 (Winter 1971), 33–36.

Dougall, Lucy (ed.). *The War/Peace Film Guide.* Berkley: World Without War
Council, 1970.
An annotated list of about one hundred documentaries dealing with war.

_____. *War/Peace Film Guide.* Chicago: World Without War Publications, 1973.
An amplification of the guide first published in 1970. Lists 225 films, mostly
documentaries, including fourteen Vietnam documentaries, but not one of
the feature films about that war.

The editors of *Look. From Movie Lot to Beachhead: The Motion Picture Industry Goes to War and Prepares for the Future.* Garden City, New York: Doubleday, 1945.
A heavily illustrated and enthusiastic account of Hollywood's war activities.

Fulbright, J. William. *The Pentagon Propaganda Machine.* New York: Liveright, 1970.
A broad overview of the Department of Defense's public relations work. For a more detailed account of Hollywood and the Pentagon, see Suid, below.

Furhammer, Leif, and Folke Isaksson. *Politics and Film.* New York: Praeger, 1971.
International in scope; contains sections on war films and propaganda.

Gallez, D. W. "Patterns in Wartime Documentaries." *Film Quarterly,* 10 (Winter 1955), 125–35.

Garnham, Nicholas. *Samuel Fuller.* New York: Viking Press, 1971.
Like Phil Hardy's book (see below), a close study of a director who keeps coming back—almost obsessively—to war as a topic.

Gassner, John, and Dudley Nichols. *Best Film Plays of 1943–1944.* New York: Crown Publishers, 1945.
Contains scripts for six films about World War II or its impact: *The Purple Heart, Watch on the Rhine, Dragon Seed, The More the Merrier, Hail the Conquering Hero,* and *Casablanca.*

———. *Best Film Plays, 1945.* New York: Crown Publishers, 1946.
Includes Ernie Pyle's *Story of G. I. Joe* and *Thirty Seconds Over Tokyo.*

———. *Twenty Best Film Plays.* New York: Crown Publishers, 1943.
Contains script for *Mrs. Miniver.*

Gessner, Peter. "Films from the Vietcong." *The Nation.* 24 January 1966, pp. 110–11.

"Glory." *The New Yorker,* 29 June 1968, pp. 24–27.
A "Talk of the Town" piece on a party for Green Berets and actors following the Manhattan opening of *The Green Berets.*

Goodman, Walter. *The Committee.* New York: Farrar, Strauss, and Giroux, 1968.
A broad and detailed account of the House Un-American Activities hearings that gave Hollywood its blackest hour and help make the film industry an active partner in the Cold War. See also Kahn and Trumbo, below.

Grossman, Edward. "Bloody Popcorn." *Harpers,* 241 (December 1970), 32–40.

Hardy, Phil. *Samuel Fuller.* New York: Praeger, 1970.

Hellman, Lillian. *The North Star.* New York: Viking, 1943.
A "classic" American war film doing for Russia what *Mrs. Miniver* did for England and *Dragon Seed* for China: involving American filmgoers in the Allied struggle.

Hoch, Winton. "The Vietnam War as Filmed for *The Green Berets.*" *American Cinematographer,* 49 (September 1968), 654–657.

Hughes, Robert (ed.). *Film: Book Two. Films of Peace and War.* New York: Grove Press, 1962.
A major collection of essays and interviews surveying the international status of the war film and inquiring into the effectiveness of films about peace and war. Representative topics and titles: Donald Richie's "Hiroshima in Film," Colin Young's "Nobody Dies" (on patriotism in Hollywood films), and Paul Goodman's "Designing Pacifist Films."

Jacobs, Lewis. *The Rise of the American Film: A Critical History.* New York: Columbia Teachers College Press, 1968.
See Chapter Fourteen, "Movies in the World War."

_____. "World War II and the American Film." *Cinema Journal,* 7 (Winter 1967–1968), 1–21.
 Also in Arthur F. McClure's collection of essays, *The Movies: An American Idiom* (Rutherford, New Jersey: Fairleigh Dickinson University Press, 1971).

Jacobson, Herbert L. "Cowboy, Pioneer and American Soldier." *Sight and Sound,* 22 (1953), 189–190.
 A brief but valuable essay on how the Western has reinforced the American military tradition.

Johnston, Winifred. *Memo on the Movies; War Propaganda, 1914–1939.* Norman, Oklahoma: Cooperative Books, 1939.
 Documents the movie climate that suggests the United States will soon enter the new war in Europe.

Jones, Dorothy M. "Hollywood Goes to War." *The Nation,* 27 January 1945, pp. 93–95.

_____. "The Hollywood War Film: 1942–1944." *Hollywood Quarterly,* 1 (1945), 1–19.

Jones, Ken D., and Arthur F. McClure (ed.). *Hollywood at War: The American Motion Picture and World War II.* New York: A. S. Barnes, 1973.
 For buffs only—provides cast list and one illustration for each of 450 films made during and about World War II. For a more useful survey, see Morella, below.

Jowett, Garth S. "The Concept of History in American Produced Films: An Analysis of the Films Made in the Period 1950–1961." *Journal of Popular Culture,* 3 (Spring 1970), 799–813.

Kagan, Norman. *War Films.* New York: Pyramid Publications, 1974.
 Published too late for description here.

Kahn, Gordon. *Hollywood on Trial.* New York: Boni and Gaer, 1948.
 On the film industry's response to the HUAC hearings.

King, Larry L. "The Battle of Popcorn Bay." *Harpers,* 234 (May 1967), 50–54.
 On war movies and reality.

Koch, Howard. *Casablanca: Script and Legend.* Woodstock, New York: The Overlook Press, 1973.
 Koch was one of the script writers for this classic film about an American who overcomes his reluctance to involve himself in World War II.

Kracauer, Siegfried. *From Caligari to Hitler: A Psychological History of the German Film.* Princeton: Princeton University Press, 1947.
 Useful for comparison in examining the interplay between a nation's life and its movies. This volume ends with a twenty-page supplement entitled "Propaganda and the Nazi War Film."

Kuiper, John. "Civil War Films: A Quantitative Description of a Genre." *Cinema Journal,* 5 (1965), 81–89.
 A quick survey of 495 films made between 1897 and 1961 and a summary of earlier research.

Landrun, Larry N., and Christine Eynon, "World War II in the Movies: A Selected Bibliography of Sources." *Journal of Popular Film,* 1 (Spring 1972), 147–153.
 Lists fifty-eight items, about ten of which are included here.

Lingeman, Richard. *Don't You Know There's a War On? The American Home Front, 1941–1945.* New York: Putnam, 1970.

On the broad social and cultural impact of World War II—on movies, the radio, magazines, etc. See particularly "Will This Picture Help Win the War?"

Lyons, Timothy. "Hollywood and World War I." *Journal of Popular Film,* 1 (Winter 1972), 15–30.

Madsen, Axel. "Vietnam and the Movies." *Cinema,* 4 (ca. 1967–68), 10–13.
Apparently the only article on the subject, excluding extremely short pieces in newspapers and the essays that grew into this book.

Manvell, Roger. *Films and the Second World War.* New York: A. S. Barnes, 1974.
Published too late for description here.

McBride, Joseph. "Drums Along the Mekong: I Love America, I Am Apolitical." *Sight and Sound,* 41 (Autumn 1972), 213–16.
On John Ford's contribution to the USIA film *Vietnam! Vietnam!*

McClure, Arthur F. "Hollywood at War: the American Motion Picture and World War II, 1939–1945." *Journal of Popular Film,* 1 (Spring 1972), 123–35.
This article was reprinted as the introduction to Jones and McClure, *Hollywood at War* (above).

Morella, Joe, Edward Z. Epstein, and John Griggs, ed. *The Films of World War II: A Pictorial Treasury of Hollywood's War Years.* Secaucus, N. J.: The Citadel Press, 1973.
Following a good introduction by Judith Crist, this book surveys about a hundred films. Most valuable for the general reader are the excerpts from contemporary reviews—unfortunately, this critical overview is chiefly limited to flag-waving blurbs meant to generate nostalgia.

Peet, Creighton. "Hollywood at War, 1915–1918." *Esquire,* September 1936, pp. 60, 109.
Ends, on the outbreak of World War II, with the prescient warning: "if we are not increasingly on our guard, a modern version of those old hate films will be upon us."

Review of Support Provided by the Department of Defense to the Twentieth Century-Fox Film Corporation for the Film "Tora! Tora! Tora!" Washington: General Accounting office, 17 February 1970.
A 67–page report issued by the Comptroller General.

Salisbury, Harrison E. "North Vietnam Spirit Found High." *New York Times,* 15 January 1967, pp. 1, 47.
A rare description of film-going in Hanoi, where the hit film depicts a Saigon youth who tried to assassinate Robert S. McNamara in 1964.

Sanders, Clinton R. "The Portrayal of War and the Fighting Man in Novels of the War in Vietnam." *Journal of Popular Culture,* 3 (Winter 1969), 553–64.
Included here for comparison. Novels about the war in Vietnam are almost as rare, relatively, as films. The publishing industry's shyness concerning Vietnam is not as obvious as Hollywood's, but just as worthy of investigation.

Schumach, Murray. *The Face on the Cutting Room Floor.* New York: William Morrow and Company, 1964.
The best study of film censorship. The chapter on "Pressures and Politics" documents the baleful influence the Department of Defense and State can wield over producers.

————. "Hollywood Division." *New York Times,* 7 October 1962, II, 7.

Good short account of early breach between Hollywood and the Pentagon.

Shain, Russell Earl. *An Analysis of Motion Pictures About War Released by the American Film Industry, 1939–1970.* Unpublished Ph.D. Dissertation, University of Illinois at Urbana-Champaign, 1972.
Available through University Microfilms, this survey locates 815 American films about World War II, the Cold War, Korea and Vietnam, analyzing them in terms of attitudes toward the enemy, the changing status of the warrior-hero, etc.

Shavelson, Melville. *How to Make a Jewish Movie.* Englewood Cliffs, New Jersey: Prentice Hall, 1971.
In spite of its flippancy, a key study of the making of an American war film on location in Israel. The problem of talking executives into making this film ("who wants to see a picture about a Jewish general?") was "like persuading them that *I am Curious, Yellow* grossed $22 million because audiences were interested in its philosophical stance against the Vietnam war."

Shearer, Derek. "The Brass Image." *The Nation,* 20 April 1970.
On the Pentagon's image-making.

Smith, Julian. "Where Happiness Cost So Little: America at the Movies in World War Two." *Journal of Popular Film,* 3 (Winter 1974), 75–78.
A review of the books edited by Jones and Morella.

Soderbergh, Peter A. "*Aux Armes!* The Rise of the Hollywood War Film, 1916–1930." *South Atlantic Quarterly,* 65 (Autumn 1966), 509–522.

_____. "The Grand Illusion: Hollywood and World War II, 1930–1945." *University of Dayton Review,* 5 (Winter 1968–1969), 13–22.

_____. "On War . . . and the Movies: A Reappraisal." *The Centennial Review,* 11 (Summer 1967), 405–18.
On what may or may not be a war film.

_____. "The War Films." *Discourse: A Review of the Liberal Arts* (Winter, 1968), 87–91.
On ideological conflicts in the period 1950–1968.

Spears, Jack. "World War I on the Screen." *Films in Review,* 17 (May 1966), 274–92.

Suid, Lawrence Howard. *The Film Industry and the Military Establishment.*
A doctoral dissertation in progress at Case Western Reserve University. Suid has interviewed over a hundred and fifty directors, producers, scriptwriters, film industry executives, and military advisors on films assisted by the Department of Defense.

Trumbo, Dalton. *The Time of the Toad.* New York: Harper and Row, 1973.
Another account of the HUAC hearings—by one of the Hollywood Ten.

Tyler, Parker. *Magic and Myth of the Movies.* New York: Simon and Schuster, 1947.
See the chapter on "The Waxworks of War."

United States Congress. House Committee on Government Operations. Military Operations Subcommittee. *Military Assistance to Commercial Film Projects.* Washington: United States Government Printing Office, 1969.
The kind of report that leaves one hungry for more information.

Wakefield, Dan. *Supernation at Peace and War.* Boston: Little, Brown, 1968.
In addition to sampling the mood of the nation in 1968, Wakefield reports interviews with Michael Wayne, who produced *The Green Berets,* and James Lee Barrett, who wrote the script.

White, David Manning and Richard Averson. *The Celluloid Weapon: Social Comment in the American Film.* Boston: Beacon Press, 1972.
Contains sections on Hollywood's response to contemporary wars from World War I to Vietnam.

INDEX

*An asterisk indicates an unreleased film or the title of a project that did not reach the screen.

229